SWINDON WORKS

1930–1960

SWINDON WORKS

1930–1960

PETER TIMMS

A gang assigned to the 'finishing off' of the royal engine 4082 *Windsor Castle* prior to the funeral of the king, George V. The royal coat of arms is about to be fitted to the locomotive running plate: a second one was fitted to the opposite side. 'A' Shop, January 1936. (Author's collection)

A fully revised and enlarged edition of the book *Working at Swindon Works 1930–1960*

I doubt if historians have done full justice to the makers of railways as the makers of nations.
Stanley Baldwin, 1927

First published 2014

Amberley Publishing
The Hill, Stroud
Gloucestershire, GL5 4EP

www.amberley-books.com

British Library Cataloguing in Publication Data.
A catalogue record for this book is available from the British Library.

ISBN 978 1 4456 4257 4 (print)
ISBN 978 1 4456 4267 3 (ebook)

Typeset in 10pt on 12pt Sabon.
Typesetting and Origination by Amberley Publishing.
Printed in the UK.

Contents

Introduction

The railway works and houses for the workers stood next to the otherwise sleepy market town on the hill. At least that's how it was in 1930. By 1960, although still more or less intact, the industry was beginning to decline and many other employers were established in the town. In the past, a nation's progress could be best measured by the transportation it produced. Designing and building efficient rolling stock, steam locomotives in particular, required a lifetime of commitment from some of the country's finest engineers. Swindon's contribution to this development was second to none and has been well recorded, but that is only part of the story of this remarkable place.

Local history has become very popular, especially that which is within living memory, making the period between the 1930s and the 1950s of particular interest. The years prior to 1930 were, of course, no less significant but belong to a period when there was little or no incentive to record events. Even after 1930, most written accounts give the impression that not much happened between the building of the first batches of Castle, Hall and King Class locomotives and the war years. Purists still have a tendency to look down on the early years of the nationalised railway and see the inevitable contraction as short-sighted. In the town, nothing much changed outwardly, and the way the works was transformed to cope with the development of the coming diesel age was admirable. In the 1960s however, the Swindon 'factory' became just another repair centre and was very nearly closed altogether.

Swindon was neither the birthplace nor the headquarters of the Great Western Railway, but it is usually the first place that comes to mind when people think of the old GWR. Most of the manufacturing and administration of the chief mechanical engineer's department was centred there. Until 1916, the department was called the 'loco, carriage & wagon' department, sometimes just the 'locomotive' department. The company continued to use these former titles on some documents right up to the 1930s. It was also the headquarters of the stores department, the central laundry and the motive power department. The latter moved up to Paddington in 1956 and a lot of the staff moved with it or took the train there each day.

The equipment used and services provided by the GWR reached a peak as early as the 1930s. This was not the case with the pay and conditions of its manual workers. Both had to improve, and this they did over the two following decades. The company also invested heavily in its manufacturing and in paybill technology at Swindon. The 1930s may have become known as the heyday of the GWR, but behind the publicity internal and external matters conspired against them. The company survived the economic depression remarkably well, and history has been kind about its record during the Second World War, but this should not detract from the scale of the difficulties they faced.

The management and board of directors at Paddington were not directly concerned with the conditions of their factory servants – why should they be? In those days it was perfectly reasonable to point out that if the conditions were unacceptable, workers were free to leave anytime they chose to. In the late nineteenth century any offers to cooperate with the men were no more than attempts to frustrate the organisation of trade unions. This attitude hastened the establishment of the Factories Act and motivated the workers into organising themselves in the workplace. Following a series of widespread industrial strikes, particularly during 1919 and 1926, things did settle down. However, where they could still exert power the bosses showed little regard for the men, even in more enlightened times. When asked to intervene to moderate the numbers of dismissals at Swindon in 1938, the chairman of the GWR, Viscount Horne, said, 'This is how the company works and these men knew that when they were hired.' This, of course, was nothing more than any employer would have said, but he could have questioned why so many men were dismissed when all the signs were that the industry was coming out of recession.

By the 1930s a few hard-fought concessions had been secured, partly because the government did not wish to see a repeat of the General Strike. The Great Western Railway ran a successful business and could not have done so by being more benevolent towards its employees, given the conditions of the times. This makes the early Swindon idea all the more fantastic: if you allow for the medical, educational and spiritual welfare of the workers, they might just serve you better.

There are certain myths that have evolved about this GWR factory, such as: 'Every male of working age, in Swindon, worked "inside".' Yes the works, as well as the railway around it, was just about the only place where men could get employment before the war. However, a significant proportion of them were needed to serve the railway community as shopkeepers, bus drivers, schoolteachers, council and church people, etc. Most writers and ex-railway staff sum up the old days as 'hard but fair'; health and safety, to use a modern term, was, they say, non-existent; when referring to the product manufactured, 'no expense was spared' is another over-generalisation. Above all, it is felt that the company they, and invariably their fathers, had worked for was an 'excellent employer'. Having studied the subject from a variety of sources, I believe that this shows that the memory is selective. I respect the fact that these people were there and I was not, but I think that writing on the basis of recollections alone could be misleading.

Various terms were used by Swindonians to describe their employer, including 'the company', 'the Western', 'the Great Western', 'the factory', 'inside', 'the GWR' and 'the railway', pronounced 'row-way' of course. Their random use hereafter serves to emphasise how equally well used these terms were.

An aerial view of the works with the CME offices in the centre. It seemed particularly fashionable to take such views in the 1920s and 1930s. Although they were effective in conveying a sense of the vastness of the site, few showed more than about a third of it. (GWR)

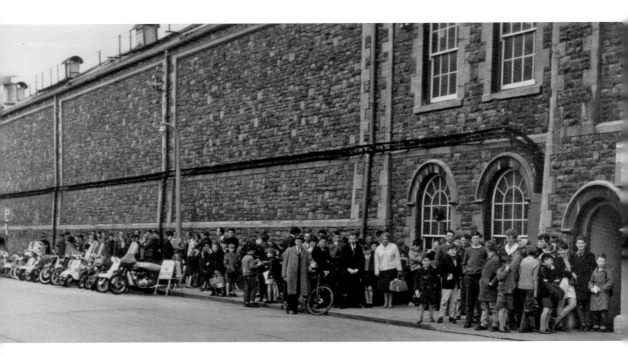

Enthusiasts waiting outside the main tunnel entrance to the works in London Street. This must have been a Wednesday just before 2.30 p.m. and taken sometime in the 1960s. (Bert Stratford collection, courtesy of David Stratford)

Acknowledgements and Sources

There are inevitably going to be parts of this subject that have been missed or not covered sufficiently. This is either because the information did not come my way in time, or because I chose not to repeat what has been published before. For instance, I have not listed steam locomotive statistics such as names, wheel arrangements, lot numbers and building dates, which can be found in many books specialising on the subject.

The recollections of my friends, ex-railwaymen John 'Jack' Fleetwood and George (everyone knows George) Petfield, got me started on this project. They introduced me to others and so it went on. I appealed through the local newspaper, the *Swindon Advertiser*, and got to meet some of the forgotten army of the offices: Dr Barbara Carter (née Dening), Yvonne Hodey (née Jones), Liz Bartlett (née Ribbins), Enid Hogden (née Warren), Maureen Marvell (née Stokes), Margaret Painter (née Eveness), Mary Parkhouse (née Almond), Dave Ellis and Jack Hartley. Jack gave me an in-depth breakdown of his working life, in chronological order – a researcher's delight. When I moved on to research workshop conditions, the following were only too glad to relive their working lives of all those years ago: Harry Bartlett, John Brettell, Bert Harber, Alan Lambourn, Peter Reade, Ken Ellis, Tony Huzzey, Gordon Turner, Dave Viveash, Doug Webb, Ken Watts, Colin Bown, Peter Chalk, Ivor Luker, John Jeffries, Roger Wise, John Walter, Vic Tucker, Mick Ponting, Mick Fisher and Maureen Fisher (née Eveness). Bob Townsend very kindly went out of his way to find me suitable photographs held by the Swindon Society; Jim Lowe was able answer the vast majority of my questions concerning locomotives passing through the works; and Ian Sawyer bombarded me with information and material relating to the works' fire brigade – thank you all very much.

The following either offered advice, put me in touch with ex-staff, or told me of their experiences of the railway town: Richard Clarke, David Lewis, Ronnie Lambourn, John Nutty, Brian Smithson, Richard Woodley, Anne Sweeney, Beryl Wynn, Roy Ferris, Mrs Parsons, Hilary Dunscombe, Kevin Weaver, Andy Binks and Joyce Walters. There were others who did not want their names mentioned but did want their memories recorded. I am very grateful to the editor of the *Swindon Advertiser* for allowing me to use old photographs from that newspaper and for publishing my appeals; to Elaine Arthurs at the Steam Museum archive; Dianne Timms for typing and computer skills; Andrea Downing for all the information, personal writing and photos from her father, R. J. Blackmore; and Richard Trewin and others at British Railways Board (Residuary) Ltd for allowing me to use official photos.

I am fortunate to have met hundreds of local railway staff over the past forty years through my work and through adverts in the local press for 'railway material wanted'.

Their stories have given me a great sense of what it must have been like. Alas, it is getting more difficult these days to obtain reliable first-hand accounts from ex-railway staff that go back to when the company name could be truly applied. I have cross-referenced technical details where possible and am as confident as I can be with them; otherwise distant memories must be classed as such and are often unverifiable. Alfred Williams's eloquent study of human predicament in 'the factory' was written when events were fresh in his mind, and there perhaps lies its true value.

As many names of workers as possible have been included because this is an account of a railway community as well as a history of events and achievements. I live in a town where the people read my books and say things like 'I didn't know old so-and-so worked there', 'I've not seen that picture of my aunt before', or 'I forgot that my foreman used to say that'. Then there have been the odd criticisms like 'that man never lived down our street, who told you that?' to which I have had to admit, 'well *you* did,' some years before. This is another example of why memories recorded earlier rather than later are the most valuable.

The staff at the Swindon Central Library's local studies section were very helpful. It is a wonderland of local history information and a humbling experience for anyone thinking that the subject is easily manageable. The staff magazines, at least those before 1948, are probably the best-kept records of this railway's social and professional activities and are less affected by the bias aimed at the general public. For me, the most interesting publication was the short-lived *Swindon Railway News* of the early 1960s. It is full of reflective snippets about characters, practices and incidents as recorded by the staff themselves. Arthur Humphries, an outstation clerk in the C&W manager's office, was the editor and when he moved to Derby Workshops' Division in 1963, no more editions were produced.

Various guidebooks produced for tour groups such as the Institute of Mechanical Engineers and Headquarters' Staff of British Railways provided information about the latest manufacturing facilities available at the time. They were produced in the works and printed in the duplication office. I have studied company rulebooks, just as every employee was required to do, as well as instruction books that were once kept in every office for 'ensuring uniformity of practice and procedure'. Certain engineering and operational details have been checked using textbooks once in the possession of the last two heads of department of the old company. The railway trade unions provided handbooks for the various sections of workers detailing conditions of service, and surviving copies provided a useful source of reference. Certain information now unobtainable anywhere else came from bound records of new work and sundry orders held at the Steam Museum, and from internal circulars, letters, publicity, telephone directories, and local rail and bus timetables in various private collections.

1

Expenditure in the 1930s

The old factory accounts' office of the locomotive department knew the importance of bookkeeping, and by the early years of the twentieth century had realised the value of accounting for all its business transactions. By the 1930s, the chief mechanical engineer's (CME) accounts department was a large one, separate from the stores accounts, which now had its own sections. The accounts department at Swindon had remained more or less independent and was allowed to run itself without too much interference from the chief accountant at Paddington. Inevitably, though, this independence was to be somewhat eroded by the 'rationalisation' that took place after 1947.

The CME department was a large one with a large budget. In the mid-1930s its annual turnover was about £14.5 million. Unlike some other departments, it did not generate much revenue itself. The money came from revenue – money raised by the company through its business operation – and capital – money raised by the issue of shares and stocks or by loans and debenture stocks. In 1929 the works' assistant chief accountant gave a lecture to the Swindon Engineering Society, breaking down expenditure into four main categories, the single largest of which was labour (wages claimed about 45 per cent of the budget). The bulk of the rest was divided between materials, work brought in, coal, gas, water, electricity and tax. The CME department had been responsible for the purchase of all the company's coal direct from the collieries, and that accounted for as much as 18 per cent of the budget. Some of the cost of the coal, as well as its movement, was recovered from other departments, but the bulk, about 40,000 tons per week, went into locomotives and was charged to the CME's running department, not the traffic department. For other uses of power, coal and coke were quickly being overtaken by electricity, but a large amount continued to be consumed at the railway's gas works. The CME's electrical assistant was responsible for the purchase of electricity for the whole company. Swindon Corporation's power station at Moredon was completed in 1928–9 and had supplied some of the railway factory with alternating electric current from the start. The factory had also produced its own electricity but, on requiring a new plant in the 1930s, decided to receive it from the municipal supply. Its own generating stations were then converted to sub-stations.

Costs for proposed 'new work' that was not classed as planned maintenance, repairs or design work were estimated. A case to carry out new work was made by a senior officer of the CME department to the Locomotive Committee meetings, where it was then fully discussed. The other departments of the company proposed work in the same way, including that which they wanted the CME department to undertake for them. More expensive work proposals were considered at the general manager's meeting, which was attended by members of the board.

The Locomotive Committee, which also covered the carriage and wagon departments, was made up of divisional superintendents and works managers, and was chaired by the chief mechanical engineer. If the estimate for costs did not appear excessive and it seemed that it might save time and increase efficiency, the work was put in hand, with the CME having the final say. Letters were then exchanged between the relevant heads of departments. New work orders were made out at Swindon in duplicate showing the date of the agreement to proceed; a correspondence reference number; the place where the work was to be carried out; a drawing number for use by the workmen; estimated costs and appropriation (the account[s] to be debited with the costs). Similar paperwork was used for 'sundry orders', which covered more minor work that was not put before the committee. For a high proportion of this CME work, Swindon's only involvement was to compile the paperwork. The following three, however, are random examples of 'new work' carried out around the works in 1939 and are taken from the order books held by the Steam Museum:

1. In February it was agreed that 'work to provide accommodation for 106 bicycles at the entrance near the West Time Office' would go ahead. The cost, estimated at £200, would come from departmental accounts. No outside contractor's name is mentioned, so I presume the 'accommodation' was made in the works. Similar work had been authorised a month earlier for inside the Redcliffe Street entrance.

2. In June 'a pre-cast concrete hut was to be provided for the (G Shop) crane testers' in place of the existing wood and galvanised panel hut. The Engineering Department would dismantle the old hut, erect a new one and install mains gas. The cost of the stove, bench and fittings came out of the CME machinery and plant account; total cost approximately £108.

3. Just after the declaration of war it was decided to 'blacken roofs of all shops and stores, also side windows where necessary, throughout the works and Stock Shed.' A good proportion of 'the factory' buildings had been designed to make the most of the natural light and had some window lights in the roofs. It was these which now required 'blacking' as an air raid precaution. The costs for this would come from the departmental account and a claim put in to the government, under whose control the railway companies now came, via the head office, Paddington.

The costs of works such as new buildings and improved facilities, as well as machinery and plant renewal, where there was a large initial outlay, came from the capital account. This was paid by head office, which would recover the money from the CME department over the anticipated life of the purchase, thus avoiding fluctuations in the available budget by spreading the costs. Both revenue and capital accounts were used to protect the considerable assets of the CME department against depreciation: revenue for repair and maintenance, and capital for replacement, like for like. The manufacture, repair and maintenance accounted for a significant proportion of the budget, so that only the additional costs of replacing the condemned stock was charged to capital. To improve and further standardise the range of locomotive types during the economic depression when expenditure was cut, suitable engines were classified as 'withdrawn' and then rebuilt and outshopped as 'new', thus qualifying for capital funding. Some spending would, in the long term, save money. For instance, after a further batch of King Class locomotives was completed, the *GWR Magazine* stated in 1930 that 'the building of large numbers of express locomotives has effected very considerable economies by the haulage of longer and heavier trains (and presumably less of them) and by reducing the number of banking engines needed.

The allowance from revenue was cut each year from 1930 to 1933, and in 1932 the company was drawing on reserves. In his book *Swindon Steam 1921–1951*, Mr K. J. Cook states,

> In the late 1920s and 1930s when revenue was low, the renewal fund (capital) was in a very healthy condition and with prices stable at that time it gave us considerable assistance in meeting our commitments ... During slump periods we had our normal allocation of money for machine tool renewal ...

As this money was only on loan to the CME department, the company must have been fairly optimistic that the economy would soon improve. After 1933 the financial situation of the department did steadily improve as business on the railway picked up. However, there was an unexpectedly bad year in 1938 on account of falling receipts for merchandise and coal movement. As a result, large-scale dismissals were announced in the works on Friday 20 May that year. Authority from the board of directors had to be sought via the chief mechanical engineer for all projects where costs exceeded £100. The board therefore had to sanction all construction, reconstruction and modifications to locomotives and rolling stock, but not the cost of ordinary repairs. Each British railway company was required to submit a statement to the Railway Rate Tribunal when it was set up in the early 1920s, showing all repair expenses for one year. From this information the figure for each company, known as 'repairs quantum', became their limit of expenditure and was adjusted each year in accordance with variations in the workload, wages and cost of materials.

Raw materials and component parts were purchased from, and manufactured items sold to, the stores department (at cost) (see Chapter 10). Around 25 per cent of the budget was tied up with work done and services rendered, through contracts between departments and outside firms. The maintenance of stationary engines, cranes and hoists at Swindon was charged to the traffic department, and likewise work carried out at docks, harbours and wharves was charged to the docks department. The drawing office did a lot of work for the chief civil engineer's (CCE) department, and the workshops made parts for the permanent way; again, the costs would be recovered from them. Locomotive power, supplied for use with CCE's trains, was debited by the CME department, as was the movement of ash and clinker from boilers, which the CCE used as hard core and to build up land. The mechanical engineers were totally separate in their role from the (civil) engineers' department: the latter were responsible for fixed structures such as buildings, lighting installations, platforms, turntable bases, canals, weighbridges, permanent way and all the company's land. There was often close cooperation between the two departments, of course, and the two sets of staff were often governed by the same working conditions and instructions. CME staff could carry out civil engineers' work on its own buildings with authority from the division engineer, and then charge them for it.

There was a statutory requirement on the GWR to keep financial and statistical accounts under the Railway Companies (Accounts and Returns) Act of 1911, and that they be made up in prescribed form to 31 December each year. Thomas Minchin, an accounts clerk at the Swindon works, presented a paper to the Swindon Engineering Society in 1921 entitled 'Cost Accounting'. In it, he attempted to explain that an accurate determination of costs had a direct effect on manufacturing efficiency; an idea that, he implies, was far from universally accepted at that time. 'Only now was the company realising the value of complete accounting because without it, inefficiencies cannot be properly identified,' he said. Careful record and scrutiny was made of all receipts and expenditure incurred at Swindon and outstation. They endorsed the paradox that for efficiency, no expense should be spared in accounting for every penny spent and earned. Mr Minchin, then a recent

Brunel medallist at the London School of Economics, pointed out that the expense of running a costing system (the assistant chief accountant's rough estimate was between one and two old pennies for every pound expended) was easily offset by the economies made. This was little comfort to the estimators (called 'guessers' by some workshop staff) in the cost offices who had to chase the reasons when actual costs exceeded estimates.

The costs of each completed lot or order were determined from materials, labour and establishment charges. Material costs were fairly easy to ascertain thanks to an organised system of storekeeping. Enough material had to be purchased to complete the job, but not too much, as that would lock up capital funds. A turnover of two and a half times per annum was claimed by the loco stores for the 45,000 or so items kept there. Other costs attributable to materials were receiving, checking and storage, and these considerations were the responsibility of the stores department. Labour costs were divided between productive and non-productive workers. The piecework accounts gave management an accurate assessment of productivity in the shops and outstation, and also kept productive workers best utilised. Labour costs could be increased by poor working conditions and poor workmanship. The latter was partially recovered by making the craftsman involved do the work again without pay up to the point where the error occurred. The attitude of some foremen was also a factor, and two published accounts of life on the shop floor at Swindon (Freebury and Williams) talk of injustices towards some men by their overseer, who knew he was accountable to no one, even if production was affected. Workers not directly employed in production were more difficult to assess for efficiency. Could they be better employed to assist production? What would the effect on output be if there were fewer of them?

Establishment charges included power, plant, rates, rent, lighting, water, coal, office sundries and anything that could not be costed accurately to a particular job. Office sundries included vast amounts of stationery, and the dramatic rise in the cost of paper in 1937 caused the company great concern. Mr Minchin listed non-productive grades of workers under establishment charges (better known now as running costs) rather than labour costs. If only for the purposes of cost accounting, progress men, clerks, typists, messengers, WC attendants and cleaners found themselves in the same category as works officials, their assistants and foremen. I wonder what the chairman of the society, Mr Hawksworth, who was at the presentation, thought of that. To be fair to non-productive workers, particularly the lower grades, where they were inefficient, it was likely to be the fault of the system to a large extent: a reluctance of those with influence to consider change. The same mentality, no doubt, that had previously ensured the product was as good as it could be without regard for cost or time.

At the GWR Debating Society in 1933 a speaker, himself a member of the CME department, said, on the subject of improving the efficiency of staff, 'I advocate raising both the standard of education necessary for entrance into the railway service and the advertising of vacancies … the encouragement of promotion from the bottom up.' On cooperation of efficiency he spoke of the danger of placing department before company as the first priority. The writer of this prizewinning essay made no mention of competitive salaries and wages in the presence of one of the board of directors, but then this great company did not need to buy loyalty.

Whether expenditure provides a good return is not always easy to determine. However, the annual reports for the Mechanics' Institute show that accounting for the Annual Juvenile Fete held in August was more straightforward. The events organised by the Mechanics' Institute paid for themselves, the company making concessions for upkeep of premises etc. From 1931 the company gave a one-off annual payment of £750 to the MI. That year, for the juvenile or children's fete, the institute paid out £664, of which the most expensive category was cake, tea, sugar and milk, all provided (nominally) free with the admission charge. This was more than £100 above the fees for artistes and fireworks, both always of the highest standard. The income from the sale of tickets, programmes, rents from stallholders and amusements' rights amounted to £772. Incidentally, the Juvenile Fete of 1931 was well remembered for the atrocious weather. The steam wagons, showmen's caravans and heavy trailers made such a mess of the waterlogged ground that the Council of the Mechanics paid £157 to the corporation for rent and the unavoidable damage caused. Normally they paid about £35 for the hire of the park. In the annual fetes that followed (the last was in 1939), the Mechanics' Council usually managed to break even because the small profit made was given to a local needy cause.

The assistant works manager said of the extent of the Swindon accounts, 'One cannot argue against the necessity of such an elaborate accounts system.' It appears, from studies such as that undertaken by Mr Minchin, Swindon was well ahead of its head office at Paddington where, at the time, cost accounts were produced as overall sets of figures and worthless for evaluation. Presumably this situation had developed because the work undertaken was not sold outside and the company had not learned to be competitive. The general manager, Mr F. J. C. Pole, said in his memoirs that his chief accountant had insisted that producing divisional profit and loss accounts would be too costly and too difficult, so this was not taken up in his time (up to 1929). However, by then it was realised that it was no longer enough for the company to know it was making a profit based on comparing monthly variations in traffic and docks receipts or maintaining a healthy general balance sheet each year. They too needed to account for all costs because, as they stood, the total costs for a given period offered no clue as to whether they were excessive, and if they were, where that excess was incurred. Like all shrewd business people, the directors of the company saw opportunities to be exploited during the most depressed years of the early 1930s. At the annual general meeting, the chairman said that economies made would continue when trade revived. Swindon, with its superior methods of costing, had not waited until events forced economies upon them.

One of the 100 large vacuum-braked vans built in 1930 for general merchandise. Until then the GWR and other British railways had preferred small consignment, short wheelbase goods wagons. They could be accommodated in sidings with sharp curves, particularly common in private firms' premises. These new high-capacity, low-maintenance vehicles, so popular on the Continent, would remain in the minority for the time being. Indeed, with the 20-ton steel-bodied coal wagons being proposed at the same time, Mr Collett's department were told that the design must retain the short-wheelbase of the 12-ton version they would replace. The main reason for this was to increase sidings' capacity. (GWR)

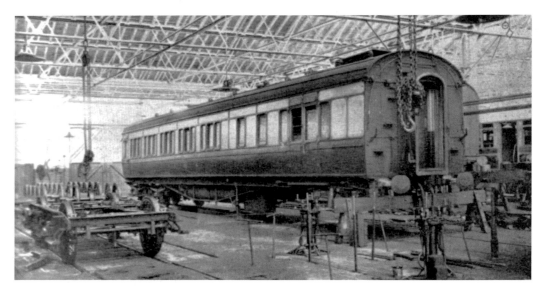

19C, the carriage lifting shop, was in an area known by the men as 'The Klondyke' because, when first built, this part of the works was remote from the other carriage shops. This shop formed part of a carriage building that had been extended, until it joined other carriage workshops to the north. By the 1930s, when this picture was taken, the original lifting shop remained in the southern part; the rest became the vacuum brake and carriage body repair area or 19D shop. (*GWR Magazine*)

2

The Economic Depression

Generally, job security on the railways was very good before the war, but in the workshops, especially among the last in, it was not necessarily a job for life. New production methods nearly always meant that less labour was required, so the men affected were moved to other work and the balance was corrected through natural wastage. But when the dividend was down the company had a policy of discharging workshop labour. Word would spread through the town when manufacturing orders were to be cut. This was usually a sign of the Western going into recession, and the 1930s began with all the worrying indicators. That was after the company recorded the highest locomotive mileage ever, in 1929, and the Loco and Carriage works were working to full capacity. The general manager, Mr Milne, set the scene in summing up the year 1930: 'We have a world-wide depression in industry, particularly in the coal, iron and steel trades from which the GWR derives about 80 per cent of its total freight tonnage.' The Wagon works had long been on 'short time' as the company reduced wagon maintenance and manufacture, while work on secondary and branch-line carriage stock was cut to a minimum. Short-time working was introduced throughout the workshops from August 1930.

On the other hand, the ongoing programme to replace main-line locomotives, carriages and wagons was almost as ambitious as ever. Of particular note was a set of 'super saloons' built to rival the luxury carriages of the Pullman Car Co. On Saturday 12 April 1930, the works was open to the public, with the admission fee going to the Railway Benevolent Institution. Examples of the latest locomotives (including the 6,000 Class *King George V*) and rolling stock were on show, and the works fire brigade put on a display under the direction of the chief fire officer, C. T. Cuss.

Plans for extending and rebuilding facilities did include financial assistance from the government as part of the scheme to relieve unemployment. During that period, the works built a plant for disinfecting coaches (known to the men as the Bug House), a 70-ton replacement weighbridge was installed in the carriage works, the locomotive weigh house was fitted with replacement balancing pans and instruments and the building extended, and a springsmith shop was built. The chair foundry had been extended and a huge new carriage repair shop was completed on land recently acquired from the council. Thousands of tons of ash and soil had to be brought in by the CME department to build up the land, and by the early 1930s a large area at the west end of the site was brought into use. A concentration yard for scrapping redundant stock and machinery and a large timber-stacking yard with workshops and sidings were built in this area – later they stored spare boilers there too.

From the company's point of view the men who produced the work could be discharged when times were hard and replaced or recalled when business improved. This could not be done to the same extent with clerical and supervisory staff. Consequently the pay and prospects of secure employment for the tradesmen was not so good and a major reason for the resentment felt towards 'them upstairs'. The years 1929–34 were the worst, with unemployment nationally rising to 3.5 million, or 15.6 per cent of the labour force. According to the *GWR Magazine* there were 13,531 employed in the Swindon factory in 1931. A year later another source said the figure was just over 11,000 (the lowest of the whole period). The short-sighted way in which workshop labour at Swindon was handled is noticeable in a report in the *Evening Advertiser* of the time. It said, 'In August of 1932, while 820 were discharged on the "carriage side", many "loco side" tradesmen were being taken on.' Although only one in three CME workers were based at Swindon, the majority of job losses came from within the town, which had by then over 3,000 registered as workless.

The Swindon GWR Chargemen's Association called a meeting of those with local influence to try to encourage them to help improve business for the railway company. They appealed to the local MP, to the Chamber of Commerce, to co-op societies, to traders and to the townspeople via the press, to help divert goods traffic back that had been lost to road hauliers. The railway companies and their staff had, for instance, become alarmed at the amount of public money being spent on the roads, which was well beyond that amounting from vehicle and petrol tax. The chargemen suggested to buyers and businesses that only goods that had been brought in by rail should be purchased as everyone in the town was more or less dependent on the GWR for their livelihoods. They were also reminded that the less the railway workers received in wages, the less they were able to put back into the local economy.

Beryl Wynn's (née Odey) father was a French polisher in the carriage works throughout the 1930s. She said, 'Although our dad always had full employment, mother had to get all the groceries "on tick" every short week and pay up every balance week' (piecework money was paid fortnightly). So it is difficult to imagine how railway families managed when the working week was cut to four or even three days and they could not fall back on assistance from relatives or the government. It was not until 1946 that mothers could claim family allowance for each child, excluding the first. For the poor souls whose 'services are no longer required', the dole queue was almost certainly the only alternative. The dole pay-out was subject to a means test, which meant an official would come to the house and assess the collateral: the family piano, the mantle clock and other non-essentials would have to be sold before any money could be claimed. Casual work would have to be sought as well, to supplement the meagre dole allowance. If it was suspected that poverty was causing a deterioration of health, a person or family might receive handouts organised by the church or civic groups. The mayor, Mr William Robins, elected in 1932, was a clerk in the factory (he later worked in the stores order office and was organising secretary of the Railway Clerks Association). Mr Robins said one of the most beneficial schemes during his term was the borough council allocating allotment land to the unemployed.

Unlike single women, men had little or no hope of alternative employment locally, a situation which allowed the company a long period of industrial harmony with its workers. The men received eight days' holiday annually, plus six bank holidays, which was all unpaid until 1938, adding to their predicament. Between 1930 and 1933 the Mechanics' Institute lost a third of its paying members. In May 1933, following an appeal by the Swindon Unemployed Association and the local Member of Parliament, the GWR agreed to allow unemployed men, and presumably their families, to be eligible for full facilities at the Mechanics' Institute at a reduced rate. The men discharged from the works over the previous twelve months were to receive free passes for the annual holiday trains, and of course this concession extended to wives and children. No doubt this proved popular for those who qualified, as it was almost no cheaper to stay at home on Trip

Day. Beryl Wynn said her father never enjoyed Trip because, like so many others, he was worried about the labour discharges that were announced a few weeks later if the company was doing badly.

The weeks following Trip holiday were bound to be difficult for the manual worker if he and his family spent the whole week away. Adams, the pawnbroker in Fleet Street, always did brisk trade at this time of year. Two local artists, one of whom was Will Thomas, had a series of farcical sketches of Trip published as postcards earlier in the century. The theme was usually the financial predicament the holiday had caused. One showed the 'annual wash' on the eve, another, the 'annual rush' to board the trains, and then the 'annual hush' afterwards depicting the wife and kids hiding behind the door when the rent collector or money lender came to call. These pathetic situations appeared comical because there was more than a little that the railway families could identify with. The effects of the depression meant that the lean times of their parents' and grandparents' generation were back, if they had ever really gone away. 'Waste not, want not' and 'make do and mend' were sayings well known to Swindon people in the years before the Second World War.

It was the men in the workshops who viewed impending retirement with anxiety and hoped they could find some sort of paying work elsewhere when they reached sixty-five. If they were unwilling or unable to pay into something like the Sick Fund Society, where a superannuation allowance was paid upon retirement, they would, assuming they lived that long, come to wish they had. Only the lowest paid would qualify for state pension payments, but not until they reached seventy years of age. Some locals said their fathers and uncles suffered hardship in retirement, even after the war, although by then, subject to a medical check, some men could continue in their work after sixty-five. Despite all this, the railway factory workers' prospects were better than those who worked in rural areas, and Swindon suffered far less of the changing fortunes characteristic of other towns that were dominated by one employer.

In his book *Swindon Steam 1921–1951*, K. J. Cook noted that 'Railway accountancy is very strictly controlled by Acts of Parliament with the object of safeguarding the interests of rail users against monopolies.' The controls included wage levels, which had been set after the First World War when the men's negotiating powers were still ineffective. In the 1930s the British economy was in no condition to introduce a minimum wage as the Americans had done for their industrial workers, among others, in 1938. The wages grades in the CME department in the 1930s allowed workers to do little more than get by, and despite a steady fall of prices in the shops, workers without a trade were below the poverty line. Over time, junior salaried staff would see their pay increase sufficiently to provide for a wife and family, unlike the manual workers who had little or no scope to improve their living standards, unless they were still working into the 1950s, when things did improve.

A mortgage offer would require an income of between £150 and £200 a year, so the newly-wed shopman would normally set his sights on renting a two-up/two-down house in an Edwardian or Victorian terrace within sight of the works. Up until the mid-1930s, the rent would be between 6 or 7s a week, or between 12 and 20 per cent of his net wages, depending on his trade. He would be responsible for the upkeep of the dwelling and all general repairs. According to Jack Fleetwood, who lived in Regent Place, homes around the town centre were getting a bit dilapidated by the early 1930s.

> Nobody had a bathroom: we brought in the galvanised tin bath that hung up in the back yard. Nobody had a flushing toilet either. There was a gap in the wall of our lean-to kitchen extension and when Dad had finished with the evening paper it was pushed through to our neighbours.

The better paid could, if they wished, buy a house a little further out. Areas to the north and to the east of the town were being developed; a semi-detached house on the Northern

Road development cost £365 and the detached version was £400. Overall, the borough's figures were quite impressive: 19,000 Swindon homes were owner occupied in 1939.

In the early 1930s, building societies were making much of the fact that houses were cheaper than ever, thanks to low interest rates and cheaper material costs, but the economic crisis meant that lending was severely limited. The GWR could arrange loans for its employees to purchase a home and offered terms more favourable than the building societies. Their savings bank required a payment per month, sufficient only to cover the interest accrued, and any amount beyond that was optional. They also had a working arrangement with the Swindon Permanent Building Society, offering slightly more favourable terms for railwaymen. The loans were directed at the staff grades, not only because they were best able to repay, but also because their employment with the company was more secure. Unless they were being groomed for some elevated position, workers in the factory were less likely to be transferred away and were better suited to take on a mortgage. On getting married, both Jack and George Petfield moved out to a council estate called Pinehurst that had been built between the wars. Their rent in 1938 was 13s a week.

The Old Town residents were generally more affluent, and consequently few wage grades lived 'up nobhill', unless parents or grandparents had the means to purchase the house. In Old Town one could rub shoulders with the managers. One of the residential roads there, Goddard Avenue, was known as Bloater Avenue because, according to its detractors from new Swindon, to pay for such expensive houses the occupiers could afford only bloaters for their tea. Jack found out that the bloater principle did exist when he worked with a bloke known as 'Granny', a moulder in the brass foundry. 'Granny' ate nothing but bread and jam at work, and whenever questioned about his diet he would change the conversation and mention his house, which was in Goddard Avenue. After the war, Jack Fleetwood told me, it became possible for shopmen of no additional means to purchase homes of their own, even though prices had gone up considerably:

> Bert Allen, one of our charge-hands, was even more frugal than Granny, although he lived in a modest place near Cambria Bridge. Bert was obsessive about economising, but he was no miser – he offered me an interest-free loan if I wanted to buy a house when I got married in 1945. People were far more neighbourly in those days and especially willing to help newlyweds, but repaying the money was a big responsibility and I declined the offer.

A familiar sight around the town was allotment fences made out of old enamel railway signs. When railway equipment was surplus to requirements, the stores department dealt with its disposal. It was all sent back to Swindon works to be reclassified as either salvageable or scrap. All metals went to the 'loco side' and timber to the 'carriage side'. If the men wanted to buy scrap items they were charged a nominal sum. Enamel station signs, and later steel coach panels, made durable fencing and kept rabbits away from the vegetables. According to Jack,

> A lot of families kept chickens or rabbits, but when time came to kill them they would often ask me to do it. Catching rabbits was a popular pastime but the ones in the Concentration Yard and Timber Stacking Ground were left alone, and consequently they became overrun with them. It wasn't that the company objected to traps, it was because they ingested a lot of wood, which made them inedible.

Rabbits could be bought from a man known as Artful Dodger, who came round selling them from a pony and cart. They were a bit cheaper than those in the shops, at around a shilling each. The skin could be sold on to Cockle Jack, the rag and bone man, for three (old) pennies (he lived in Regent Place and would repair shoes too, if required). Horsemeat was available as a cheap alternative during wartime, if not before, and some people ate pigeon too.

The GWR employee, if he or she was the main provider for the family, could take advantage of cheap coal (minimum 2 cwt) or scrap timber from the company, delivered to the door by a private haulier using a cart pulled by a shire horse. Delivery men often had a deformity or infirmity and could not pass the medical test to go 'inside'. It might be that they had been invalided out of railway work in times past. Some enterprising retired workers made themselves a handcart and put a sticker in their front window advertising 'factory wood delivered', for a small fee of course. In the 1930s wood tickets cost you a shilling a hundredweight, a little more if you required delivery to one of the surrounding villages. By the 1950s it was half a crown, and coal was a little bit more. In the Second World War the cheap supply of household coal was stopped because of alternative demands on the ships and trains that carried it. Workers and their families then had to burn wood to heat their homes.

Scrap timber could be collected from the wood wharf by Whitehouse Bridges, thus saving the small haulier's fee. Like all second-hand materials, wood was classified as either serviceable or scrap. The official instructions to employees who graded it were 'care should be taken that timber disposed of as firewood or "refuse" is such as could not be used with advantage for company purposes.' What they called 'refuse' timber was better quality for use at home or in the garden. Most of this type of scrap came from the bodies of withdrawn wagons. In 1947 the railway engaged W. F. Cole of Hunt Street to deliver timber, if required, within the town, and F. L. Belcher of Kingsdown to deliver to the outlying districts. Coal was to be delivered by the railway's own transport. This must have been hard on the people who had relied on making a few coppers from those customers. Other useful scrap, such as flue tubes from locomotive and other types of boilers, could be purchased at a shilling apiece. Two or three of these tubes fixed together made a sturdy washing line, although when it was available, signal rodding was preferred as it didn't rust so quickly. Jack said that sometimes, after paying, you could discreetly swap the flue tubes and take out new ones.

In at least one way, the economic situation directly created some extra activity in the loco works. Because of the decrease in the South Wales coal traffic, the GWR found itself with a surplus of 2-8-0 tank engines. These had been designed primarily for working in South Wales, hauling coal trains between the collieries and factories or ports. So quickly did the downturn affect the operating conditions that a batch of new 2-8-0Ts still being built would not now be needed in the Welsh coalfields. There was, however, scope for producing new engines to work medium- and long-distance coal trains worked by Aberdare Class 2-6-0 tender engines that were due for replacement. Swindon therefore rebuilt batches of 4,200 Class 2-8-0s into the new 7,200 Class 2-8-2s. For the gangs working on the conversions, including apprentice Hugh Freebury, they were 'a profitable source of activity', while 'some departments were still very short of work.' From 1934 until the work had to stop because of the war, fifty-four had been rebuilt. The alterations included fitting larger side tanks and extending bunkers so as to carry nearly as much coal and water as tender engines and extending the main frames to accommodate a trailing radial axle. The new locomotives weighed a massive 92 tons, making them the heaviest steam locos that would be lifted by the overhead cranes in the 'A' erecting shop.

By 1938 the company was slowly recovering from the recession and there was work available for skilled and semi-skilled men generally. It was, therefore, a shock when about twenty-four men on the 'loco side' were 'under notice to go', and some short-time working was introduced in March for wagon workers. There were threats of further cuts and by July well over a thousand were to go due to go on the 'carriage and wagon side'. This was due to building programmes being completed and no further orders placed. However, the company would soon have to completely rethink its short- and medium-term plans as war became ever more likely.

THE TRIPPERS' RETURN.

Above: A gang of men installing a new wagon weigh table in what was called the locomotive yard sidings because of its proximity to the engine shed. It would be used to weigh wagon loads of scrap metal that had been put through the shears in a building in the scrap yard behind F shop. The weighbridge house where the balancing table gauges would be read was a converted signal box. The date of this picture is about 1929 or 1930 when men were starting to fear for their jobs. Another photograph taken at the same time shows these men standing outside a Pooley mess van with 'For use in the Swindon district' stencilled on the side. All of this gang, except 'Nobby' Newbery (on the right), a works' labourer, were were employees of Henry Pooley and Sons Ltd, the weighing machine company. (S. A. S. Smith, courtesy of Ray Eggleton)

Left: One of a series of Edwardian postcards illustrating the plight of Swindon families who dared to take a holiday, courtesy of the company. The sentiment in this cartoon situation could equally be applied to 1930s Swindon. (Author's collection)

Top: The conversions of 42XX class 2-8-0 engines to 72XX 2-8-2s provided much needed work for some men on the 'loco side' in the 1930s.

Middle: Communal alleyways ran behind all terraced houses in the town and were known locally as 'backs' or 'backsies'. This picture shows the 'backs' in the railway estate; all these houses would have been occupied by railway families. (Swindon Society, courtesy of Bob Townsend)

Bottom: The stark discharge notice given to the 'last-in' when things were bad. They were also given to some apprentices coming out of their time and I think this may be the case here. Wiremen are now universally known as electricians, and as such G. E. Evans would probably have been employed on connecting up electric motors for machine tools and installing electric lighting in the works as gas was gradually replaced. (Author's collection)

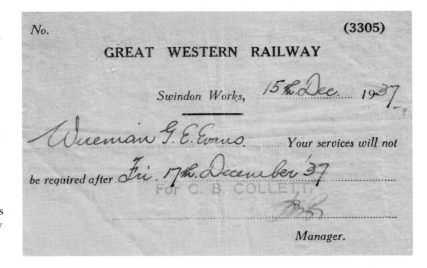

No.   (3305)

GREAT WESTERN RAILWAY

Swindon Works, *15th Dec.* 19*37*

Wireman G. E. Evans .... *Your services will not*

be required after *Fri 17th December '37*

For C. B. COLLETT,

Manager.

3

Pay and Negotiations

Standard salaries, wages and hours of duty had all been established at Railway Rate Tribunals set up under the Railways Act of 1921, and became known as 'national agreements'. The agreements were based partly on the ordinary annual expenditure figures set by the tribunal for each of the four main railway companies. Tribunals set up to deal primarily with railway staff pay would be supplied with verbal and written evidence from both sides. The unions' representatives would argue that their members and their families suffered unreasonable hardship, and even ill health, and deserved a better share of the profits, a shorter working week and paid holidays. For the Management Negotiating Committee, the Great Western's chief accountant, Mr Cope, and others would present the statistics for the annual expenditure and revenue, and argue a case for moderation. Separate agreements for the CME workers, such as footplatemen, supervisory staff, clerical staff, women and girl workers, and conciliation staff, but excluding shopmen, were worked out, and subsequent challenges to the application of the terms of agreements were 'interpreted' at an industrial court.

Subsequent pay adjustments had to be agreed by the Central Wages Board or, on appeal, by the National Wages Board, bodies set up by the joint railway companies consisting of a panel of representatives from all sides. The wages boards became increasingly unpopular with both unions and management. The problem was the constitution of the boards, which were expected to sit as judges and remain impartial, and as a result became slow and laborious. In particular, the deadlock over the need to further reduce earnings in 1932–33 because of the dire economic situation showed the shortcomings of settling these matters through the wages boards. The railways suggested that negotiations at a local level might be the way to determine questions relating to pay rates in the future, so in early 1934 the machinery, as established under the Railway Act of 1921, was terminated.

A new machinery of negotiation emerged to cover major issues of standard salaries, wages and hours of duty through 'discussion or negotiation'; the former terms 'conciliation and arbitration' were now omitted from the vocabulary. Before any matter could be dealt with under the machinery, it had to be first referred to the railway company concerned through the appropriate channels. The improved means of communication offered did not mean the company had gone soft: they instructed their officials to scrutinise 'the book' (what we now call the small print) carefully before conceding to proposals or alleged injustices. The memorandum included a detailed disciplinary procedure, although there was no provision for negotiations over this, or matters of management. The stance towards those accused of serious misconduct was also retained, despite union insistence on a proper hearing. The company rulebook of 1937 stated that anyone guilty of misconduct and dismissed 'forfeits any right to wages to any period subsequent to the completed week preceding his dismissal or suspension prior to dismissal'.

Any dispute that came within the scope of the new local machinery, but was not resolved in favour of the men, could be referred to the headquarters of the trade union concerned. They could raise the matter at a higher level or go directly to the general manager, Mr (later Sir) James Milne. Agreements reached and minuted through the various channels became operational from the beginning of the next complete paybill period, or from such a date settled for the purpose. If the matter was still not resolved, the parties could go to arbitration through the Railway Staff Tribunal, formerly the industrial court, for a decision.

Of the workshop men working for the GWR, 50 per cent were in the CME department and the remainder were divided between the (civil) engineers, docks department and the signal works. Skilled men in railway workshops could be engineers, coachbuilders or construction workers, and had been paid at rates set for each craft and governed by the fortunes prevailing in those industries. District rates, as they were now, were not related to other manual railway workers' rates. As the name implies, they varied depending on local conditions.

At the shopmen's industrial court hearing of 1922, both the railway companies and the National Union of Railwaymen (NUR) were keen to bring their shopworkers' rates in line with those of other railway workers, as had happened so successfully during the First World War. However, they disagreed about how future increases in the rates should be negotiated. The NUR wanted pay rates, as decided by the court, to be subject to the sliding scale, as was the case with the conciliation grades. The railway companies' view was that the rates, fixed on the principles set by them, should vary with the national variations of the engineering trade; the Amalgamated Engineering Union (AEU), and other craft unions that still represented many of the railway shopmen, naturally wanted things to stay as they were. The court would not come down on one side or the other, but recommended the establishment of local machinery to incorporate pay issues.

The GWR had begun to offer facilities for the establishment of shop and piecework committees in the same month they were making their representations to the court, and within weeks of Mr Collett becoming chief mechanical engineer. Swindon men received a circular in February 1922 offering the option of local committees if the majority of men in each area wanted it. They would be made up of shop stewards and representatives of all grades, irrespective of trade union membership. Matters of piecework, welfare, discipline and improving working methods were within the scope of the new machinery, but not pay. The management saw the committees as a way of 'securing good mutual understanding with the men'. There was even an appeal committee if matters could not be settled, but initially not all sections of the workforce took up the idea, as some saw it as undermining the union process that they had fought long and hard to secure.

In the late 1920s, following the general strike, with a worsening economic situation and increasing competition from road transport, all sides were looking for the opportunity to present their case and receive a fully considered response, and not to repeat the confrontations of the past. The railway companies, no doubt under pressure from the government, reached agreement with the unions and extended the negotiating powers of the shopmen's committees in 1927. The GWR then issued circular No 3053 to each man summarising the scheme. Only then, five years after it was recommended by the industrial court, did the scheme 'afford facilities for the discussion of questions relating to rates of pay, hours of duty and general conditions of employment of railway shopmen. The 'discussion' would be carried out on behalf of those in dispute by elected representatives, with other committee members appointed by the company. These 'facilities' were to be known as shop and works committees.

A few months earlier, while this document was being worked out, the locomotive *King George V* was sent to America. The general manager, Mr Pole, and assistant general manager, Mr Milne, accompanied the party and spent some of the time gathering information about aspects of American railway working with a view to improving the Great Western. On the subject of employees' conditions of service, they wrote, upon their return, 'It was gathered that when the railways of the United States were under government control, all negotiations were conducted through the unions. On decontrol however, the Pennsylvania Railroad devised what is known as the "Pennsylvania Plan", under which conditions of service etc. are negotiated only with elected representatives of the men, except in one or two grades where there are highly organised trade unions. Following this lead the majority of railways have definitely broken with the unions.' It seems likely then that the GWR management thought the introduction of the committees would break the men's loyalties to the unions.

Throughout the period of this book, rates of pay were expressed in shillings and (old) pence (for those too young to remember, there were 12 pence to a shilling and 20 shillings to £1). I see no point in giving the present equivalent monetary figures to earnings. Included are recollections about the home lives of former railway families, and their limited means speaks for itself. Rates of pay referred to the weekly not hourly amount payable, excluding any bonuses or allowances. The enginemen and firemen had standardised rates of pay, unlike the shopmen. Every type of workshop trade had attracted a different rate for the job on account of separately negotiated agreements that had been worked out locally and were known as district rates.

In the late 1930s, when it became more commonly known as the cost-of-living allowance, the bonus paid was 16s 6d for all skilled and semi-skilled employees and labourers in the shops. Shopmen were graded according to their experience and the type of work they were engaged on. A grade 1 man could be paid up to 8s more than the man next to him. Workshop men in industrial towns and cities, including Swindon, were paid more than men in smaller towns and rural areas because of increased living costs. Workers in the London area got a little more again. A patternmaker was paid more than a fitter or skilled turner (lathe operator). A toolmaker was highly skilled and respected, but his rate did not reflect this. Much of the metalwork done on mills, slotters, planers, shapers, borers, grinders, drills, capstan and turret lathes was simple and repetitive and required only limited skill. At that time the metal machinists were classed as skilled, although that skill was acquired with experience and little formal training. Because of this, these grades were easier to replace than the journeyman, and the company could pay them less. The time-served turner, for instance, undertook specialised work and was paid more than those who just finished the outside diameters of locomotive or carriage wheels and axles.

A first-year apprentice received 14s a week, which included a war wage of 4s. Out of that he may have had a sizable deduction to repay his training fees and the loan that paid for his tools. No doubt the remainder barely covered what mother or landlady expected for bed and board. As he approached his twenty-first birthday, and possibly a letter stating 'your services are no longer required', he would be getting 28s, including 8s war wage. As is well known, many ex-apprentices later returned and could expect a journeyman's rate of between 38 and 48s, depending on age, experience and the type of work undertaken. Adult pay rates started at the age of twenty, excluding apprentices. This had gone up from eighteen in the early 1920s.

Of the skilled shopmen of the 1930s and early 1940s, in 'Area 1', which included Swindon, most were eligible for the 46s rate. This included coach body makers, loco erectors, cabinetmakers, fitters and electricians. Some trades, such as wheelwrights, painters, wagon riveters and coach trimmers, were regarded less highly and were paid less.

Peter Reade said his first pay when learning to be a blacksmith was 30s, the starting figure for a smith's striker. After three years learning the trade, he would be eligible for the 38 to 46s rate. Most of the semi-skilled rates were between 30 and 36s, but they were better paid initially. If the work was heavy, such as boilermaking, or involved hot metals as did that of the stamper and drop hammerman, the wages were equal to those of many skilled grades. A semi-skilled grade-1 wagonbuilder's or springmaker's rate was also equal to that of the lower end of the skilled man's pay range. When starting new work, materials, nuts, washers and split pins had to be drawn from the stores and specialised tools were issued from the tool store. Two grades worked in the shop stores: the stores issuer and the storesman. The issuer was in charge, and the storesman was his general assistant. Their wages were worked out as a percentage above that of the grade-2 labourer in the same area. The rate for the stores issuer was between 29 and 44s. Depending on his grade, the storesmen received between 27 and 31s.

School leavers did not go straight inside at fourteen years old, so Jack Fleetwood started work as an errand boy at the Wiltshire Bacon Company shop in Regent Street, Swindon, next to the new Savoy Cinema.

> After a 'twelve month' [period] I went into the works, starting in the R Shop scraggery machining end faces on nuts [other railway works put boys on very similar work at first]. For this I got 12s 6d on the short week and 18s to £1 on the balance (piecework payout) week.

This was 1937: previously piecework bonus was not paid until the person reached the age of eighteen, although their work was taken into account. Jack knew the foundry labourers at Swindon as 'the 31 shilling men'; the semi-skilled were 'the 39 shilling men' and by the start of the war, a semi-skilled iron moulder was 'a 47 shilling man'. Jack was learning the craft of brass moulding and was rated, for the purpose of pay, slightly less highly than the men who produced (generally speaking) heavier iron castings.

Most men in the workshops rarely had the chance of 'Sunday time', which was time-and-a-half of flat rate, but they did get to work nights, thereby getting the higher rate of time-and-a-quarter from 10 p.m. to 6 a.m. At Swindon and elsewhere, with the gradual introduction of more reliable electrical machinery, a maintenance fitter would be paid to be on call at home at night, with someone being sent out to knock him up if required. Promotion to chargeman or inspector was considered an honour and was a good move towards becoming the foreman, but otherwise the small increase in pay did not tempt everyone to take on the extra responsibility. Promotion to foreman offered a man the opportunity to progress up through a lengthy seniority scale and the salary increases that went with it. All the company's supervisory staff, including the CME department foreman, were on the same salary scale, which was made up of five classes. Clerical staff were also on the same scale, excluding the lower half of their class 5. The foremen were paid their salary in weekly parts. A junior foreman was paid between 65s and 81s, depending on the number of men he had under his control and the length of time in that position. At the top end, the chief foreman, the man in overall charge of several areas and large numbers of men, would receive between 120 and 130s; more than double that of the tradesman or staff grade 4s in his charge.

Men who worked at railway electrical generating stations were normally paid enhanced rates. The electrical powerhouse at Swindon supplying its workshops, however, was not considered by the industrial court in 1922 to be of sufficient capacity, and the skilled workers therein were paid rates set for ordinary electricians. The plant became a sub-station when the works started receiving most of its electricity from the municipal supply in the 1930s. The dozen or so works' full time fire-brigade staff received 58s at ordinary grade plus an on-call allowance. Gatemen and watchmen were classed as semi-skilled, but were paid no more than a labourer, with a minimum of 30s.

In the offices, male workers up to the age of eighteen were officially referred to as 'junior clerks' and females were 'girl clerks'. At Swindon their senior colleagues preferred to call them 'office girls' or 'office boys'. They did little clerical work and plenty of errand running and odd jobs. In the mid-1930s, boys could start a year earlier than girls, at fifteen years old, on a salary of £35 per annum. Girls began their clerical careers on a wage of 17s 6d per week. Possibly uniquely among railway grades, this worked out equal to the annual salary of their male counterparts of the same age. The rates of pay for male clerical staff, published periodically by the NUR and the Railway Clerks Association, showed that in 1937 a junior clerk received an annual salary of £80. This had risen to £192 by 1948. There was a £10 annual increment following each birthday to a maximum salary of £200, although they should have been promoted into a higher class before reaching this limit. Mr F. G. Richens of the CME department said, in a lecture he gave to the GWR Debating Society in 1934, 'The automatic wage advancements up to the age of 31 make no distinction between the keen and the apathetic employee.' Women clerks, sometimes called W1s, were paid weekly and started on 30s, with the most senior female clerk receiving a minimum of 70s per week in 1937.

The course of progress up through the grades depended on age, experience and qualifications. Promotion was usually from within the department, if not the office. George Petfield says he does not remember anyone coming in from outside to fill a more senior position from 1944 until the 1960s. Grades 5 to 1 excluded ancillary office staff employed exclusively as timekeepers, messengers, assistants and those who supplied information to the clerks making out the paybills. At the top of the pay scale, the senior males (apart from those reaching the 'special classes') in class 1, with a minimum of five years in that post, were awarded £335 to £350 in 1937 and £460 to £490 in 1948: the higher figures were discretional. Beyond grade 1, promotion to 'special A' up to 'C' was as high as the most ambitious person could hope to reach before retirement. The salary for 'special C' was about £500 per annum in the mid-1930s, increasing slightly after two years' service. In 1948 this had risen to a starting figure of £600.

Office staff had been entitled to holidays with pay well before the shop workers. They also received their money in full from the company for a limited period when out sick. Staff grades 2 to 5 got twelve days' paid holiday, plus Good Friday and Christmas Day, but not until they had a minimum of ten years of service. Those in classes 1 and 2 got fifteen days, and those in 'special classes' received eighteen days' paid holidays. As well as the concessionary rail travel awarded to all workers, senior clerical and supervisory staff got first-class rail passes when they had completed two years of service.

In 1939 there were increases in the minimum wages of conciliation workers to 47s for men and 36s 6d for women. From 1 January 1940, it was agreed with the three rail unions to make a war wage advance of 4s per week to adult male conciliation grades or £10 per annum to male salaried staff, and 3s per week to adult females on the staff. When Peter Reade joined the company in 1939 working as a hammer driver, he was sixteen years old and so received the standard rate for juniors of that age, which was 10s, plus a small percentage war bonus amounting to about another 5 per cent. The war wage bonus was introduced in 1915 and was retained in principle and name throughout the inter-war years and on into the next war. This cost-of-living allowance amounted to 10 to 15 per cent extra (the higher percentage given to the lower paid) after the first twelve months of war. It was funded by the government and continued to be reviewed twice yearly; the rate of increase required to keep pace with the cost of living accelerated as the war continued.

The 1940s, despite all the upheaval, were to be more lucrative and secure for the men and women not called up than the previous decade. Now the amount of extra time required at the workplace was excessive, with twelve-hour day or night shifts on six days of the week. For some there was even the option of working the Sunday as well, but as the workers started to show signs of fatigue, it became counterproductive and a limit was imposed. Despite continuing increases in cost of living and rates of income tax, the buying power of the pound became fairly stable throughout the second half of the war. There were only the basic items available in the shops, but for those used to struggling to make ends meet, these were better times. The rationing of consumables started at the beginning of 1940, but there had already been shortages. Bread, cigarettes and beer never went 'on ration', but shopkeepers kept their limited supplies aside for their regulars. In the middle of 1941 it became necessary to ration clothing, and the following year it was sweets. Barbara Carter remembers running down Milton Road towards 'the factory' because she was often late. She said,

> At the bottom opposite the Medical Fund building you sometimes saw a queue of people which disappeared around the corner into Faringdon Road. That could only mean one thing: Blackwell's sweet shop actually had sweets for sale. For some workers the temptation was too much and they arrived late clutching a bag of wartime sweets.

John Brettell started his career as an office boy in 1941 and received the standard 8s a week. 'Although I was down as working in D Shop I actually spent my time in the Newburn Carriage Sheds,' he said. The Royal Engineers had taken over most of this building, which was only two years old. The railway staff that were there came over from D1 and D2 shops. When John started his apprenticeship on his sixteenth birthday, he too got the 10s rate, but the bonus had by then, two years into the war, gone up to 65 per cent. Years later he managed to get a copy of his personal record card when the staff records were all being relocated. This shows precisely how an apprentice fitter and turner was paid in wartime and how the war wage almost reached 100 per cent. At each birthday the wages increased: 1942 = 11s 6d plus 7s; 1943 = 14s plus 8s 10p; 1944 = 19s 6d plus 17s 2d; 1945 = 23s plus 21s 9d.

It was reported in the local evening paper that apprentices at the works had become increasingly dissatisfied with their pay scales. This came to a head in July and August of 1941, and they held meetings to decide what to do about it. Engineering apprentices in the shipyards at Clydeside and elsewhere, they said, were getting higher rates. They were also unhappy that women and dilutees coming into the workshops at Swindon were getting more after nine weeks training than lads who had been training for three or four years. They decided to approach the Amalgamated Engineering Union. If they would take up the case, it would be referred to the executive council and the shopmen's council and they would take it up with management. It appears to have all come to nothing, presumably because their money did soon go up as already mentioned.

In 1942 the trade unions submitted pay claims for minimum-rated conciliation and salaried staff. As usual, the workers' representatives, the unions and the national shopmen and electrical councils put in for more than they would be prepared to settle for. The *GWR Magazine* reported that with effect from 9 March, the Railway Staff National Tribunal would grant the following: the total war wage to be increased to 4s 6d per week for adult male conciliation grades who earned the minimum 48s industrial rate. Adult females (age twenty or over), taking the place of men, received the same rates and increases as the minimum-rated men. Class 5 male clerical staff would receive one extra annual increment of £10 to a maximum of £210 per annum at the age of thirty-two years. The Class 4 maximum would not exceed £220. The Class 2 female increment would rise to 2s 6d per week to a maximum of 62s 6d at thirty-two years of age. Only the salaried staff increases were guaranteed until the war's end. The tribunal left it to the two sides to consider the effects of this upon the pay differentials of the higher grades.

Within days of the end of the war, and with the backing of the new Labour government, an agreement was reached between the railway executive and the unions for improvements in standard rates of pay for all grades; an increase in the war advance; concessions in respect of annual leave; and the Sunday rate increased to time-and-three-quarters. The unions' claim for a forty-four-hour working week was resisted, but only until June 1947, when most CME grades would work five eight-hour shifts and a four-hour Saturday morning per week. The one week or six days' paid annual leave entitlement for all wages staff was to be doubled from 1946. This was in addition to receiving days off with ordinary rate pay for working Whit Monday or August Bank Holiday.

In 1947 the salaried staff's ordinary rostered working hours were reduced from forty-eight to forty-two per week, to be worked as five long and one short turns, or six equal turns. Those in classes 2 to 6, the special classes, and female class 1, were to be granted fifteen weekdays' annual leave instead of the twelve previous.

War bonuses were replaced by higher basic rates by 1950. Beyond that, the pay scales continued to be complex, despite the 'reorganisation' of 1948, with neither side willing to make the concessions that streamlining the rates would require. There were further improvements in overtime rates, lodging allowances and annual leave entitlement; time off to attend a funeral; new minimum rest intervals between turns of duty; and financial assistance for demotion and redundancy. The junior conciliation grades' scale started at 39s per week for fifteen-year-olds and up to 66s for nineteen-year-olds. Women were paid 2s less throughout the same range. Equal pay for women in the offices did not happen until after the introduction of the 1964 Sex Discrimination Act.

The average weekly earnings of railwaymen had doubled in the ten years since 1938 with a reduction in the working week of four hours. In the same period inflation had eroded the value of money by 72 per cent. Between 1948 and 1953 railwaymen's pay slipped below that of other industries.

In 1949 the men's side of the Railway Shopmen's National Council put in for an all-round increase of 10s a week and improved rates for Saturday working. More than 10,000 Swindon men would be affected by this. It was rejected by the Railway Executive as there was a pay freeze on at the time on account of the devaluation of the pound. Even the TUC advised the unions to show restraint. Despite this, the NUR, the Confederation of Engineers and Shipbuilders and the AEU put in for a pound a week increase. The negotiations became protracted and in January 1950 the unions asked for an increase in the minimum wage from 92s 6d to £5. Mr Pearce, the Swindon district secretary of the Amalgamated Engineering Union, pointed out that the cost of living and profits were up and so was production within the industry. The RE eventually agreed to pay rises if they were linked to schemes for reducing costs, but the unions resisted this because it would mean redundancies. In February 1951, with a new Minister for Labour, Aneurin Bevan, an agreement gave all wages and salaried staff a pay rise, broadly equivalent to 7.5 per cent. The new British Railways' management said in a declaration issued to every employee that 'Only part of the extra £12 million to be spent on salaries and wages can be recovered from savings effected under nationalisation, this means that in order to find the money passengers and senders of goods by rail will be asked to pay more.' Another stipulation of the pay increases was that 'opportunities of reorganisation and technical progress must be given full scope'.

Harry Bartlett moved from fitter and turner in 15 Shop to the 'carriage side' cost office in 1957. By this time orders for carriages were being diverted elsewhere, causing a surplus of labour in the carriage works. Harry started on 233s as a temporary estimator. As a journeyman he had been getting slightly more, but now he was on the staff and would climb the new pay scale by annual increments.

There is no mention of the 'special classes' in the National Union of Railwaymen pay rates for salaried staff before nationalisation. So it is likely that this was the start of lower management in the GWR and anyone promoted above grade 1 was presumably expected to sever all union loyalties. Only senior management were above a 'special C' grade and only they were not paid in cash. They received an annual salary by way of a bank cheque sent down from Paddington with a representative of the chief clerk. Alan Peck noted in his rough book, while working in the drawing office, that the vacant post of outstation materials assistant to the loco works manager was being offered with a starting salary of £650. This was in 1949 and presumably this position, which interested the twenty-nine-year-old Peck, was then paid at the minimum starting figure for senior staff. Later, as its unofficial archivist, Mr Peck wrote the only complete history of Swindon works. The CME's chief accountant Mr Gardner said in his lecture to the Swindon Engineering Society in 1929, 'The salaries figure is of course subject to constant scrutiny in that additional staff are only appointed after careful consideration and advances (increases) in salary are only made as authorised by the Board of Directors.' Established management positions were rarely, if ever, considered dispensable on the Great Western, but there would be questions asked about increases in personal expenses or why certain sections of a department wanted to increase their manpower.

The first reference I have found relating to piecework in GWR documents dates from early 1909. This company was not among the first to offer financial bonuses to improve output, even though it was shown to work. Manual workers in the CME department were either on piecework or day work, or sometimes a combination of the two. Men on piecework were paid a bonus, calculated as a percentage of their daily wage rate and paid out once a fortnight (converting the piecework figures onto the paybills fortnightly instead of every week greatly reduced the work for the accounts department). The percentage received depended on the productivity averaged out over the week, between all the gangs working on a section within the shop or outstation. A man could expect a fairly consistent weekly bonus, known as 'the balance', as long as his work was not held up before reaching the gang. Every job in the CME department had to be priced at every stage (or detail) or, if the job was repetitive, given a time allowance. Piece rates were set to allow the worker not less than 33.3 per cent of his basic day or time rate. This figure had been more generous than other railway companies, until the industrial court ruling of 1922. The balance represented the amount by which the total value of the piecework certificate exceeded the basic rate earnings of the gang during the fortnightly period. In the workshops the shop clerks issued the store's order forms and drawings with each batch of work to be undertaken. The inspector, a staff grade 2, was responsible for checking the standard of work produced and seeing that the order was completed. Tables showing the various rates were held by the chargeman of the gang. Some jobs required teamwork to complete, as in Peter Reade's case: it was he, as the blacksmith, who earned the bonus for his strikers and himself, as they could only work at his speed. The blacksmiths were exceptional in that they would work out from the drawing how much material they required and price up the job themselves. 'Although most smiths did every type of work in the shop, it was usual practice for the man who set the price to do that particular job,' said Peter.

I do not have actual piecework prices or times of any CME shop work, so the following example from running shed times shows how the piecework bonus could be earned. At Old Oak Common in 1931, a fire-dropper was allowed thirty minutes for clearing the grate of each Metro tank and other small shunting engines, and shovelling out the ash-pits. He was allowed sixty minutes for the larger 4-6-0 classes, forty-eight and fifty-four minutes for intermediate types, and ninety minutes for ROD freight engines. These times varied at other sheds depending on the facilities available. In theory, if he worked hard he would accumulate time. For instance, if throughout the turn of duty, he had worked on six small locomotives at thirty minutes each and nine large ones at sixty minutes, he had totalled up twelve hours. So his day balance is 50 per cent because he had accumulated four hours beyond his eight actual hours worked, or a half again. If Jack Fleetwood's memory is correct, one eight-hour shift in the iron foundry was allowed for a semi-skilled man to prepare ten moulding boxes and pack them with sand, to cast five or six locomotive firebars per box. His piecework time allowance was ten hours and twenty-five minutes. Therefore, the time difference for him equated to 30 per cent. A good weekly balance in the case of a 'factory' man at least, would be around 50 per cent, but an average was around 35 per cent of the flat rate, or about 16s for a skilled man in the 1930s. Jack said the average balance figure was more like 50 per cent by the middle of the war, and in the 1950s the unions had negotiated conditions whereby much higher payments again could be achieved.

The detail piecework rates were reviewed by both sides whenever working arrangements changed. The men might claim that a time allowance was, in practice, unprofitable and therefore as a gang they could not hope to achieve their quota. If working practices or wage rates changed, the men were likely to seek a review of the piecework rates, but they knew if they made too much fuss, the work-study people would be brought in. Although the piecework committee was expected to settle differences, I have seen several letters showing that the chief mechanical engineer himself occasionally intervened. The CME's name usually appeared on notice-board circulars and letters relating to departmental working conditions. This added weight to the instruction, but it was one of the CME's assistants who normally dealt with labour relations and conditions. Mr Collett and Mr Stanier had, in turn, spent time dealing with disputes over pay and piecework, as did the CME's outdoor assistant Mr Crump. They would have to meet with the men's representatives, especially when the delicate matter of cutting pay and piecework rates was necessary. According to letters between the depots and the management at Swindon, matters concerning piecework were expected to be sorted out locally and when Swindon did intervene, they did not usually settle things in favour of the men. Altering detail piecework prices was not something the company entered into lightly (see letter from Mr Rodda, the divisional locomotive superintendent at Worcester, who became works manager at Wolverhampton loco, carriage and wagon works in 1929). While pay rates were largely decided independently, the company presided over all other payments, unless they formed part of a nationally agreed wage settlement. In the early days, when the Great Western had a choice, they dispensed wages every two weeks so as to minimise the man-hours devoted to its preparation. Piecework payments, being an arrangement set up by the company, could not be legislated on from outside so that remained a fortnightly payout.

Despite all the man hours compiling the figures, piecework was a clever way for the company to maximize output. Apart from the chance to earn a bit extra, no gang wanted a reputation for consistently achieving less than other gangs and therefore reducing the overall balance. On the other hand, there might be some benevolence shown to a fellow who was genuinely not 'up to the job'. Harold Stoker, a fitter, turner and erector in the 1920s and 30s, had developed a sight defect like his father before him. His gang did make allowances for him, presumably with the foreman's knowledge, so that he kept his job. The other reason to make up the wages with bonuses and allowances was that it made the men think twice before taking time off sick. A day-rate was paid as an alternative to piece-rate, to non-productive workers. They received their bonus as a fixed 13.75 per cent of the flat wage. Day-rate workers included watchmen, gatemen, electricians, beltmen and WC attendants, although the latter two were phased out during the 1940s.

Besides the overtime rates of between time-and-a-quarter and time-and-three-quarters, certain work attracted other financial allowances for permanent and temporary staff which had been negotiated through sectional councils or workshop committees. Conditions attached to wage increases often included the loss of an allowance, and so it was that the dirty work allowance was discontinued in the 1920s. Individual cases where conditions were particularly unpleasant were still considered for extra payment by the local committees. A bonus of 3s was paid to men who were part of a 'breakdown gang' on each occasion that they were called upon to go out with the breakdown train in an emergency. Normal overtime payments were, of course, paid in addition to the call-out payment if the crew were required outside of the normal working day. Where men who were not regular members of a breakdown gang were called upon to augment those re-railing an engine or vehicle, or clearing debris from the track, they were also entitled to the 3s bonus. Outstation men often worked longer day or night shifts, and could claim travelling and breakdown time where applicable, as well as the food and lodging allowance, which was 2s 6d per week before the war.

The resident workshop staff could not claim the allowances for food and lodgings like some of their colleagues who worked away, and no doubt this was pointed out when negotiating piecework. Before nationalisation, there was a small annual payment made to the qualified first aider of the shop. With this, he had to replace all the supplies he used, such as bandages, iodine, absorbent lint and smelling salts. The remainder might cover some of the piecework bonus he would lose while doing ambulance training and practising first aid. He also received an extra free travel pass every time he passed the annual test. Technical, clerical and supervisory staff could claim travelling expenses when on company business and lodging expenses when away from their home districts on relief duties. Items that could be claimed in personal expense accounts and entered in the paybill as petty disbursements included travelling, laundry, postal and telephone charges, removal allowance and cab hire for conveyance of cash to and from the bank. Allowances and enhanced rates for clerical staff and most other grades in the CME department were given for temporary duty in a higher grade, lodging and travelling. Holiday and sick pay of course, only included the 'cost of living allowance' (until phased out), on top of the basic wage.

Another way a bit extra could be made was for a worker to come up with a way of increasing efficiency in his workplace. A 'suggestion scheme' had been in operation on the GWR since 1913, the first on any British railway. A financial incentive was offered if a person could convince his superiors his idea would save the company money. There was always scope for improving working methods to reduce paperwork, speed up production or reduce the amount of scrap (known by some at Swindon as 'shxxxers'). Carefully drawn diagrams with text were required for consideration by a committee and, to avoid any prejudice, the identity of the person submitting a suggestion was not disclosed. The scheme was apparently a long drawn-out process. Alternatively, some men put forward ideas directly to their foreman who, in some cases, took all the credit himself. This would have caused resentment and suppressed further efforts.

A standard system of adjusting wages was used in the 1930s. It was started during the war when inflation was high and the railways were under state control. Before that, the GWR had prepared their own graph showing the rise and fall of the cost of living as determined by Board of Trade statistics, which they used to adjust the wages. Wages were higher in the 1920s than in the 1930s because of inflation caused by the First World War, but of course the buying power of currency was reduced. During this period the Ministry of Labour published a 'cost of living' index figure based on a quarterly review. The GWR, like other British railways, was bound by the index and would adjust the cost of living allowance (usually referred to as the war wage bonus) accordingly. This was known as the 'sliding scale arrangement'. The lowest paid grades were given special consideration (something they didn't get with the cuts in the standard wage rates between 1928 and 1936). The index figure at which the bonus became payable was set lower for those on the lower rates. Wages had been falling steadily with the sliding scale arrangement since a peak in late 1920, and the COL index figure reached its lowest point, compared to the baseline year of 1914, during the recession of the early 1930s. From the first few weeks of the decade until July 1938, the figure did not rise above 60.

Management and government hoped the sliding scale would break the cycle of what they saw as unreasonable demands followed by labour disruption. As early as 1924 it seemed that this might not be the case, moving an anonymous writer to submit a letter to the *GWR Magazine* in response to the unrest. He or she pointed out that the financial advantage was already offered to railwaymen and that the railway pay rates compared very well to those of the other great industries, 'so much so that there was a tendency for the position of railway workers to be held up as an argument for improving conditions in other trades'. It was also pointed out that the shopmen lost a smaller percentage of their war wage when the COL index figure went down (their wage adjustments were not linked to the sliding scale). The letter went on to imply that the rank and file should remain loyal to the company during a downturn in its fortunes, and warned of the very real danger that increased wages expenditure could mean job cuts and increases in fares.

The popular monthly *GWR Magazine* was produced at Paddington and the editor was appointed from the general manager's staff. Sir Felix Pole said in *His Book* that 'the *GWR Magazine* played an important part' in the family spirit promoted by the company in the early 1920s. The publication of the professional and recreational achievements among all ranks, for a small subscription, undoubtedly improved the sense of family. When disputes became news, however, the widely read magazine's 'appeals to reason' must have eroded the men's support considerably.

In 1931 the company's chief accountant said that the wages bill had increased by 150 per cent from 1913, while passenger traffic was not more than 20 per cent above pre-war numbers and that more could not be taken out of the industry than was put in. The Great Western Railway, along with the other railway companies of mainland Britain – the Southern; the London, Midland & Scottish; the London & North Eastern; and the London Underground – applied to the Wages Board for a further reduction in the wage rates, as the cost-of-living allowance had all but disappeared. Traffic and docks' receipts continued to fall and reductions in the wages bill would help the railways to remain competitive. The first reduction in the gross wage had been agreed with the unions in August 1928 as a temporary measure. The rail unions and the National Shopmen's Council agreed to the cuts in return for some assurances against job cuts and reduced working. They also submitted other proposals to the board and to the railway companies, which were rejected. Officers and staff with salaries of £350 or more per annum had their normal pay increases deferred with the possibility of a reduction at a later date, while directors' fees, salaries and wages had already been reduced by 2.5 per cent during 1929–30.

The conclusions of the National Wages Board, published in March 1931, included increased rates for conciliation and workshop grades in respect of day and night overtime, night duty, Sunday and public holidays. Although with working hours being cut, few in the department would benefit in the foreseeable future. Only in cases where double time had been paid was there a reduction in the rate, to time-and-two-thirds. Conciliation grades had lost 2.5 per cent of their basic earnings in 1928: now they would lose a further 2.5 per cent from earnings in excess of 40s per week. For example, a man earning 50s would lose a total of 1s 6d, made up as follows: 1s 3d being 2.5 per cent from the whole 50s, plus 3d being 2.5 per cent on the amount over 40s. Salaried staff wages had been reduced by the same amount, and they would lose a further 2.5 per cent on earnings above £100 per year. Workshop grades went from 2.5 per cent to a straight 4.25 per cent cut.

In 1932 yet another reduction in its wages bill was the only solution to improving the company's financial position during this time of severe economic depression and to honour its commitment to shareholders. Railwaymen's salaries and wages in real terms were still significantly higher compared to the baseline year of 1914; in fact, higher than the average outside the industry. The joint railway companies proposed an all-round percentage reduction taking the amount to 10 per cent since 1928, and not surprisingly direct talks with the unions to this effect failed. The 10 per cent cut was never introduced because the situation had eased before the Wages Boards could come to a decision. There were no further moves to increase the reductions which, with 'partial restorations', lasted well into 1937. By 1938 the COL index had climbed back to 60 per cent above the pre-war (1914) level, with 25,000 Western men receiving wage increases thanks to the reversal of the rate cuts and the sliding-scale arrangement.

With every adjustment to the pay rates and bonuses, the CME department at Swindon works GW6 received notification from the general manager's office. Their accounts department then prepared new figures and a further letter was sent via the divisional superintendents for the information of the local paybill staff. These letters explained how the changes would affect the various sections of workers in the department and were usually signed by either the chief clerk to the CME, the outdoor assistant, or sometimes the principal assistant to the CME. Notices from the general manager, Paddington, for display at depots and cabins, then followed.

Manual workers and others, whose remuneration did not exceed £250 per annum and who were not members of a superannuation scheme, had to subscribe to the National Health and Pensions' Insurance. Every insurable employee had to hand in to the company a current insurance card and pay a contribution each week. In 1936 men aged sixteen to sixty-five paid 10d and women paid 7d per week. The GWR matched the contribution, making the individual's total stamp 1s 8d and 1s 2d respectively. If the insured employee was a member of either the GWR Staff Friendly Society or Locomotive Running Department Staff Approved Society, they would contribute 1d less and the employer 1d more. Sickness benefit (claimable after twenty-six weeks of contributions) was 9s per week for men, increasing to 15s after 104 weeks. Women's benefit was proportionately less.

Thus all workers in the CME department became members of the Medical Fund Society, but Swindon people paid extra for local facilities such as the dispensary and baths. Family men paid the maximum 10d per week and this also covered any children under sixteen, while retired members without dependents paid the least – a halfpenny. Members had access to a whole range of medical and health services, unlike those in other schemes elsewhere in the country. The book *A Century of Medical Service*, a history of the MFS, shows that the subscription fees charged in 1947 remained unchanged from the 1930s. This may be because in the later period, prior to the takeover by the National Health Service, the fee was separate from sick pay deduction. Bernard Darwin's book also gives the company's contribution to the MFS as £1,750 for the year 1947. On top of this, they, and not the subscriptions, paid the salaries of the medical staff. Later came the National (Health) Insurance, which George Petfield remembers paying at a fixed amount of 6s 9d in the mid-1950s.

Those same employees whose total rate of remuneration was £250 per annum or less in 1936, had to be insured against unemployment. When the worker commenced employment, he or she had to obtain an unemployment book from the labour exchange and hand it to the company. The rates and concessions were the same as for the National

Health and Pensions' Insurance, and the two were known collectively as National Insurance. Contributions were payable every week that wages were received, including paid holidays and sick leave with pay. The other compulsory deduction was income tax; the paybill clerks were frequently reminded of the importance of entering the necessary particulars on wages income tax cards. Occasionally the company was advised of a court order taken out against a man to retrieve unpaid loans or fines through the paybill.

The 'privileges' offered to Great Western men – the reduced rail fares, the apprenticing of a worker's son, or the cheap coal and wood – all came at a price, regardless of whether the man and his family took advantage of them or not. Up until 1927 the men in the workshops had been paid according to rates set by their various crafts throughout the industry. Because these rates were calculated outside the company where these 'privileges' were not given, a fixed sum deduction was made as a 'differential'.

A person may be indebted for coal, firewood or scrap timber provided by the company for private use, and this was deducted automatically every balance week. The various deductions were calculated to be taken either weekly, as was health insurance, unemployment insurance and savings bank payments, or fortnightly, as were payments for coal, wood, life insurance, medical fund and Railway Benevolent Institution subscriptions. Gas supplied by the company for household use and the mechanics' sub were deducted every four weeks. Those paying in for railway convalescent home cover were 'stopped' every three months, and payments to the casualty fund were taken annually.

Membership of the Mechanics' Institute was readily subscribed to by most Swindon workers because, between the wars, 4d per week allowed them and their families to apply for a free pass and travel on one of the annual holiday (known as Trip to the masses) special trains. After the war the men successfully negotiated through the Works' Committee that Trip train travel would be granted to all employees and not MI members only. Unlimited reduced rail fares, known as privilege tickets, were available to all employees and covered the workman's trains. Again, after the war, it was conceded that railway staff could commute to Swindon Junction or Town, free of charge. Besides Trip, one further free travel pass was given to each employee, which was increased after nationalisation and included one or two British Railways passes (known as 'foreigners'), depending on their length of service. A card was issued to past and present employees authorising them to obtain free and privileged tickets at the works booking office from 10.30 to 11.00 a.m. any weekday morning.

The Helping Hand Fund had been aiding deserving cases among past and present workers since 1924. They held fundraising events and collected contributions, then allocated financial assistance where needed. It was claimed to have been the only scheme of its kind on any British railway. As with other optional charity contributions, the worker could choose to have payments deducted at source. One of the advantages was that if he chose not to give, this remained confidential. The famous male voice choir, the GWR (Accounts) Staff Gleemen, were sufficiently popular to record some of their songs for the Parlophone Company in the early 1930s. They donated the royalties from sales to the GWR Helping Hand Fund.

There were many organisations offering benefits to Swindon railwaymen, including the GWR Loco & Carriage Department Sick Fund Society, which had offices at 6 and 7 Oxford Street. This was the approved society for health and pension insurance, and about 50 per cent of local railway staff belonged to it. For a fee of around 6d per week the wise investor could insure he would 'get by' if and when he found himself 'out on the club'. There was no shortage of private insurance available for accident, unemployment, retirement and death. The Boiler Makers Iron and Steel Shipbuilders' Society had a local branch secretary in Swindon to deal with industrial injury compensation, as did other staff and trade associations, and successful claims were paid via the railway's wages department. The GWR had arrangements with various pension and benevolent funds such as the Ocean Accident and Guarantee Corporation, which was promoted through the staff magazine. Here the subscriber paid an extra 1*d* for the insurance edition of the monthly magazine, and received a range of death and accident coverage while working or travelling on the GWR.

All salaried staff were required to join a pension scheme, such as the Great Western Railway Salaried Staff Supplemental Pension Fund, the GWR Salaried Staff Retiring Allowances Fund or the GWR Female Clerks Pension Fund. The employee paid between 4 and 6.75 per cent of their salary from the time of joining a scheme until their retirement, with the company contributing a like amount. The fixed percentage contribution depended on a medical examination and how old a person was when they joined. No one was admitted as a new member over the age of 39 years. Every member who attained the age of 60 was, on leaving the service, entitled to a capital sum and an annuity for life: the values of which depended, of course, upon the completed years of membership.

In July 1941 the various pension and superannuation funds, including the GWR Engineman and Fireman's Mutual Assurance Sick and Superannuation Society, became known collectively as the GWR Superannuation Fund. The next of kin of a superannuated man who was 'called up' received the difference between his forces pay and his normal railway pay, less the contribution. When, from about 1942, it became clear that the war was not going to finish quickly, the directors of the company, as trustees, suspended all new applications. George Petfield in 22 office, along with all new appointments at that time, had to wait until 1945 to join the fund. George remembers some of his colleagues joining the London & North Eastern Railway (LNER) scheme after nationalisation because they offered more favourable terms. Some men with families paid into the Widows and Orphans Fund to ensure some financial cover if they, as the breadwinner, died before those who depended on them. The shopmen did not have a superannuation scheme until as late as 1954.

Fixing plywood roofs to 12-ton wagons. The piecework rate was eight roofs completed per gang, per shift. Notice the suspended cradle for holding tools. (GWR)

With a locomotive firebox suspended from a swing jib, Elma Howard is 'holder up'. She is employed between the 'rivet hotter' and the man using a Fielding & Platt fixed riveting machine. This was labour intensive because it was important to have the rivets at the right 'heat' when the opposing head was formed. Elma lived in Percy Street. (GWR)

Looking down the main shopping street in the town, Regent Street. The Wiltshire Bacon Company on the right was where Jack Fleetwood worked as an errand boy until he went into Swindon Works aged fifteen. (Author's collection)

GREAT WESTERN RAILWAY.

GENERAL MANAGER'S OFFICE,
PADDINGTON STATION,
LONDON, W.2.
June 27th, 1938.

Circular No. 3496.
(R1/38,396)

RATES OF PAY OF RAILWAY STAFF.

The official cost of living index figure having fallen to 55 per cent. above pre-war level, the following reductions have to be made in accordance with the sliding scale arrangements as from July 1st, 1938, in the rates of pay of staff in the undermentioned groups:—

SECTION OF STAFF.	REDUCTION IN COST OF LIVING BONUS OR WAR WAGE. *Per Week.*
Adult conciliation grades (including those embraced in railway dock and steamboat staff agreements of August 4th, December 1st and 2nd, 1920, and March 19th, 1921, and Canal Staff embraced in agreement dated September 1st, 1926):—	
Where the amount of cost of living bonus is 1/- or more	1/-
Where the amount of cost of living bonus is less than 1/-	Balance to be withdrawn.

The grades of adult conciliation staff in which cost of living bonus will be payable as from 1st July, 1938, are shown in the schedule which accompanies this circular.

Adult male wages staff not in conciliation grades, to whom the war wage of 25/- per week applies ...	1/-
Women to whom the war wage of 13/- per week applies	1/-
Charwomen who are in receipt of war wage, and are not in receipt of a consolidated rate:—	
In receipt of wage (excl. war wage) under 10/- per week	6d.
,, ,, ,, ,, 10/- per week and over	9d.
Charwomen who are in receipt of a consolidated rate :—	
In receipt of consolidated wage under 18/- per week	6d.
,, ,, ,, ,, 18/- per week and over	9d.

The paybills for the week ending Saturday, 2nd July, 1938, are to be made up on the new rates and the amount accrued at the higher rate in respect of the four days due is to be entered below the rate of each person affected, e.g.,

Reduction 1/- per week	... ...	8d.
,, 9d. ,, ,,	... ...	6d.
,, 6d. ,, ,,	... ...	4d.

JAMES MILNE,
General Manager.

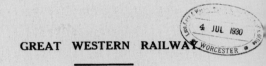

GREAT WESTERN RAILWAY.

4 JUL 1930 WORCESTER

NOTICE TO THE STAFF.

Rates of Pay of Railway Staff—Sliding Scale.

In accordance with the Sliding Scale arrangement, an adjustment in Rates of Pay will operate from July 1st, 1930, the cost of living index figure having fallen to 54 per cent. above pre-war level.

SECTION OF STAFF.	AMOUNT OF REDUCTION PER WEEK.
Adult male staff in conciliation grades ; railway dock and steamboat staff embraced in agreements of August 4th, December 1st and 2nd, 1920, and March 19th, 1921 ; and Canal Staff embraced in agreement dated September 1st, 1926:—	
Where amount of cost of living bonus is 2/- or more	2/-
Where amount of cost of living bonus is less than 2/- {	Balance to be Withdrawn
Adult male wages staff not in Conciliation Grades to whom the war wage of 26/- per week applies }	2/-

PADDINGTON STATION,
June 28th, 1930.

J. MILNE,
General Manager.

Above left: A private notice detailing the reduction in the staff's rates of pay.

Above right: A notice to the staff informing them of the reduction in their pay.

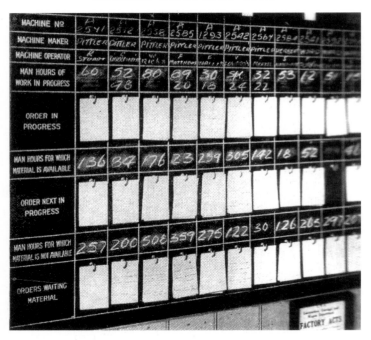

The loading board in T shop office showing machine work 'in progress' and 'in hand'. Note the Factories Act notice below. (GWR)

INCOME TAX YEAR 1944-45
CERTIFICATE OF PAY AND TAX DEDUCTED

Fleetwood J   CHECK No 6148

(Name of employee and Works No., if any)

Code No. at 5 April, 1945
(Enter "E" if an Emergency Card
is in use at 5 April, 1945)   *14*

District
Refce. (if any)   *65371 703*

	Gross pay			Tax		
	£	s.	d.	£	s.	d.
1. Pay and tax in respect of previous employment(s) in 1944-45 taken into account in arriving at the tax deductions made by me/us						
2. PAY AND TAX IN MY/OUR EMPLOYMENT ...	*344*	*4*	*2*	*76*	*18*	*0*

I/We certify that the particulars given above include the total amount of pay (including overtime, bonus, commission, etc.) paid to you by me/us in the year ended 5 April, 1945 and the total tax deducted by me/us (less any refunds) in that year.   FOR F. W. HAWKSWORTH

....*W.J.B*.........Employer

....Date

TO THE EMPLOYEE. Keep this certificate. It will help you to check the Notice of Assessment which the Tax Office will send you in due course.

P60   *£5-13-0 AFTER TAX*

Jack Fleetwood's P60 certificate for the year ended 5 April 1945. (J. Fleetwood)

There were three types of electric Muldivo calculators used at Swindon from 1936; earlier models were hand operated. Muldivo was the name of the British importer and distributor. (*GWR Magazine*)

Dinner break in R machine shop in 1924. As with most workshops, the machine shops still required men to work at benches using handtools. (R. Hatherall, courtesy of R. Clarke)

GREAT WESTERN RAILWAY.

COPY.

WO.

Chief Mechanical Engineer's Department,

DIVISIONAL LOCOMOTIVE, CARRIAGE & WAGON SUPERINTENDENT'S OFFICE,

Telephone :
WORCESTER 530

PRIVATE.

Swindon.   WORCESTER.

Please quote this reference—
49714
13.

Sat. 3rd December 1927.   Your reference—
3273.

Dear Sir,

Shop Committee - Worcester.
——

I am obliged by yours of the 30th ultimo, but must
inform you that the functions of the Shop Committee do not
embrace any discussion of detail Piecework prices, and you should
be careful to avoid entering into such discussions.

There is no objection, however, to discussing detailed
piecework prices with representatives of the Shop Committee who are
members of the grade concerned, but the obvious course to take is
for piecework prices to be discussed with the individual Chargeman
responsible for the work, this question always being considered
in the nature of a contract between the men doing the work
and the Management.

If the men wish to detail the matter to anyone it must
be to a representative of their own grade upon the Shop Committee,
for these new committees cannot hope to successfully function
as a whole if they endeavour to settle detail piecework prices.

Yours truly,

For C.B. Collett.
(Sd.) W.A.S.

H.C. Rodda Esq.,
Worcester.

A letter from Mr Rhodda concerning piecework prices. (Author's collection)

4

Paybill Production

The massive task of producing the individual paybill accounts for all the workers in the department had become partly mechanised by the early 1930s. Twenty-five years later the best possible methods of processing the accounts, and in particular the paybills, given that they had to be completed every seven days, was still a top priority. This is why one of the first computers to be used in industry was installed in the works. The GWR had always employed the best technology available for its wages production. Had they chosen not to, other methods would have failed to interest the railway press and the historian could have been forgiven for thinking the whole subject was unremarkable. Of the period, 1937 was a good year for the company, but there was a large increase in the cost of salaries and wages. For every £1 taken in receipts, they paid out 11s in salaries, wages and personal expenses. This was not only the largest single item of expenditure, it was larger than all the other costs put together. The wages bill for the CME department was around £6.5 million; they could not afford to be unremarkable in the way it was handed out.

From September 1936, the start of the morning shift in the workshops was changed to 7.55 a.m. instead of 8.00 a.m. Monday to Saturday. The factory hooter was activated by mains steam. It was sounded an hour before the start time in the morning, to help people to rise in time for work. Then there were short blasts, ten and five minutes before the start of the morning and afternoon shifts, and a longer blast at the actual start time. Dinner time was one hour, which started at 12.30 p.m. Office staff were not governed by the hooter and their times varied slightly. The afternoon shift finished at 5.30 p.m. and when the Saturday shift was in operation it finished at 12 noon. When twelve-hour shifts were introduced during the war, the day shift finished at 7.55 pm as the night shift began.

The system at Swindon allowed the man in the workshops up to half an hour after the last hooter to 'book on', with loss of pay of course, but after that he or she was sent home for the day. Before the war all latecomers had to see the foreman before starting work, knowing that he had the authority to dismiss a man over bad timekeeping. Most of the men were rarely, if ever, late or off with sickness, and many shops had someone that claimed never to have had a day out ill in all their years 'inside'. Peter Reade's old foreman Mr Titcombe, for instance, retired from the stamping shop in 1949 claiming he had completed 51 years of service without a single week's absence through illness.

The method of recording the men's attendance and punctuality in the Swindon workshops was by allocating each a brass timecheck, sometimes referred to as a 'tally' or 'ticket', stamped with his paybill number. The idea probably originated in the mining industries, where metal checks and boards were a reliable way of knowing who was below ground. A board with numbered hooks to hang the checks was fixed to the wall near the entrance to the shop; larger workshops had more than one board. The checkboards varied in size and design but they could all be closed with a sliding glass cover. Like most wooden fittings and fixtures 'inside', they would have been made by the works' carpenters. Before the final hooter sounded for the start of the shift, each worker would be required to remove his check, and only his check, and retain it. The 'checky', usually a shop labourer, was responsible for closing the glass cover at the start of the shift, thereby excluding all latecomers. Coloured penalty checks, showing a quarter or half an hour's pay to be forfeited, would be placed on the hook of anyone not conforming to this procedure, unless they were on nights or working away, in which case alternative checks would cover their hooks in their absence.

In Edwardian times 'losing a quarter' or 'a half' meant not being allowed to start until after the breakfast or dinner break. At the end of the shift, the men would have to return their checks, which in the event, were usually thrown at the wooden tray beneath the board. The poorly paid checky, who gladly worked extra on either end of the shift to earn a little more, would retrieve all the checks and return them to the correct hooks. The checkboard system was, according to the company rulebook, 'worked according to local arrangements'. The only condition that came down from Paddington was that the checks never left the premises. Years earlier the reverse happened: the checks were handed in when the owner was at work and kept by him after 'knocking off'.

After the commencement of the shift, time office personnel would record the remaining checks and note any penalty or alternative checks placed on the hooks by the checky. This information was then compiled at one of the time offices. There were time offices east, west, at Rodbourne Lane, another on the carriage side and one for the running shed staff. George Petfield, who worked in the wages office, doesn't remember receiving the time-keeping records from the time offices, only direct from the chargeman from the shop, so he assumes the system was altered before 'his time', which began in 1951. Completed paybill sheets were returned to the shop offices every week to be signed by the foreman, who did not always have the inclination to check too closely what he was signing. The chargeman also used the checkboard to determine the attendance when compiling the piecework sheets. Jack Fleetwood's chargehand in the iron foundry would withhold some of the piecework account 'in the back of the book', then claim extra for the men before Christmas and Trip . Up until the late 1940s the time check was also required to be handed to the lavatory attendant when going to the toilet, as a maximum of ten minutes was allowed: more than that and a quarter of an hour's pay was lost.

Salaried staff did not have to use a checkboard system, and their start and finish times were staggered slightly from the workshops. All salaried staff in the shops were required to sign in at one of the time offices before the start of the shift in the morning. Some workers on irregular shifts, such as maintenance engineers and those not allocated to a particular shop, were required to use the check system at one of the time offices. There was an unwritten law that allowed staff grades to arrive up to two minutes late and to leave two minutes early, while the men in the shops expected to wash their hands and perhaps change their outer clothes during work time before going home. The use of the checkboards for timekeeping at Swindon works lasted right up until the 1970s, when time stamp clocks and punchcards were brought in. The latter were nothing new and had been in limited use elsewhere on the Western for many years. The works had tried them themselves, well before the 1930s, but the idea was not taken up, probably because the early design was unreliable. The fire station did use a time clock recorder: one of the few places in the works to do so. As an office boy in the east time office in 1953, Alan Lambourn would go and collect the clock rolls from there once a week.

An amusing story recalled in the *Swindon Railway News* involved Mr K. J. Cook, who was at the time the loco works manager. The story goes that Mr Cook came into the shop and noticed an area of floor near the checkboard had sunk a little, and remarked with a smile that it was 'probably due to all you chaps hanging about round the checkboard at the end of the day waiting for the hooter to blow'. He didn't get away with that one: 'T'aint caused by the weight o' money we gets, any'ow,' said a voice from the back.

When working 'outstation', the person in charge usually collected the timesheets from his men and recorded any lateness, overtime and leave. Sometimes these details were phoned in direct to their workshop office. A signed copy of hours worked was returned to the individual before payday and he had to have it ready for inspection if required when collecting his pay. Whenever possible, arrangements were made for the outstation gangs to sign on and off under the supervision of a local station or department, if they were not arriving direct from Swindon.

At the works on the day before payday, the 'checky' would collect paychecks from the cash office. The person issuing these checks was provided with a tick list showing the names and numbers of men to be paid that week. The checky or other designated person was responsible for distributing the checks and satisfying himself as to the identity of the payees. By the 1930s paychecks were mainly made of copper, except the stores checks, which were of an alloy, often referred to as 'white metal'. Some shops had the check drilled so that they could be collected from the checkboard on payday. As with the timechecks, each had the pay number stamped on the face. Blocks of numbers were allocated permanently to each shop and not to the workman. The hundred or so workers in the iron foundry had pay numbers from 5700; the chair foundry from 6000; the brass foundry from 6100 and so on. Most sets of numbers were four digits, some less. Jack Fleetwood remembers that 'in the early days, a charge of five shillings was made if a man lost his check. In later years "ol checky" always seemed to have a few blanks that could be die stamped, thus avoiding the charge.' Clerical, supervisory and other salaried staff did not have to hand in a paycheck, but they still needed a registered pay number. All paybills were identified by the recipient's name and number, which would be required in any discussion with the wages department.

In 1951, George, by now a grade 4 clerk, moved to the loco wages office. This occupied the top floor of the loco managers' office block. The wages office on the carriage side was also in close proximity to their managers' offices. The only time these two sets of staff worked together, prior to the amalgamation in June 1952, was during the paying out, when all available staff were used to cover every shop simultaneously. The loco wages office was split into various sections: George was in Bert Broad's section, one of three dealing with the locomotive works; other sections covered mechanical productions, motive power, salaried staff and stores. Each had eight people including a section chief, for which two large desks were positioned back to back with four people working each side. Staff worked in pairs: George worked with Kathleen Foster, who had recently moved over from the C & W wages office; they later became husband and wife. Between them they would deal with all the timesheets sent in from the iron, brass and (track) chair foundries, and they were also responsible for issuing pay numbers to the new starters in those areas. The office as a whole was responsible for about 5,500 shop-based workers alone, so it was quite a coincidence that George dealt with Jack Fleetwood's timesheet in his earliest days in the loco wages office. Whether George was born with it or developed a great capacity for detail in the course of his work, I do not know, but if I asked him if he remembered someone in a workshop fifty years ago, not only was he likely to say yes, but he would often give their pay number as well. For instance, the three men in the oxygen plant then were Alfie Church, Alf Dunman and chargeman Arthur Stanley: 3476, 3479 and 3410 respectively.

The locomotive and carriage wages offices both moved into the CME block when they amalgamated. The carriage wages was then sited in the old 'make up' area next to the cash office and run by senior clerk Billy Gunter. The loco office was across the corridor on the east side of the building. There was now one clerk in overall charge of the two, collectively known as the central wages office. This was Bill Sargeant, with Fred Hook and later Luke Roberts as his assistant. At this time Mr Roberts was looking after the administration of the wartime Comforts Fund, which was being continued to assist the casualties who were still in hospital or at home recovering. George's first section in the central wages (loco) included George Tomes, who was in charge, Ray Jackson and Oliver Porter. He dealt with wages staff timesheets as he had done before, but now it was for the K.C. (coppersmiths) and K.T. (tinsmiths) shops, as well as stamping and steam hammers: a total of about 250 workers.

The clerks worked six feet apart at double desks: their only aids were 'ready reckoners' (books of rates tables) and adding machines, of which each office had two or possibly three. Timesheets and piecework sheets were sent in from the workshops, and clerks working in pairs would work out the individual entitlements and stoppages and add the totals in spaces provided on the sheets. They would first calculate the gross pay according the individual's rate then, from that, the percentage tax deductible using tax tables and the individual's tax code. Then together with the piecework bonus, overtime and more than thirty types of possible deductions, the totals were transferred on to wages' cost slips. The slips were then sent on to the machine room as 'time returns': the same system being used for material costs. The methods used to arrive at these figures had not changed for many years, except as George Petfield said:

> By the time I started in the wages office, the information from the timesheets went straight on to Powers punchcards. The punchcards were, as they had been for years, approximately 7" x 3" and had the worker's pay number printed on them. They worked on the Hollerith system whereby pencil marks would indicate where the combinations of holes were to be made by the machine. A second card used throughout the year kept a running total for each person.
>
> In the wages office you got to get out and about a bit more than in other types of accounts work. If there was a problem with a timesheet, I usually found it easier to go and see the worker who had submitted it. However, this was not always possible because many discrepancies were due to excess payments claimed by outstation workers.

Men working outstation did not have their timesheets checked like the shopmen, where any such problems should have been picked up by the shop clerk. They relied on the foreman to check when he signed it, but he was less likely to spot an error than the clerk. If the workman was not happy with his pay, he might go along to the office where the relevant clerk could usually point out why he had not received what was anticipated. Sometimes a little extra overtime took the man into the next tax bracket, making him liable for a higher rate of tax on the whole amount. Understandably, he then felt cheated, and thought twice before volunteering for extra work next time. The rate of tax increased at five-shilling intervals in the 1940s and 50s.

At paybill offices all across the system, the figures for CME workers were compiled according to their own method of timekeeping. The time returns were sent on to the divisional or chief officer, together with the correct coded form detailing any deviations from normal working hours. Anticipated hours to be worked after 6 p.m. on the Friday and before the end of the working week on Saturday could be added to the time returns (now usually referred to as the paybills), as Friday was when they were forwarded on. If those estimated hours turned out to be different than the actual hours, the divisional or district officer had to be advised by first thing Monday morning via a coded form so that if possible, the paybill could be amended before being sent to the chief accountant at Swindon. If it was not possible to amend the paybill, any over-entry had to be deducted at the pay table and the amount paid back through the daily cash account.

Producing the weekly paybill was a problem of recurring urgency at the works. It was the Western Region's biggest commitment at Swindon outside manufacturing. George recalled the pressure under which the department operated:

> Everyone involved with wages knew their duty. It was the one job in 'the factory' that must not and did not get behind. Consequently, overtime in the wages' sections was not something regularly required to allow catching up. If anyone involved with wages was off sick or on holiday, their work had to be covered and the deadlines met. The rate of sickness was very low in our department and sometimes staff struggled in when they were clearly not fit. There was psychological pressure to do your share and not to leave it to your colleagues: besides, the 'sick record' was always a factor in assessment for promotion. Despite the importance of the work, there was a tendency for clerks elsewhere to look down on wages work: that was until they came to work here.

Liz Bartlett (nee Ribbins) worked in this office for a while, and remembers that her section included Malcolm Avenell and Walter Shepperd, as well as George Petfield. Other clerks in the office in the early 1950s included Frank Horn, Clem White, Ashley Manhair, Reg Drake, Mike Cousins, Eric (Tub) Loveday (who could take off the radio comic Tony Hancock), Eric Martin, Dave Bunce, Percy Harris and Bob Fox, who came from Weymouth. Among them there was a beekeeper, a Shakespearian actor and a flying instructor. Several were members of the Railway Correspondence and Travel Society, and one was a football referee. (William Russell, who worked elsewhere in CME accounts, was another amateur referee. He took charge of the 1924 FA Cup Final and an amateur cup final.) Dave Bunce ran an office shop, supplying biscuits and chocolate at cost price; George said that this sort of thing had to be conducted very discreetly and would not have been tolerated by management at all. Mike Cousins bussed in 14 miles every day from Lechlade. This small Gloucestershire town did have a station – in fact his father was the stationmaster there – but there was no direct line to Swindon.

George remembers some of his colleagues for the military campaigns they fought or the regiments they were attached to; this impressed the younger generation in those days. One fellow was at the Dardanelles, another at Gallipoli: others were remembered as ex-Royal Engineers or Royal Artillery. Some bore physical and mental scars, but most continued working until normal retirement age. Fred Boucher had been a Navy regular before arriving in the loco wages office during the Second World War. Fred had been injured during the Battle of the River Plate and despite continuing ill heath, spent thirty years in the department. One poor fellow suffered from a speech impediment due to shell shock in the First World War, but was still in the works offices forty years later. Another casualty from the 'first lot', Frank Witts, arrived back at the office very late after dinner one day. He said he had jumped off the bus at the medical centre and his lower leg prosthesis came off. This caused a female nearby to faint, leaving Frank to deal with both problems at the same time. Walter Shepperd and Reg Drake were typical of many clerks who had been in the accounts department since before 1914: they had done their bit in the Royal Flying Corps. Many young men in the works were recruited into aircraft production in the First World War, while others arrived at Swindon for the first time following the rundown of the Air Force at the war's end.

Swearing was rarely heard in the loco wages office unless something went very wrong. Then it was usually directed at someone on the other end of the phone, followed an apology all round – especially pronounced if females were nearby. For some reason few women, or W2s as they were known to the company, worked in loco wages compared to other areas.

When the boss was out of the office some people would make private calls. George remembers one chap entertaining the office as he became ever more irate with someone in the booking office at the station: 'The imbecile keeps quoting me times of trains to Lemster and I want to go to Leominster.' On another occasion the calm of the office was shattered when someone rang the AE shop office looking for Mr Duck, the clerk in charge: 'I understand you've got a duck down there called Mr Clerk,' began the inquirer quite innocently. There was quite a mix of characters to break the monotony: the quiet ones with a dry sense of humour; the practical joker; the extrovert; the shy and nervous types. One chap had a habit of kicking his shoes off under the desk when working. Knowing him as a rather sober, aloof type who would be unimpressed by the joke, someone managed to get the shoes away and hide them. 'Unfortunately for him, the victim was then summoned by the works accountant to undertake a special job, but still no one owned up to the prank,' said George. He eventually turned up for the appointment in a tatty old pair of shoes he kept in his locker. On his return, of course, the shoes were back under his desk.

Most types of accounting were carried out using machinery in the CME accounts, stores and mileage sections. Nearly 40,000 paybills and payslips were totalled up and printed by machines in CME accounts for the carriage and wagon engineers, chief accountants, chief mechanical engineers and motive power superintendents' departments. Each had sections dealing with paybills, as well as pensions, retirements, free and privilege tickets. Although the stores superintendent's accounts were compiled separately, it was for some reason, the CME staff who undertook the task. Ultimately all accounts came under the control of the chief, and later the regional accountant at Paddington.

Percy Richards MBE, a senior clerk at Swindon in the 1930s and 1940s, presented a paper to the GWR Engineering Society entitled *The Application of Modern Machines to the Production of Accounts and Costs of the Chief Mechanical Engineers Departments.* In it he said:

> In the early 1900s, the accounts were kept in bound books; written with elaborate copperplate figures. Next came the 'slip system' which, by means of separate documents for wages and materials expended on each job, made it possible to analyse expenditure by hand sorting of the slips. Later again, the company was persuaded that the 'punched card system' was so far advanced as to make an extended trial desirable, if it was to keep abreast of the times. Up until then, the question of capital outlay was measured only in terms of clerks and stationery. The first experiments with machines were applied to the costing of repairs to individual engines, boilers and tenders. These were done by Powers-Samas machines and proved eminently satisfactory.

Barbara Carter worked with Powers-Samas machines 'inside' for ten years, but still associates them mainly with the different stages of locomotive repair costs; they were also used for material costs. Other mechanised accounting covered train schedules, fuel costs, goods inwards, stores transactions, statistics, manufacturing costs and so on. Burroughs adding machines and Hollerith punchcard machines had been in use at Swindon since before the First World War. Barbara said that 'An early tabulator with a mechanical starting handle was kept at the back of our office. I remember working on it in the 1940s.'

The works at Swindon was one of the very few industrial sites prepared to invest in the best equipment and training to achieve efficient accounting. Indeed, the company is thought to have been the first railway in this country to have used the advanced Powers-Samas system. At first, however, the company was reluctant to be influenced by the early successes of outside firms and apply the technology to paybills because, having so many variable deductions, paybill figures had always been difficult to mass produce. The numerous deductions due to the many additional facilities offered to employees and the varying periods between payments taken made the GWR system particularly complicated. Mr Richards said: 'Now [1936] with something approaching £30,000 invested in these machines in the last seven years, it will be appreciated how much of a reasonable return on the outlay can be shown.' It is not possible to ascertain from this account, or probably and other source nowadays, the chronological development of punchcard application to paybills. However Mr Richards does say that 'The production of the weekly paybills at Swindon had still not quite reached the full potential of the Powers-Samas punchcard capability, but was going through the final stages of trial.'

The wages office clerks totalled up the piecework figures, converted them to percentages payable to each man, and then sent them on to the machine office. The fortnightly piecework account was calculated by Muldivo automatic electric calculators, from information on the piecework certificates. There were thirteen female operators who had to be kept fully occupied in order to justify the £150 initial cost of each machine. These calculators had to be imported from Italy and worked on the unfamiliar metric system. The female operatives, after intense training, became highly skilled and articulate with this system. For instance they had to be able to decimalize pound sterling, at sight, to six decimal places. Of the three copies of each certificate received by the operatives, two were returned to the shop after checking and evaluation: one went to the relevant chargeman and one to the shop office for cross-referencing. During the four-weekly accounting period, the Muldivos had to perform a large amount of further calculations arising out of manufacturing costs, process accounts output, overhead charges, South Wales docks wages, and statistics.

Cost slips arrived from the wages offices where they had been priced and evaluated, and costs made to balance with the paybill totals. Now referred to as paybills, the slips gave the figures for the period up until the previous Saturday dinnertime. The information was then transferred to punchcards which were designed with 45 columns grouped together to indicate, when used for paybill production, the account charge-code, the workman's ticket number and wages cost. A combination of holes was made in each card by semi-automatic punching machines and these represented a person's gross pay. Any mistakes made to the punchcards by the machines could be corrected using a hand punch. Other punched cards were set up for fixed and variable deductions. These were then added and tabulator machines converted the information on the cards back to numbers and figures.

By 1936 the actual production of the paybill, giving a net figure for payment and a cash slip, was performed by three Underwood-Sundstrand accounting and payroll machines. The earlier model of this machine required that the completed paybills went through a Burroughs listing machine for production of the payslip. Each shop in turn was handed over to an operator who took information from a combination of timesheets, machine cards and deductions lists. The printed bills were returned to the wages offices to be checked and finally sent on, two days before payday, to the chief accountant and chief cashier. A summary sheet accompanied each batch of bills and detailed the total cash to be drawn. Paybills were also produced for money due for pensions and retirement allowances.

The latest electric calculating machines were installed at Swindon works from the early 1930s, starting with comptometers and, for the piecework figures, the Muldivo calculators. Previously the ladies had been using mechanical comptometer adding and calculating machines, which were retained and used in the mileage office for many more years. The machine room also contained National Ellis listing machines, Ormig duplicators, Electromatic typewriters and Addressograph machines, which printed names and pay numbers on to blank (skeleton) paybills and timesheets.

By the early 1950s there was a machine room especially set up for paybills. It was behind the cash office on the east side of the CME building, separate from the other mechanised accounts. Liz Bartlett started work there at the age of seventeen, using National Cash Register machines. She said not all work done there was automated:

> Among other things, girls at desks had to work out the 'cash analysis' for the cash office and stick stamps on National Insurance cards. Shortly after I arrived we amalgamated with the carriage and wagon side. Mr (Bill) Sargent was in charge of the new central wages machine rooms and Miss Gapper was my section chief.

The publicity said that the Western Region was among the first undertakings in the British Commonwealth to make a complete study of electronic accounting. Powers-Samas of Croydon manufactured and, as a combined effort with engineers from Swindon, installed electronic accounting machines in this railway works. They were put in the Central (Carriage) Wages Office where staff had formerly sat at desks working to the same ends. The British-made electronic multiplying punch (EMP) was the first machine of its type. It began running in 1954, 'requiring only a few minutes training', and experience with it served to emphasise the advantages to be gained using electronic methods. The installation of a Powers-Samas 'programmed controlled computer' was behind schedule 'so, as an interim measure, a Hollerith computer was installed, which was quite straightforward,' said Liz. George, in the wages office, was not so keen on the temporary equipment:

> We had to stay late one night awaiting some figures from the Hollerith. We waited till 9.15 p.m. then went over to the Locomotive Hotel and had a pint. When we returned there was still nothing forthcoming, so I went home at midnight. Ron Alexander and another clerk stayed until 4 a.m. so they could get the information needed and not hold up the paybills.

Another intermittent problem with this equipment was that men were being paid either bonus or flat-rate money, but not both: the machine might then inexplicably issue a tax refund, as if by way of recompense. This happened to chargeman Bill Dando, who informed the office he was on his way over and wanted the matter dealt with straightaway. With this done, Dando, the A Shop fitter/erector who had accompanied the locomotive *King George V* to America in 1927, concluded his meeting with, 'Call this automation? I calls it all-to-buggery.'

The Powers-Samas computer was delivered in 1956 to begin running under local conditions. A large window had to be taken out and the PCC was suspended from a jib and hauled through by men pulling on a rope. Arthur Ruggles said that Z Shop where he worked, were engaged to do this using an old pre-war road crane. It was quite an occasion by all accounts, with managers and personnel from G Shop and Z Shop (transport) all seeing the equipment safely inside and upright.

The computer section would be staffed, more or less from the old paybill machine section, and all clerks were to be trained in turn. The new machinery was to do the work in a fraction of the time, but initially with only the paybills to do, there would be just six operators. Liz said:

> Mr Sargent got us together and assured us how much easier our working lives would become, but at first it was hell. The punchcards were stacked in the computer's magazine but would not be processed if the holes (now called encoded data) were slightly out of line or if the edges of the cards were worn. We had to work overtime to get the cards finished and sent on to the tabulators. We all wished we could have stayed with the Hollerith system.

Mr Sargent came over to run the electronic accounts room. Jeanette Clark was his secretary, Jack Parker was section chief and Gladys Ackrill was the senior female. Some of the others that Liz remembers in that first computer section were Charlie Kimber, who came up from Keynsham, George Brunger, from the wages office, Dennis Vance, Sheila Keen, Tom Fisher and Reg Sumbler. Liz Bartlett left the railway in early 1961, by which time Frank Maslin had taken over as the section chief.

The application of this futuristic equipment created interest well beyond the factory walls and for a time the operators enjoyed some celebrity status. Later publicity claimed that 'In early 1957 the computer took over the massive task of complete CME department paybill production. Shortly afterwards, all the department's accounting was fully computerized.' According to the *Western Region* staff magazine, 'The machine rented from Powers-Samas reduced the amount of staff working on paybills from 100 to 60 with a saving of £10,000.' George Petfield's time in this office ended with computerisation, which made much of the work done by the wages offices obsolete.

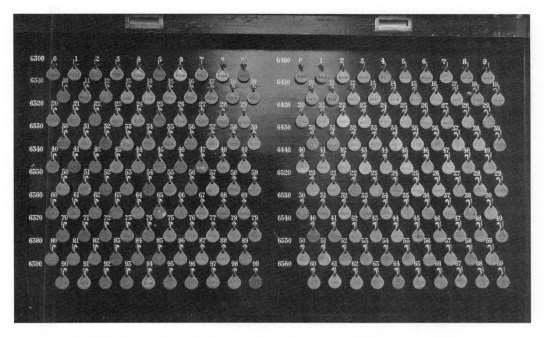

On the back of this photo of a workshop checkboard is written, 'T Shop 9/2/09.' There are two sets of numbers painted on the board so perhaps the brass finishers shared their board with the adjoining Brass Foundry. (Author's collection)

Powers-Samas punch card machines used at Swindon in the 1930s and 1940s for the production of paybills and material charges. Maintenance was provided by service mechanics and electricians employed by the manufacturers, who were permanently on site. (*GWR Magazine*)

This was 40 office in the 1930s; the machinery section was behind the photographer. Two of the girls in the front are Nancy Verrinder (left) and Molly Adkins; behind them are Marjorie Gooding (left) and Ethel Fletcher; in the next row back are Beryldene Hunt (left) and Enid Munden. (Central Library: local studies section)

The loco wages office sometime between 1952, when it was combined with the 'carriage wages', and 1956. Fred Boucher and Walter Sheppard are seen in the centre, facing the photographer. The section dealing with workshop stores wages was off to the left. (BRW)

The CME machine room paybill section at Christmas time in 1953 or 1954. Left to right standing: Barbara Tuck, Mary Beckhelling-Williams, Bill Sargeant, Audrey Sharland, Fred Hook (from loco wages office), Liz Ribbins, Janet Hooper, Doreen Freeman. Left to right sitting: Betty Fincham, Florence Gapper, Rosie Jones, Doreen Huff. (Liz Bartlett)

Liz Bartlett was the clerk chosen to be photographed with the new computer for the Western Region publicity in 1957. Cards punched with basic data are about to be placed into the magazine. They were processed at the rate of two per second and arrived in the receiver at the front end. This was a staged photograph; before actual use the panels would need to be replaced. (Liz Bartlett)

The electronic machine room in 1957. As well as the PCC in the background, there were a key punch, a sorter, an interpolator, a reproducer, an interpreter and two tabulators in use here. (BRW)

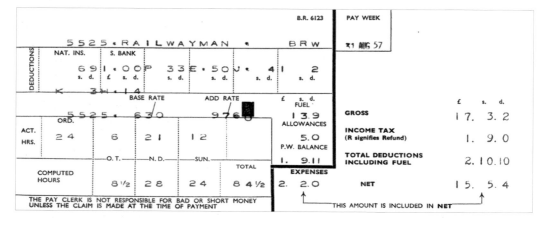

The later type of Powers-Samas punch card, the medium by which large volumes of information were processed. Unlike the machines, the layout and size of the cards changed little from the 1930s until they became obsolete in 1959. (Author's collection)

A sample payslip for 1957. (Author's collection)

5

Payday

The story of how the money for wages arrived at the works was thought worthy of space in the *GWR Magazine* on more than one occasion. Presumably the writers were given full access to observe the proceedings and quote official statistics, but these articles were never meant to be a definitive study or historical record. They written in the days when such quaint and timeless rituals were not recorded for posterity as, unlike nowadays, there was no reason to suspect that progress would soon change them for something less interesting.

Every Friday morning (Thursday from some time after 1941), a Mercury tractor from internal transport left the works hauling a steel and iron-framed box mounted on a chassis. It was bound for Lloyds Bank in Regent Street about three-quarters of a mile away to collect the money for the workers' wages. At the bank, the money was ready to be transported in canvas bags and strongboxes. It was important that exactly the right number of coins of each denomination was received. This was achieved by sending a 'coin analysis' up to the bank earlier in the week. The works cashier or a deputy arrived at the bank independently at 9 a.m. to oversee the loading of the money and to sign and exchange the paperwork. Men from the works security were also present during the loading, and no doubt the local bobby was about too. Together with its commitment to other businesses, one can imagine the frenzy of activity at the bank in advance of each payday.

The withdrawal amounted to the net earnings for all the weekly-paid men: the manual workers (wages grades), the office/supervisory workers (staff grades) as well as the Swindon footplatemen and shed grades. The latter came under the motive power superintendent's department, a subdivision of the CME department. About 11,500 workers were based at the works in the mid-1930s, of whom about 60 per cent were on the 'loco side'. The works' population increased after the war and went down again in the 1950s. For the period of this study, however, conflicting figures have been published about how many were employed at the works at any one time; similarly, only a vague reference, made for publicity purposes, can be found regarding how much money left the bank each week. According to the GWR's published figures, the total wages bill for the CME department was £6.6 million in 1935 and £8.8 million in 1941. Something over 25 per cent of the CME's wage bill was paid out at Swindon works. Allowing for stoppages and excluding managers' salaries, the actual amount of cash leaving Lloyds Bank each week must therefore have been around £25,000 in 1935. The amount for 1941 works out at around £35,000, but this is contradicted by a *GWR Magazine* of the period, which claimed that 'about a ton of money, sometimes close on £50,000 left the bank' each Friday. It is possible that the contradiction between these 1941 figures reflects the sums before and after the considerable overtime payments. The report also makes the point that the majority of the money made up the wages of those actually producing the work.

Once loaded, the petrol-driven tractor, which was licensed to run on the public road, would slowly tow the load down Bridge Street. Lloyds Bank was at the near end of Regent Street, on the corner where it crossed the old Wilts & Berks Canal, now disused, and, at that point filled in. There were two riders: the driver and another man in an elevated position 'riding shotgun', as the locals would say. They turned left into Faringdon Road and through the GWR estate, passing the Mechanics' Institute on the left in Emlyn Square. Alfie, the watchman on the old gasworks gate, told George that he used to ride shotgun on the pay run. When asked if he was ever worried about being held up, he said, 'Look, I've been shot at all across North Africa. If they wants the money they can have it.'

In the early 1940s, with the increasing volume of road traffic, a one-way system was introduced on some roads in the town centre. The pay wagon then suffered the indignity of a long detour up around the Town Hall and back down Commercial Road and Milton Road to reach the GW cottage estate. Bank and railway officials motored back to the works ahead of the pay wagon. They did not escort the tractor and its precious load, as seen in the photograph, until the late 1940s or early 50s. By this time men of the works security (watchmen) were no longer flanking the procession, but conspicuously watching the proceedings from a distance. After being demobbed, Bert Stratford remembered 'following the money' back to the works and wondering what would happen if an organised attempt was made to steal it. Enid Hogden (née Warren) occasionally rode on the pay run between 1944 and 1948, probably deputising when the regular person was unavailable. She remembers the tractor moved at walking pace, and amazingly does not recall any additional security staff at that time. At the bottom of Emlyn Square the tractor would turn left and then almost immediately right, the articulating transport being narrow enough to pass easily in through the double doors of the main entrance to the works. When motor escorts were later used, they were left outside and the occupants followed on foot. The doors were then closed behind them and locked by the gatekeepers until the dinner break. In the mid-1950s, Dave Viveash worked in Dunn & Co., the hat shop, before going 'inside'. He said: 'We always watched the pay wagon go past the shop on Thursday mornings, pulling the red trailer. In the pub later, the lads would speculate on the chances of stealing the money and getting away with it.'

At the far end of the tunnel under the mainline, this route, which was also a fire engine right of way, took a left turn up a steep slope. Here the tractor came into its own again and was the other reason for using this sluggish transporter, the works' equivalent to the Scammell 'mechanical horse'. At the top of the slope the vehicles turned right, past the door into the East Time Office and the Progress Office. Then they passed No. 3 Accounts and the outdoor machinery depot, to stop outside the cash office. This route was well known to visitors then, and is still there today, now open to the public.

The iron moneybox that was used in the later days of the GWR was still sitting in the old iron foundry when the works finally closed in 1986, and still had GWR painted on each side. It was considered as an exhibit for the Railway Museum, but was found to have rusted beyond restoration. Photographs of the pay wagon are uncommon; what there are show that at least two different types of moneybox were used from the early 1900s. The pay wagon had been drawn by a shire horse, possibly up until 1938; no doubt this was where the nickname 'money hearse' originated. This was at a time when a few horses were still being used around the factory for pulling trailers and shunting wagons, and here again they were superseded by Fordson tractors in the 1930s. After the 1950s, private security vans would deliver the money via the main gate in Rodbourne Road.

The contents of the pay wagon were manhandled into the cash office and the doors locked. The cash office should not be confused with the wages offices, where the information for the paybills was compiled. The chief cashier, his assistant and a couple of clerks who were resident there dispensed the money to clerks brought in to make up the individual wages. All the time watchmen stood guard outside until the money was distributed to the shops and departments. On other days the small partitioned area at one end of this large office was the only part occupied. The staff would handle financial transactions between the workers, the works and the bank. Wages could be collected from this office at other times by prior arrangement.

Enid Hogden started work in the cash office at the age of sixteen. She had just done six months as an office junior in 22 Accounts and would not become a clerk proper for another two years. Ernest Habgood was chief cashier in the 1930s, but by the time Enid arrived in 1942 George Eynon was in charge. It is likely that Mr Eynon had previously been the clerk in charge of the GWR Savings Bank sometime after Oliver Tidball retired in 1932. He remained in the cash office throughout the 1940s and 50s, although George Petfield thinks that an Isaac Carter took over for a period within that time. Enid said that Mr Eynon was a meticulous man: 'Mr Mainwaring in *Dad's Army* had a very similar manner to our chief cashier, but he was a nice man.' Cyril Davis was the assistant cashier, and clerks Joan Thatcher, Phyllis Peddle, Beryl Breakspear and Jean Moses were all in the office at various times during Enid's six years there. When she left and moved to the South Coast, Enid found the wages in similar work a lot lower than in the Western. She said, 'I nearly had to take a job with the Southern Railway' (as it continued to be called, despite recently being nationalised). When contacting old Swindon colleagues recently, Enid found them saying, 'Oh yes I remember you: you were the senior clerk in the cash office.' 'Fancy that, sixty years later I find out that I was in charge,' she said.

Because paybill production time had been cut since before the war with the introduction of new machinery, wages' staff became available on payday, where previously they were borrowed from elsewhere in accounts. After 1952, when the loco and carriage wages offices merged, they had enough staff of their own for 'cash office make-up', as it was referred to (George Petfield told me that there were 115 staff in the central wages office at the start). Dozens of men and women clerks, mainly from the lower grades, were brought in to make-up and pack the individual wages. Enid remembers a senior clerk from the General Managers' Accounts being present. He had arrived earlier by train to oversee proceedings and deal with other matters that might have arisen between the two departments. She said: 'One of us was sent up to the bank with the pay wagon and at that time there were just the tractor driver, the clerk and the man from Paddington.' His weekly visit to the cash office ceased quite early on, possibly due to reorganisation in 1948.

The shops knew it was no good sending their office boy along to the cash office on an errand that day, as it was very unlikely he would be seen. Staff were allocated table numbers and worked in pairs, calculating the total amount of cash required for each batch of earnings in the correct denominations, and drawing this from the cashier. The cashier and his assistants were busy breaking down the money, receiving the requisition slips and dispensing the cash through one of three hatches in the partition. The cashier's clerks were each given a particular type of coin to dispense. Barbara Carter remembers she was in charge of the threepenny bits on her visits to cover for absentees. On the make-up side, George Petfield remembers being sent down for a trial run to see how it was done, before making up the wages for real the following week. He said: 'You had to have your wits about you to keep up with the others. After collection the notes and coins were further broken down into individual net wages by the "maker-up". They were made-up in blocks of thirty-eight, but I cannot now remember why.'

Clerks worked from summary sheets, which listed the net totals against workers' names and pay numbers, and it is possible that these sheets held thirty-eight entries. George remembers when the clerk Ted Scott, who was working near him, kept recounting a bundle of a hundred £1 notes and making it £101. With a witness, they accepted that there was indeed an error. They also noticed that two notes had the same serial number (this was in the days when £1 was a good proportion of a person's wage). The whole roll had to be returned to Lloyds Bank.

The clerk then placed the individual amounts around a circular wooden tray to his or her left, wrapped in the payslip. The tray was turned clockwise on a central spindle as more amounts were added. A second person sat opposite and checked each wage then put it in the correct pay tin or envelope. The 'checker' took longer than the 'maker-up', so the tray filled up until it held about twenty-five sets of wages. This gave the latter time to go round and load the packed wages into strongboxes. A photograph of the cash office taken in 1911 shows that this procedure was the same as George remembers it in the late 1940s, although the old revolving trays did go shortly afterwards. The pay tins were about 2 inches in diameter by 1¼ inches high. They had the recipient's number painted or stamped on the push-fitting lid. Care had to be taken not to get notes caught between the top of the tin and the underside of the lid, which might then jam tight. New notes presented other problems by being difficult to separate, causing vital time to be wasted. The filled tins were placed in numerical order into the shallow boxes, which were padlocked when full. Mr Richards of the accounts machine room had said that counting money by hand and packing it into tins was out of date in the 1930s, and that 'Machinery was now available, that dispensed correct sums of money at the push of a button.'

Staff grades had always received their money in paper packets, and shopworkers' pay was packed in individual tins. In the late 1940s, when £5 notes started to be included, they did away with tins in favour of a buff-coloured envelope, and later a cellophane packet. The envelopes were much better to handle. They had the person's name and pay number printed on them and you were told to check the amount before opening the packet, which was not easy. Derby works on the LMS were using envelopes with transparent windows by the mid-1930s, but my source does not make it clear whether this included the shop-floor workers. If a discrepancy was found and the recipient could show beyond reasonable doubt that he or she had been 'short changed' according to the payslip, it was the policy to call in the police. It was no doubt a reflection of the times that although there was a lot of people handling a lot of money, George only heard of this happening once and even then no one was ever suspected of dishonesty.

The designated shop labourer would go the cash office and collect the pay. He would lift the boxes containing the pay tins on to one or a pair of sack trucks, and with a pay clerk, walk back to his workshop. In some cases this was quite a distance, but again I have not heard of any incidents that breached security. As with the making up of the wages, clerks from elsewhere in accounts were borrowed to help with the paying out; even then there were not enough clerks for every shop. All the female clerks I have spoken to went out to assist with the payout at various times. It is thought that this was done by men only before the war. Jack Fleetwood said:

> The payout of the wages in the workshop was mockingly referred to as 'the ceremony'. The pay table was brought out into the shop and assembled in advance. The wages arrived at the shop with the minders, where they would rendezvous with the shop clerk who was waiting to assist the pay clerk. Some men were already lined up, waiting as the pay clerk unlocked the tin boxes but did not take out the pay tins. The foreman appeared at the top of the office steps and looked at his watch. If he was slightly early or he sensed any impatience, he would

disappear into his office again before proceeding down to the pay table. Workmen would start to shuffle their feet and the foreman looked at his watch again, waited thirty seconds, and then with a nod of his head the clerks would start paying out. The men were, by now, all lined up in pay number order. The office boys were the first to slap their paychecks on the polished brass surface. The shop clerk called out the number on the check and the pay clerk ticked the sheet and issued the tin. The check was then sent down the slide into a round tin under the table.

The pay clerk had to certify the paybill sheet so that it was clear by whom each man had been paid. After all the attention and care spent on producing the correct payments, the payout appeared to be very hastily done. The idea was that it did not take any more than five minutes of work time. Men could be seen standing around tapping their upturned tins or sometimes poking a screwdriver in to release the coins and notes before dropping the tin into a basket. Harry Bartlett remembers 'Grabber' Greening of 15 Shop struggling with his pay tin because he had bad arthritis in his hands. Jack said:

> In the earlier days if the hooter finished blowing before all the men were paid, they would have to wait until the afternoon, which meant a nice little stroll to the cash office where the staff were anything but pleased with the interruption. The following week the foreman would not leave it quite so late, but it was difficult to get the last man away before the hooter blew.

Newcomers were paid their anticipated wage at the end of their first week, with any adjustments being made the following week. If a man was not happy with the amount he received, he explained the problem to the shop clerk. If the clerk could not settle the matter then, and only then, could the man speak to the relevant wages clerk. At the close of the payout, unclaimed wages had to be balanced by the pay clerk with the amounts outstanding on the paybill sheets and with any unissued paychecks. The pay clerk would then make his way back to the cash office with the locked tin containing the paychecks, the pay sheets and any unclaimed pay. This was then enveloped or boxed if not already done and entries written in the unclaimed wages register.

George Petfield remembers that following a severe fire in the nearby oxygen plant, he assisted the paying out in the P1 Shop. Whole sections of the roof were covered by tarpaulin in this, the shop where loco boilers and their fittings were steam tested. 'This was January 1945 when I was a junior clerk,' said George. With the shopmen paid, the wages staff could deal with the salaried staff during the afternoon. In pairs, wages and other clerks delivered their money to them personally in the offices and shops. The strongboxes were now fitted with dividers which held dozens of the lighter wage packets, instead of tins, and could be easily carried around by hand. George said that one pair of clerks went off to pay the carriage works' salaried staff: another to pay the CME personal staff: a third pair dealt with the accounts staff, and so on.

Outstation staff would collect their wages from the works at the end of the week, the following Monday morning, or when they could, depending on their travel arrangements. Men on nights collected their wages from the weigh house office or the west end of A Shop on the loco side, depending on where they worked. On the carriage side they went to the carriage stamping shop. The running shed men on nights collected their pay from the machine room office where the paybills were prepared and printed. A worker unable to collect could nominate another to receive his paycheck and wages. If a person lived near someone 'on the club' (out sick) they could, if requested, go to the invalid's foreman or office chief, collect an order form and sign and withdraw the wages on his or her behalf.

Jack Fleetwood remembered that local businesses were all geared up for the extra payday trade:

Knees the newsagent and tobacconist across the road from the works tunnel entrance had a problem when the average shopman's pay reached £5, because men would rush into the shop with their note and ask for five or ten Woodbines. The change soon ran out, so the proprietor began lining up the cigarettes together with the right change for a £5 note on the back shelf, ready for the dinner-time rush. This transaction also allowed the workmen to sort out how much change to put in their pocket before handing over the money to their wives.

Jack never actually saw a wife meet her husband at the factory gates and take his wages, as some had claimed to have witnessed: 'I did see the Roman Catholic priest outside during Friday dinner-time, waiting for recompense from Irishmen not seen at Mass the previous week.' Local children too could often be seen waiting to collect their 'Friday penny' from their father.

Regent Street from Bridge Street with Lloyds Bank on the right. The men in the picture suggest it was either lunchtime or a Saturday. (Author's collection)

The iron body of a later pay wagon, found in the works during clearance in the 1980s. (B. Harber)

The pay wagon returning from the bank to the works in the 1950s. 'There was mild panic in the town on one occasion when a private vehicle got between the wagon and the accompanying car,' said George Petfield. The tractor for this run was regularly driven by Clem Manning at this time. A second man, a labourer, was chained to his seat and instructed to pull on the handbrake lever if the tractor ran away on a slope. (BRW)

Clerks Pam Whitworth (left) and Pat O'Neil making up pay packets in 1956 or 1957. (BRW)

Mr Eynon, the chief cashier, watches as new clerk Pam Sheppard counts out money to Dick Minihane. On this occasion Dick would have been one of the clerks sent down to make up wage packets. (BRW)

The shop and wages clerks 'paying out' in one of the workshops with the foreman in attendance. (BRW)

6

Workshops and Output

GWR supporters boast that, at the Swindon works, basic and raw materials such as hard and soft woods, iron and steel, oil, fabrics, leather, water and power went in, and locomotives, carriages and wagons came out. This was, in one sense, true, but to provide the manufacturing facilities on this scale there was a huge reliance on plant, machinery and stores, which had to be brought in from specialist firms.

The diversity of manufacturing skills practised in one works was impressive. Some might say excessive and outdated because it was not always cost-effective to make every component within their capability. It was the job of the assistant CME to compare, with the help of the accounts department, the cost of manufacture with the cost of buying in. Mr Gardner, when assistant chief accountant to the CME, said that his department covered work being done for other departments, private firms and other railway companies, and this tends to confound the myth that Swindon looked after itself alone. Jack Fleetwood said: 'We did do some work for the signal works at Reading and their people did tend to be very particular about the standard of workmanship they required of us.'

The manufacturing capabilities of this railway factory were only realised outside when they were required to undertake orders for the Ministry of (War) Production, particularly during the years 1941 to 1944. Much of the work for the war effort was very different to the type of mechanical and timberwork they were used to, and tested their capability, skill and resourcefulness. Not only did the works satisfactorily complete all that was asked of them, they took on work that could not be done elsewhere and usually delivered ahead of time. The loco works' manager during the war, K. J. Cook, was awarded an OBE in 1946 for organising the war work undertaken during his term of office.

LOCOMOTIVE AND ROLLING STOCK

The building of express and other main-line engines in the 1920s and early 30s had reduced the GWR's reliance on ageing and underpowered locomotives. This increased availability and allowed the company to withdraw more engines than they were building. As steam locomotives become more expensive to maintain as they get older, this meant significant savings for the CME department. They were then able to concentrate on updating, designing and rebuilding the smaller classes. For instance the works built one hundred large 2-6-2 tank engines of the 5101 class, for passenger stopping trains. In 1932 the first of a new 0-4-2 pannier tank was outshopped: the 4800 class. These were light enough for all rural branch lines and replaced the ageing 517 engines. Some were built with auto-gear and automatic train control to pull or propel auto-trailers. The most numerous type built in the 1930s was the 0-6-0 PT for light passenger trains. Several variations of these were designed to suit different operating requirements. Again some were fitted for push-pull working, with the engine in the middle if using more than two trailer cars.

Besides the overhaul of locomotives at planned time or mileage intervals, the works built or rebuilt between 100 and 150 locomotives per annum in the 1930s. With the slowdown of locomotive development and the standardisation of classes, however, fewer types were being rebuilt by this time. Swindon received some batches of smaller classes from private builders and disposed of the displaced engines by cutting them up and selling the scrap, or occasionally selling small engines to minor companies for further use. Most repairs to locos, carriages and wagons between planned overhauls were done at the company's depots or other works.

At the height of the economic depression in 1933, the *GWR Magazine* tells us that 134 mainline or suburban coaches were built, excluding specialized vehicles such as Post Office vans and brake vans. More than a third of the existing passenger carriages were still lit by gas at this time. The number of wagons constructed that year was 1,392. In the following year, 1934, an increase in revenue allowed the company to replace and increase its rolling stock considerably. They built a total of 246 coaches and 2,470 wagons. The company also took possession of 5,000 20-ton mineral wagons built by contractors. The wagon works, like other departments, sometimes subcontracted orders because they could not handle the work at that time. They would also have to buy in specialist work such as the new glass-lined milk tanks that were fitted on to Swindon six-wheel underframes. Two new sets of coaches for the *Cornish Riviera Limited* were built and went into service in 1935, the company's centenary year. Just after the Second World War, Swindon produced the first track relaying trains, designed by Ken Webb, in the drawing office.

CARRIAGE CONSTRUCTION

The accepted terminology seemed to be that carriages were 'constructed' while wagons were 'built'. In peacetime Swindon received a large amount of timber from abroad. Consignments arrived mainly through the docks at Cardiff or London and was transported by barge to Brentford. It was then examined by the company's inspector before being accepted. Wherever possible the company policy was 'to utilise timber grown in the British Empire if cost and quality were satisfactory'. Rock elm and hickory came from North America, as did yellow pine which, together with New Zealand pine, was used for making patterns. Pine also came in from Canada, mahogany from Borneo and West Africa, while oak and teak, from Poland and Burma respectively, were used for carriage frames. Usually purchased as logs and trees, the timber was sawn down in the sawmill and artificially seasoned in the drying shed before being cut to manageable sizes and sent out to the shops. Most woodworking shops on the carriage side had their own sawmill and could cut the timber down further to their own requirements. Occasionally it was received from the supplier as ready-cut boards if their own facilities could not cope, or a good price had been secured. One of the few woods used at Swindon for its engineering qualities was lignum vitae, a wood so dense it won't float. It was used to make brake blocks, bearings, shafts and pulley sheaves. Hardwood blocks, including lignum vitae, were kept in the guard's van of a train along with the jack to secure a temporary repair to axle boxes, excluding the locomotive, where the white metal bearing had broken down. Mansell wood wheels had been used extensively for carriages (with steel tyres and bosses), but this practice had ceased by the 1930s. The wooden segments were reclaimed and made very durable floors in some areas of the carriage shops.

Before an order for a new batch of coaches was undertaken, the availability of materials sufficient to complete the work had to be ascertained from the stores department. It was important that the work would proceed simultaneously in the various workshops and that all the main component parts came together without hold-ups.

Timber for coach bodies was sawn from logs in the sawmill and further trimmed using a milling machine. The body frames were assembled using hardwood and steel members. By the 1930s considerable changes of production methods for semi-steel (composite) coach bodies had taken place. Extensive use of jigs had reduced the use of handtools to a minimum and mass production methods of machining and assembly had cut production time considerably. After being marked out by machine, 16-standard wire gauge (equal to 0.064 inch or 1.6 mm) steel outer sheets were sheared to shape, then another machine punched the holes.

All the assembly and machining of new wheels and axles was carried out in 16 Shop, which also dealt with repairs sent in from the carriage lifting shop and 13A (carriage frame) Shop. A Benrath wheel-balancing machine and several Craven tyre-turning lathes with auxiliary grinding heads were in use here. To check for cracks, two Hughes supersonic flaw detectors were used on axles before they were pressed into wheels and machined. The wheelsets were then sent to 15 Shop where a gang of about fourteen men did the bogie erecting. Ever greater use was being made of jigs and templates to produce bogies by pressed steel construction. The bogies and underframes (from 13A Shop) were assembled and steam heating pipes fitted, together with the brakegear and drawgear, from the carriage smiths' shop. 15 Shop was the largest C&W workshop, with about 800 men employed, the majority of whom were fitters.

The complete underframes were then shunted over to the body shop where the coach bodies were lifted on to them. Coach finishers fitted all the furnishings and windows: the internal doors, seat frames, panelling and luggage racks came in for fitting from the finishing and polishing shops. (Once a day a short train called the *Royal* ran between the two areas of the carriage works bringing parts for rebuilding and taking away parts for refurbishment). Trimmers laid linoleum and rugs and finished the upholstery, then electricians fitted dynamos, batteries and other train lighting equipment. All internal surfaces were then cleaned and polished. Finally the vehicles went by the electric traverser to the adjacent carriage paint shop to be externally cleaned, painted and have transfers and varnish applied. There were a total of thirty-four carriage painters, including those painting coaches taken out of service in 24 Shop. Each new coach received three coats of paint and three of varnish, which took seven days to complete.

From the 1930s to the 1950s the materials used for carriage bodies and frames changed from mainly wood to mainly steel, but timber was not being superseded to the same extent in wagon and non-passenger vehicle bodies. By 1930 galvanised steel panels were fitted to all new carriage stock and to those coming in for overhaul. They were very durable and improved the fireproofing. Horsehair was a valuable commodity, so it was removed from old seats and recycled. It was put through a carding machine over by the carpenters' shop. The machine, operated in the 1950s by Jack Huckin, pulled the hair apart or combed it, then washed it. It was then bagged up and sent over to the trimmers in 19A Shop for re-use.

WAGON BUILDING AND REPAIRS

The underframes of wagons were constructed in 13 Shop. As with carriages, the frames were erected using parts made in the smiths, wheel, machine and fitting shops. The two solebar members were fixed in a jig to secure the wheelbase, then such things as axleguards, spring shoes, transoms, buffer trimmers, stanchions and headstocks were riveted or bolted to them. The frame was then squared up and riveted to an underframe. Next, it was lifted by electric hoist for wheels, axleboxes, tie rods, drawgear, buffers and brakework to be fitted then painted with red lead before the body was added. Doug Webb, who worked in 13 Shop from the late 1940s onwards, recalled:

> I worked with chargeman wagon plater Mervyn Iles to start with. Mr Jordan was our foreman and Mr Dobson was the wagon builders' chief foreman. It was very noisy there, as much of the assembly was done by riveting. As a fitters' mate, I would take components over to the 'loco side' for grinding or heat rivets in a nozzle hand forge. No one else liked going up ladders, so I spent a lot of time changing pulley blocks that were suspended from swinging jibs. While I was there, a very sophisticated scissor-riveting machine was purchased for 13 Shop. It was only then found to be far too heavy for the frame that was intended to support it from above. This expensive piece of equipment lay in a corner of the shop for years and I heard that it had eventually gone for scrap. I remember too, steel link chains made in the factory that were used for hand hoists: we used to bury them in the ground outside to make them rust. This stopped them sliding through the blocks and pulleys too freely.

Wagon bodies and merchandise containers were built and repaired in 21 Shop. After the war wagons received complete overhauls rather than just repairs when necessary. Roads 1 and 2 at the north of the shop were for new builds: roads 3 and 4 were for overhauls and the other two roads dealt with repairs between overhauls. The workshop was 600 feet long and wagons moved through the building on a belt system to emerge at the end, built, rebuilt or repaired. In the 1950s the wagon works as a whole delivered on average 300 wagons per week back to traffic: the most numerous types dealt with were 12-ton open and covered goods wagons, ventilated vans, cattle wagons and brake vans. The weekly wagon building capacity was, by 1957, equivalent to one hundred 13-ton open-top types. They were also busy throughout the decade converting hand-braked vehicles to vacuum-braked.

FOUNDRY WORK

Jack Fleetwood was in the foundry all his working life, and told me:

> With its furnaces, Swindon could sort and recycle all the company's scrap iron (with or without additional pig iron and coke) and other ferrous metals, as well as some alloys. And it seemed as though we were self-sufficient. Recycled ingots were analysed in the laboratory then, if necessary, returned to the furnace with additional metals to produce the required composition.

According to the company's figures, the iron foundry produced between 9,000 and 10,000 tons of castings annually in the 1930s, with approximately 1,700 tons of non-ferrous castings coming out of the brass foundry. There was no steel foundry on site, so carbon steel ingots and billets, steel bar and plate were brought in to be tested, inspected and either hammered, rolled, drop forged or stamped, then machined and heat treated. Locomotive and other steel wheel centres were also produced outside.

In the iron foundry, old broken castings and bars of new pig iron were melted in the cupola, a small blast furnace. When the fire in the furnace had burnt up, the blast was gradually increased to raise the temperature sufficiently to melt the metal. (Moving molten metals to the moulds, by hand, was potentially dangerous. Jack said he could never understand why the heaviest jobs in the brass foundry, where there were no lifting aids, were furthest from the furnace). The dross was skimmed back as the metal was poured into a hollow shape or mould, which when cooled produced a solidified form equal to the space. A sample might also be sent to the laboratory to check the composition. The moulder's job was to produce the hollow, and the usual way to do this was by closed box moulding. For this a loose pattern in the shape of the proposed finished piece, and slightly oversized to allow for shrinkage, was pressed into one half of the box filled with packed sand. The other half, also filled with sand, was pressed hard down on top and the two were clamped together. The pattern was then carefully removed by separating the box, so it was important that the sand was of the right consistency to bond together. Jack told me:

> The type of sand we used varied depending on the work. It would often need further grinding and sifting if it came straight from the quarries. Until after the war, sand additives were mixed in on-site too. Red, green and sea sand had such things as oil, coal dust, clay, plumbago powder or treacle added. The right balance had to be made between binding the sand and leaving it permeable enough to disperse hot gases. Horse manure too, was used. (It wasn't until about 1950 that shunting wagons with horses was completely phased out in the works; then they had to buy in manure.) Sand mixing was done in an apple mill or, if large amounts were required, by hand using a good polished shovel. Most was used only once or reused as packing sand. In the brass foundry petrobond was bought in after the war. This was fine sand, which therefore produced a smooth finish.
>
> A wagonload of red sand regularly arrived outside the brass foundry from Kidderminster. Labourers were then normally paid two hours' overtime to shovel the sand out of the 12-ton wagon and move it into the shop. Because of the terrible weather conditions in the winter of 1947, the steel doors on the sand wagon were frozen solid. The men made a fire underneath using the contents of the furnaces that were emptied that evening so they could start unloading in the morning. What they didn't realise was that the floor of the vehicle was made of wood and it burned through and collapsed. The contents remained inaccessible but now the line was blocked too. After much head scratching, it was realised that nothing could be done with the crippled wagon and its load until the weather improved weeks later.
>
> If the casting was to be hollow or have any cavities, cores would be added by the coremaker, and channels to let in the molten metal and allow the hot gases to escape were added. Locomotive combined cylinder and saddle blocks were probably the most exacting work undertaken in the works foundries and required the best quality cast iron. Up to twenty-six separate cores could be used, but I never saw a 'scrapper'. Assorted (plain) scrap was used for loco and carriage brake blocks, which were known as slippers.
>
> During what was probably my first winter in the foundry I thought I was going to die of cold. The older hands said, 'Just go and ask Foreman Webb for some extra heating,' so I did. His reply was, 'Work a little harder – that will warm you up.' When I came out of the office, the men were laughing their heads off; they had caught another naïve newcomer.

Another method was 'bedding-in moulding', where the mould was packed into sand in the foundry floor then covered by a top-part moulding box. This avoided the need for expensive bottom-part moulds, particularly when making bulky irregular castings. Open sand moulding was a similar method but did not require a top box. Large castings, weighing several tons, took more than two weeks to complete because of all the preparation, and afterwards the cooling, fettling and cleaning (fettling involved grinding off any ridges left from where the two halves of the mould met). All the moulds had to be ready by early afternoon as this was when the furnaces, which were lit first thing in the morning, would be ready. With heavy castings being hoisted around and molten metal splattering unpredictably, the foundry was full of hazards, even for the resident workforce. So imagine the amazement one Wednesday afternoon, said Jack, when 'a woman with a pushchair got separated from the guided tour and came wandering through the shop'.

It was not uncommon for railway companies to keep successful methods of production to themselves. For instance, Swindon never recorded the process they used for making their 'yellow brass', which is still admired today on surviving locomotives and rolling stock. Arthur Lawrence worked in the brass foundry in the 1920s and 30s and would occasionally have to attend a court of law in connection with the brass that was made 'inside'. In a legal dispute over ownership or liability, Arthur or others from the foundry and laboratory would have to swear under oath that the material in question was works brass. The source of this information is Arthur's daughter, but unfortunately she never knew specific details.

The usual sequence was for castings to have various machining operations performed and be partially assembled and then, if they were locomotive parts, go on to the erecting shops. As well as moulders, other types of workers in the foundry were known as dressers, furnacemen, knockers-out, cupola men and ladle runners. Behind the iron foundry was the chair foundry, where semi-skilled men produced track chairs and other castings for the permanent way. The chargeman chair-moulder in the 1950s, Harry Johnson, said his forty-three men were the best paid of their grade in the factory. Jack said of the chair foundry: 'The work was hard and tedious, and the conditions were dirty and cramped.'

ALSO MADE IN THE LOCO WORKS

Apart from supplying motive power for the traffic department, the locomotive works produced and repaired an impressive range of other mechanical items for the GWR, such as pumping and hydraulic machinery, sheet metal fabrications, patterns, ticket issuing machines, merchandise containers, different types of road vehicle bodies and electric motors for overhead crane mechanisms. Bells were also produced on the premises; these were not cast, said Jack, but pressed out of sheet metal:

> Those we made in the foundry were of silver bell metal, an alloy of (eighty parts) copper, tin, zinc and lead, which was expensive to manufacture. We made bells for the company's shipping, for fitting to traversing tables and to dock shunting engines. We made smaller bells for signalling equipment and the ATC boxes in loco cabs. If it was a matter of replacing a part that could be cast, we did it. If a large steam hammer or press developed a crack in its frame, a mould was made of the part and a new piece, sometimes weighing several tons, was made. If a roll needed replacing in the rolling mills we would cast a replacement. We also made some of our own moulding boxes as well.

Not all of the company's castings were produced here, though: the engineering department made the lineside signs and nameboards displayed around the system. The official policy was that Swindon only cast larger batches of such things: otherwise they couldn't compete on cost. Signal and train lamps were made or repaired in the loco works along with such diverse things as chains, nuts, bolts and rivets, and they may have made their own steel wire and hemp rope. Machine tools had been made in the factory many years before, and two cylinder borers of 1865 and 1881 were still going strong, with the addition of electric motors in place of the old overhead counter-shafting and belt drives, until the end of steam on the Western.

Dozens of types of chains and lifting tackle were made here, so they also had to produce the stores' catalogues that went with them. Some constructional work at Swindon, and throughout the department, was done by CME men or contractors with the approval of the Chief (Civil) Engineer. The company's engineering handbook stipulated that iron and steel brought in for such construction must conform to British Standard Specification No. 153, dictating that a high minimum quality of steel was required, and that where practical all materials should be of British manufacture.

ALSO MADE IN THE CARRIAGE WORKS

Artists and photographers had designed those little pictures that were in every compartment on the trains, and they were framed and glazed in the carriage works. As well as their contribution to railway carriages, carpenters and cabinet makers produced station furniture, trolleys, platform barrows, sack trucks, ticket and label racks, and the fixtures and fittings needed throughout the railway company. No doubt the check boards used for determining the men's attendance had been made 'inside', and it's possible the wood and even the marble roll of honour plaques were made here too. Fitting the upholstery on to coach seats and furniture was done by trimming shop personnel. They also worked with leather to produce such items as tablet pouches (for single-line working), dispatch bags and straps of every description. Bricks and rope had also been made in the carriage side at various times. For men who had been injured while working for the company, wooden artificial limbs were produced by a man at a bench in 7A (Finishers') Shop.

From the middle of the 1930s, with the introduction of chemical additives and solvents for refining, significant improvements were made to lubricating oils and methods of application. Oil could be blended, and used oil cleaned and refined, in the oil works, which had been in use since 1915. (Reclaiming oil was highly specialized; even minute traces of water in lubricating oil could reduce its effectiveness.) They could also produce coolant and hand soap here. Paint from the works' paint mills, putty, grease and the ten tons of soap powder used each year in the company's laundry were also made up on the premises. I've heard it said that candles were produced from tallow somewhere in the carriage body shops.

Some unlikely items were made here, including some not fashioned by the workforce at all. Birds were attracted to come into some of the workshops, especially those with high roofs, and there are stories of them building nests inside. If the location chosen left the birds vulnerable, the men could become very protective towards them. The following was recorded by R. J. Blackmore in 1960 concerning George Higgs, the new sawmills foreman who retired in February 1959:

> In the spring of 1958 a blue tit built a nest in a sashbox of the giant bandsaw. George who ever loved to point out every footprint and every semblance of wild-life near his mill, was delighted. He immediately had a board of the sashbox removed and replaced by glass so that the whole business of family rearing could be observed. Bird lovers who got to hear about the tit, made a surreptitious way from nebulous recesses of the engineering shops to see the intrepid bird; far from being rebuffed by George, they were treated as if they had come from the press, and granted every facility for taking photographs if they were so disposed. George's heart was sad when the crane driver accidently struck the nest just a few hours before the whole family would have been complete.

BOILERMAKING

Locomotive boiler barrel construction involved cutting heavy steel plate and feeding it through bending rolls to form cylinders, the tapered sections requiring great skill to get right. The inner copper and outer steel firebox wrappers were formed under hydraulic presses from single pieces cut out with a template which reduced the number of joints, as these were the weak points. Hundreds of steel and copper staybolts would hold the two together. Dozens of fire (flue) tubes to carry hot gases from the firebox through the boiler were held by tubeplates at either end of the barrel. The tubeplates and firebox throat plate were sheared to shape and flanges formed under a press so as to allow fixing by riveted seams to adjacent structures. The cab sides and roof were also riveted and fitted up by boilermakers, using jigs.

In the 1930s the maintenance of locomotive fireboxes was reduced considerably by the introduction of welded seams in place of riveted lap joints. Welding copper fireboxes by oxyacetylene torch was however very uncomfortable and slow for the gangs of men trained to do it. Because copper is a very good conductor of heat, the insides of the fireboxes being worked on became very hot. Two men worked simultaneously for a short period and were then replaced by another two. At the same time the copper plate around the seam had to be hammered to counteract the effects of shrinkage. As a child in the mid-1940s, Mick Ponting noticed that his neighbour, Mr Heath, who lived opposite him in Whitby Grove, arrived home early each day from the factory. He asked his father, a boilermaker, why this was, and was told: 'Old Charlie Heath welds copper fireboxes, and through the works Committee it was agreed these men should work shorter shifts.'

Doug Webb's father was a skilled man, a chargeman wire rope splicer, but Doug had an older brother who became an apprentice boilermaker, leaving him to become a labourer. Doug started in the boiler shop alongside Rodbourne Road, like his brother, in 1936. The head boiler foreman at that time was Mr Eburne. Doug said: 'I started as a "water boy"; as the men worked on fireboxes and boiler barrels I poured water over the cutting tools to keep them cool.' Some of this was done from the inside, so Doug had to work with a candle and a box of matches signed out from the stores. Until the early 1930s, drilling out staybolts on boilers in for overhaul was slow and costly. Drill bits would go blunt and break regularly, so French Wageor electric drills were brought in. They were very powerful and had a forward thrust driven by compressed air. Like similar equipment used for drilling and reaming holes once the stays were out, the new drills hung in suspension from above and could be operated by one man.

Working on steam boilers was very noisy because of the use of hydraulic riveting guns against the heavy plate barrel and box fabrications and the manual hammering of rivets that were inaccessible to the machine. Much of this work relied on co-operation between men and they communicated by hand signals. The noise was such that it soon caused hearing problems, and it is well known locally that a retired Swindonian with indistinct speech and a hearing aid was likely to have been a boilerman 'inside'. As well as V Shop (boilermakers), Doug spent time in P1 Shop, where the completed boilers, weighing anything up to 24 tons, were taken to have their fittings attached. They were then tested with steam from a master boiler, thus avoiding the need to fire them up in the normal way. A two- to three-inch layer of asbestos that had been soaked to form a paste was then added by the 'plasterers' while the boiler was still hot. This ensured it dried out thoroughly and quickly. A tunnel, through which the boilers were taken, connected the two workshops, one either side of Rodbourne Road. 'The irregular bursts of high-pressure steam soon played havoc with your nerves,' said Doug. The men could apply for other types of work in the vicinity and vacancies were displayed on the noticeboard. Doug did manage to move and was then based in the nearby 'tube house' with chargeman Ernie Fisher and his assistant Jesse Pettifer. Here the fire tube ends were machined to fit the tube plates: one end was stretched and the other narrowed. 'I still found myself in the boiler shop a lot of the time but the balance (piecework bonus) was better here. Another thing I remember about the tube house was the dust coming down when the rats ran along the pipes overhead. This made the woman that were here in the war feel uneasy at first.'

Doug saw one poor fellow, a 'hooker on', crushed by a boiler when the slings suspending it gave way. He thought this was about 1937 or 1938: 'I can't think of his name but I remember he lived in Princes Street. The mood in the shop was very subdued for the rest of the day.' By coincidence a similar story appeared in a recent newspaper feature that resurrects news that was published 'on this day' in years gone by. From this I am fairly sure that Doug was referring to Charles Wheeler, aged 50, who was due to marry an Eva Humphries in a few weeks. The date of the accident was given as 1 March 1940. After witnessing this and seeing a friend suffer a nasty injury when some scrap iron fell on his arm in the rolling mills, Doug decided he had had enough and, with his father's blessing, left the works shortly afterwards.

STAMPING, SMITHS AND STEAM HAMMERS

Peter Reade was not a local lad but had an uncle who lived in Swindon and worked 'inside'. Peter was looking for alternative employment and told me that 'The idea of working with steam locomotives seemed exciting to me, so Uncle Charlie (Pipkin), a C&W upholsterer, got me an application form for the Swindon factory.' The company preferred newcomers to have an older relative already in their employ who would vouch for them. The rule that only sons and daughters of workers could apply for work in the Western had presumably been relaxed when the need for labour increased. After an interview and a medical examination, Peter started in F (loco-side smiths') Shop in 1939, along with some other chaps who were all about his age. The work of the smiths was, by diverse means, to heat steel ingots, blooms or wrought iron and forge it, usually by hammering. This work was carried out in F and F2 Shops. They were separated by an area where the big steam and drop hammers (30 cwt up to 6 ton capacity) were used to forge such things as locomotive coupling rods, connecting rods and extension frames. Peter said:

> Donald Grant, Bill Tidmarsh, Gordon Glover and I all trained to be steam hammer drivers. We were each put with a gang of four men working the smaller 10 -to 20-cwt hammers. As drivers we set the hammers (the extent of the downward thrust) and controlled the amount of steam admitted to power the blows, according to the smith's instructions. An experienced smith would often communicate with his mate (the driver or striker if hand forging) by nodding his head: the more pronounced the nod, the heavier the blow. Later we progressed to the larger hammers. Down the sides of the shop were blacksmiths' forges, each with an open tank of water (called a bosh) to cool the blacksmiths' tongs. The steam hammers and furnaces were down the centre of the shop, and half way down both shops was a large circular saw that was used to cut through hot metal.

Other areas in the smiths' shop included stamps or drop hammers, chainmakers, springsmiths and a gas welding section. The other types of heat treatment done by smiths elsewhere was that of normalising, annealing, hardening, quenching and tempering of components and tools. Carefully controlled heating and cooling was usually done to produce the high-tensile, toughened, hardened steel and iron needed to resist wear and the stresses of tension and compression. Cutting tools, rope wire, couplings, buffers, tyres, axles, brake blocks and springs were all heat treated here.

F and F2 Shops each covered an area of about 33,000 square feet. The floor was just earth, which was sprayed with water every now and again to keep the dust down; components were stacked on steel plates. Despite the heat from the forges and furnaces, it could be very cold and draughty in winter, especially for the hammer drivers. The foremen in the smiths' shops during Peter's time were Alfred Legge (springmakers and chainmakers), Frank Mason (smiths), and Mr Titcombe (steam hammers and stamps). Herbert Parker was the chief foreman over these areas until he retired in 1939 with fifty years' service. 'In the early days of the war a lot of younger men in the smiths' shop, as elsewhere, volunteered and were accepted into the armed forces before we found ourselves in a reserved occupation. Four of us hammer drivers tried to join the Navy but were turned away for being underage,' said Peter. Later in the war, when they were thinking of putting women on to steam hammers, Peter and others were asked if they wanted to learn the art of hand forging as a blacksmith. They jumped at the chance and, after three years of 'working on the other side of the anvil', they were able to call themselves skilled tradesmen.

The men wore leather aprons and pads to protect against flying sparks and embers. The 'inside mate' got the metal to the right heat: he was the senior striker and was on a slightly higher rate of pay. The blacksmith held the work while strikers hammered it alternatively. The smith moved it and turned it, thus controlling the form it took. Various types and sizes of hammers were available depending on the work. Most blacksmiths had one or two strikers and some jobs required even more. They had to make all their own tools and were always in demand to make items for use at home (known as foreigners), such as pokers, chisels, axe heads and even iron gates. Most foremen were quite firm in their dealings with the men but in return for the odd 'foreigner' for themselves, within reason they turned a blind eye to the practice. The railway work of the loco side blacksmith included fashioning cab fittings such as regulator handles (known 'inside' as starting handles) and brake levers. Engine piston rings were also roughed out by the blacksmith before being machined.

On the carriage side there were seventy-six skilled smiths in the early 1930s: besides the furnaces and hand-forging facilities they had the use of two hot saws and nine steam hammers. By 1948 there were 109 C&W smiths: their work included making parts for brake systems and fittings for goods containers as well as numerous tools used in the works and elsewhere on the railway. A lot of coupling links were manufactured by the carriage smiths, using a pneumatic 5-cwt hammer.

Peter joined the Amalgamated Engineering Union as a lot of the smiths and strikers were members of it. Their own union, along with those of several other crafts, had been amalgamated to form the new AEU in the 1920s. Peter said: 'To pay my dues, I used to meet a bloke in the pub down by what was still known as the old Golden Lion Bridge.' The company would not allow such transactions to take place in the factory before the 1940s. Other men remembered in Peter Reade's shop were 'Spud' Taylor, Frank Ellis, Peter Vizard, Alec Leach, Eric Bradley, Ken Pinnegar and Jim Poole, who came over from the C&W side and was a big union man. A number of people, including Peter, have pointed out that it is not easy remembering names as many workers were only known by a nickname.

ROLLING MILLS

Another 'hot shop' was the rolling mills. Doug Webb worked here as a 'puller up' in the 1930s when Billy Davis was the foreman. 'It was hell in there,' Doug said, 'Very hot and, until you got used to it, very dangerous. I had no choice, as a labourer I could be moved from one shop or area to another.' The puller up got the steel billets and blooms into and out of the furnaces by sliding them along on rollers. Steel used in the rolling mill was either in the form of purchased billets or old carriage and wagon axles that had been melted and recast. Large pieces of white hot metal were slid across the floor, which was lined with iron plates, and for this reason, no outsider dared walk through the shop. The iron used was grade C, which was made from assorted scrap, and A and B iron, which came from selected scrap and had also been melted down.

One or two 'shinglers' used large pairs of forceps to turn white-hot iron under a 70-cwt steam hammer. By the 1930s this was believed to be the only place in the country still using this method. They wore face guards, white smocks, leather aprons and iron boots while handling the mass between hammer blows. A third man controlled the rate of the blows with a lever at the side. After the metal was compressed sufficiently it was slid across the floor by a 'rougher' or transported on a truck by a 'coacher'. The work was then passed quickly through roughing rolls and back through finishing rolls, which squeezed it into a long bar. Setting the rolls and seeing that the drawn metal became the correct profile was the job of the 'roller', and he was the chargeman. The finished rolled iron or steel was either taken to the benches to be straightened or was cut into sections, causing a spectacular show of flying sparks. All this had to be done before it cooled too much and hardened. The mills themselves consisted of a 10-inch and a 14-inch roll, each driven by a stationary steam engine built in the works in the nineteenth century.

LOCOMOTIVE ERECTING

Of necessity, the buildings within the works were constructed and enlarged haphazardly over more than one hundred years. Consequently many were out of date and certainly not laid out to serve production efficiently. Only the A Shop appeared to harmonize the different stages of locomotive stripping, rebuilding and new building. Even then, this was only achieved after a major rethink of the way each stage was carried out by Mr Millard and his bosses in the early 1930s. A Shop was divided up into AW (wheel section), AM (machines), AV (boilers) and AE (erecting bays). At the eastern end of a shop was the engine test plant and, when in use, would have the wooden No4 dynamometer car alongside providing additional recording apparatus. After the extensions to A Shop in 1921 to take the larger locomotives, there were enough extra-capacity engine pits, electric traversers and overhead cranes to deal with 400 larger-type engines annually. Some smaller classes of engines went into the B Erecting Shop up until the workshop space was needed for building diesel multiple units.

The movement of all components through the shops was scheduled in the progress office. All hold-ups were chased by the progress staff, the object being to bring all parts together for assembly at the right time and not have men left waiting on others. In the 1930s the method of overhaul was altered from 'strip and rebuild' on the same pit with the same erectors to a sectionalised flow system, usually referred to as 'the circuit'. This required the locomotive to be lifted and lowered into different sections from stripping to various stages of rebuilding. In his book: *Swindon Steam 1921–1951*, Kenneth Cook tells us that the installation of the Zeiss optical equipment for aligning locomotive frames and the machinery for grinding the hornblocks 'forced upon us a complete alteration to our system of locomotive repairs'. Hugh Freebury, who was there in the run-up to the changeover, said in his book *Great Western Apprentice* that there was strong opposition to this from the men.

Locomotives requiring works' attention usually arrived at Swindon overnight. If necessary, steam locos were turned, while in steam, to face London and parked at the east end of the works. Once inside the erecting shop those for overhaul were stripped down and the frames and cylinder blocks cleaned by hand using scrapers: all smaller detachable parts were taken to the 'bosh'. Here they were immersed in a tank of boiling caustic soda solution to remove dirt and oil (which could be recovered) before being inspected and sent on to various shops for repair or scrap. The boshing plant was renewed in 1939/40 and moved close to the stripping pits. It was then served by a Wharton 6-ton overhead crane capable of dipping a bogie truck complete or the largest pairs of driving wheels. Bill Harper, Roy Gibbs and Len White worked here as labourers in the 1950s. The surfaces of piston valves and internal passages of cylinder blocks, among others, needed decarbonising while boiler parts including fire tubes and superheater flues needed to go for descaling.

New engine frame members and cylinder blocks were received from W (Machine) Shop and assembled on 'new work' pits. One end was lowered on to timber baulks and the other on to jacks so that they could be set level ready to be squared up. From now on the building sequence was the same as for rebuilding engines after overhaul. The cylinders, extension frames and angle irons were fitted before the boiler, cab, steam fountain and reversing handle were fitted. Connecting, coupling and piston rods and other parts that made up the valve gear had been machined and heat treated in the furnace, then cooled in oil, making them both hard and tough to resist wear and stress. The cylinder block and smokebox saddle castings had been machined using cylinder borers and a radical planning machine respectively. Steel tyres were heated in a special furnace in the shop floor of the wheel section. The wheel centre was lowered into the hot tyre, which had expanded: as it cooled the tyre shrank on to it and held fast (old tyres were also taken off by heating in the same way). A new or reconditioned boiler from V Shop, with fittings attached and tested in P1 Shop, was then fitted into the frames. Lowering the locomotive on to its driving wheels was the last major job to be done by the erectors.

The most costly locomotives to build in the mid-1930s were the four-cylinder Castles, costing around £5,000 each. The boiler with the firebox fitted was the most expensive of the major components at slightly more than £1,000. The 4,000-gallon tender cost a further £1,000. Other locomotives in the erecting area had been taken out of service for various types of overhaul, depending on the mileage since the last visit and mechanical condition.

John Brettell finished his apprenticeship in 1946 and started in A Shop on Georgie Gardener's gang. They fitted the boiler, valve gear and motion bars. 'Next to the work of building and stripping boilers, locomotive erecting was generally considered the most undesirable area to work in because it was heavy going,' said John. The stripping pits were where the dirtiest and heaviest work took place, and Dave Viveash had expected to start there when his time came in the 1950s. Instead he was sent to work with Harry Bown and Arthur Iles, aligning the cylinders and horn gaps in the main frames in the early stages of locomotive (re)building. From there he moved to horn grinding, which was done in conjunction with the optical alignment of the frames, and again the work was relatively light and clean. The Zeiss optical method of lining up the frames had first been used on the German state railways. It considerably reduced the time previously spent on this work and increased the time between the maintenance of the motion parts. Dave's next stop was valve setting with Bob Jarvis: 'They thought they were a bit above the other gangs in the shop, but it was not as difficult as they tried to make out.' George Petfield said that Ernie Nutty, the senior technical assistant in the 1950s, could listen to a locomotive move away after (re)building and say what adjustments, if any, were needed to the valve settings. This was the last procedure carried out before the engine went out to the weigh house for wheel balancing, then trials.

In the weigh house the locomotive was driven on to balancing pans and the weight on each driving wheel was taken in turn. The leaf springs had been over-tightened before leaving the erecting shop so that now they could be slackened to make all the readings the same (it was impossible to get enough torque to do it the other way round). With this done, the adhesion would be improved and the wear on the bearing surfaces such as the big-end bushes was minimised. The GWR relied more on an ageing express passenger fleet of locomotives between the 1930s and the 1950s than the other companies. Consequently, the amount of time spent in the works or stopped at depots increased and availability decreased.

O SHOP: TOOL ROOM

Engineering tool rooms would normally make their own jigs, and perhaps gauges, but not usually drills, taps, dies, milling cutters and reamers. Their manufacture was more specialised, but Swindon could make the lot, and made them by the advanced method of grinding the cutting surfaces of hardened blanks. This was during the war when the usual suppliers could not meet the demand and such things became difficult to buy in. The tool room was the showpiece of any engineering works. At Swindon there were 100 machine tools for such things as thread grinding, jig boring, gear cutting (or hobbing) and tool tipping, as well as 140 skilled tool and gauge makers.

For a visit of the Mechanical, Electrical and Carriage & Wagon Engineers in May of 1953, some of the more impressive work carried out was noted in the tour guidebook:

A high standard of workmanship with close tolerances for engine parts depends on accurate tools and gauges coupled with constant checking (calibration). In 1929 a Lindner thread grinding machine of German origin, the first on any British railway, was installed mainly for the production of boiler stay taps. The results were very successful; the cost of manufacture of the stay taps was less than half the price asked by the trade and the output of new and repaired boilers was considerably improved by their use. In 1930 a second similar machine was installed and all taps were, afterwards, produced by this method. A fixture was developed in the shop to enable all types of dies and chasers with flat threads, to be ground on the machine. A suitable hardening and tempering procedure was developed and special measuring instruments installed in the inspection section which included the following: 1) an optical machine called a Hilger projector, which could magnify profiles of threads, gauges, etc., by 50 times, enabling an accurate check on the shape, to be made. 2) A horizontal O.M.T. Omtimeter with which it was possible to measure accurately to 1/20th of a 'thou' (1/1000th of an inch) on external and internal measurements. 3) A Sigma screw diameter and radius measuring machine which could measure diameters of threads to an accuracy of 1/10th of a thou up to a diameter of 4in. 4) An Edgwick optical dividing head that could measure angles to an accuracy of three seconds of a degree, was used for checking jigs, gauges etc. 5) An Edgwick diamond hardness tester, used for checking the hardness of various items manufactured in the Tool Room. 6) A Spekker steeloscope (also made by Adam Hilger Ltd) was installed during the war to enable rapid checks of the special alloy steels which were used extensively in the manufacture of war work, and by its use it was possible to identify the alloys of steel used and to give approximately the percentage content of the alloying metals.

Early in the war the Ministry of Supply arranged for the transfer of a Lindner jig boring machine to be installed in the Tool Room in a special enclosure. Later two thread grinding machines were brought in from the makers: The Coventry Gauge and Tool Company Ltd. One was a universal thread grinding machine for internal and external work with a capacity up to 8in diameter x 18in in length. The second was a Matrix machine to take similar diameter work up to 40in in length.

Mechanical clocks used in the works were made by well-known makers but repaired on site in a workshop next to Foreman Bill Holland's office, above O Shop. As was often the case, O Shop offices were above the shop's tool store. Dave Ellis worked in O Shop in the 1950s and remembers that Fred Gabb was 'chargeman clock repairs' and George Reason was the other senior person on that section.

MACHINE TOOL INSTALLATION

Erecting new machinery was a regular occurrence in the Swindon workshops through a policy of continuous renewal. If a case could be made by the works managers that production was being affected or that costs were excessive because of outdated machine tools, then it was likely to be acted upon. The preferred manufacturer depended on reputation, and shop floor supervisory staff would have an opinion on this too. Makers' catalogues showing the latest products were received and retained as a matter of course. The model chosen would depend on the type of work to be undertaken and price. Machine tool manufacturers had their own rail access and would dispatch direct to the receiving workshop in sheeted open wagons. For the purposes of accounting, the paperwork was handled by the stores department.

At the chosen site in the workshop a hole was dug in the floor. This may or may not have been the site of an outgoing machine. Works bricklayers, with advice from a machine tool fitter, excavated a space for the baseplate using a template made by a D Shop carpenter. Next the brickies laid a suitable foundation of brick or concrete or both. Meanwhile the main component parts of the machine were lifted from the wagon outside, by crane. They were moved into the shop by the 'heavy gang' using rollers, ropes and levers. Under no circumstances was a crane to be used to winch the loads along. Once set on to its foundation and loosely bolted down, the machine was fully assembled. Wedges of steel and timber were then driven under and around the base to bring the structure into alignment using plumb lines and a spirit level. The bricklayers then prepared a strong mortar mix and poured it into the cavity around the base.

This type of work was often done after the Friday day shift had finished or during the annual holiday shutdown. A general arrangement (blueprint) drawing and a manual would accompany the cargo as aids for future maintenance by works fitters. An export packing list of parts was included with machinery to be assembled on site. Every machine tool in the works was given a number, which was fitted to it on a cast plate. This identified it for maintenance and for company records.

This photograph shows King Class locomotives of the 1930 batch in the early stages of building. These are the pit roads of the new work section at the top (north) end of the AE shop. On the right, the main longitudinal frame plates have arrived from W shop and are laid flat for jig-drilling. Next they will be stood upright for cross members to be temporarily bolted on, ready for the frames to be set level and squared up. With this done the whole assembly was secured by stiffeners and the buffer beam, forming the foundation on to which the locomotive was built. The horizontal jib crane supporting the hydraulic riveter could be swung to serve up to four engines being erected on the two roads. A method of arranging component parts and tool equipment to be used seems to be non-existent. The coming 'overhaul circuit' would, to some extent, improve this. (Authors' collection)

This is one end of the north bay of the Iron Foundry where the heavier work was undertaken. It was equipped with 5-ton swivelling jib cranes and a 20-ton overhead crane that ran the length of the shop. The foreman in the trilby hat, Charlie Webb, watches as high-grade molten iron is poured into core barrels to produce cylinder castings. (BRW)

A set of loco driving wheels mounted in a quartering machine. The opposing crank pins are being machined to achieve exact positions 90 degrees apart. A number of operations had already been done to the wheel centre castings and axles to reach this stage. Firstly the bosses had to be bored out and keyways cut. The axles were ground and pressed into the wheels hydraulically, together with the keys. On a wheel lathe, the rims were then turned ready to accept the tyres which would be expanded by heating and shrunk on using a gas furnace specially designed for the purpose. A key called a Gibson ring was driven into a recess between the tyre and rim to further ensure it held fast. The wheel diameters could now be finish turned before holes were bored and crank pins pressed home. (BRW)

Alignment or 'squaring-up' of locomotive frames was done at the start of building or rebuilding. The man on the left will measure the distance from the front (outside) cylinder face to all the axlebox guide faces in turn using a telescope. The other man is lining-up a collimator which enables the telescope to take a reading. The measurements of guide faces relative to cylinders determined how much was to be ground off or added to the faces. The objective was to have the centre lines of the axles, when rewheeled, at absolute right angles to the cylinder centre lines and at the correct distances along them. (BRW)

The roof label boards that were so much a part of the 'Western' were produced in the Carriage Works: the painting and lettering being the job of carriage signwriters in 8 (carriage painting) Shop. This coach is one of the rear portion of the post-war 1.30 p.m. Paddington to Penzance service. They were detached at Newton Abbot to become a short train for the Torquay line. (Ken Ellis)

Hydraulically lifting a bogie up to a carriage from below floor level in 19C Shop. (BRW)

Moving carriage wheels and bogies using a 7.5-ton Wharton electric crane, which took its power from overhead lines. (BRW)

A wagon repair line in 21 Shop. (BRW)

A machine tool in R Shop salvaged from a German ship after the First World War: so the story goes. (R. Grainger)

A mobile tank removing used coolant from a Churchill plain grinding machine. Another tank would go round and refill the machine tools. (BRW)

A line of Ward No.10 combination turret lathes in R (machine) Shop. (BRW)

A large locomotive connecting rod is being checked with calipers between blows as it is forged under a 4-ton Massey steam hammer. (BRW)

5 cwt. PNEUMATIC POWER HAMMER "WITH SLIDES"

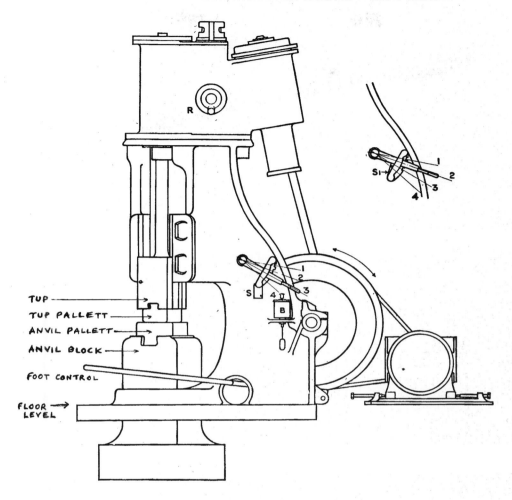

A diagram of a machine tool from the makers' manual: one of which was delivered to the Carriage and Wagon Works' Smithy in 1932. It would have been used to forge relatively small masses of iron and steel such as components for carriage and wagon drawgear, brakegear and carriage bogie frames. The hot metal to be shaped was held on the anvil pallet while the tup pallet rose and fell as either a single blow or as continuous (automatic) blows. A section of the carriage and wagon smiths' shop was almost continuously manufacturing 3 link couplings. For this the 5cwt hammer was used to form and close the links by hammer welding.

Apart from being ahead of its time as regards operating versatility, there was nothing remarkable about this particular piece of machinery compared to others being erected in the works regularly. However, for some reason the paperwork that accompanied it from B&S. Massey Ltd of Openshaw, has survived. From this it can be seen that: the machine arrived towards the end of July 1932 in 33 separate parts; it cost the GWR £306-16s-6d; its height above ground was 9ft; the drive was powered by a 17 horse-power electric motor. Inside the cover of the manual is handwritten: A.H. Munden, 15 Shop, and I assume he was the machine tool fitter responsible for maintaining this equipment at some period.

7

Workshop Grades

With sons following their fathers into the works in the time-honoured way, many men had an unbroken family line of railway ancestors going back well before the turn of the century. The staff magazine of 1954 recorded the case of Chargeman Steward, an erector in A Shop whose grandfather came to Swindon in 1852, like so many at that time, from the north of England. The grandfather's son worked 'inside' all his life, and his grandson (Steward), along with his two sons, who were both still in A Shop and would put in many more years yet. Bert Harber's father William had come down from Wolverhampton to be apprenticed in the locomotive works in the days when the time served was seven years. When Bert started, his father was in AM Shop, his three brothers and three uncles were also in the massive A Shop, a fourth uncle, Ralph Morkott, was boilermaking; only his father-in-law did not work 'inside', having left some years before.

SHOPMEN

Labourers and newcomers to the workshops could join the National Union of Railwaymen, the Transport and General Workers' Union or the Amalgamated Engineering Union. After a period in post they were eligible to join a union representing their craft, and that's what some shopmen chose to do. There were about thirty-two different types of crafts represented at railway shopmen's negotiations. Patternmakers, plumbers, foundrymen, coppersmiths, braziers, metalworkers and electricians all had their own societies within the Federation of Engineering and Shipbuilding Trades. According to the Swindon and District Directory for 1938, there were ten local branches of the AEU with a total of 3,000 members, most of whom would have worked 'inside' at that time. Each branch met regularly and most had a room set aside at a specific public house or working men's club. One met at the main Mechanics' Institute and another at the Labour Exchange.

There was a definite divide between workers on the loco side and those on the carriage and wagon side, and it was rare to move from one side to the other. On the loco side, fitters stripped and assembled components and made sure moving parts worked with each other. Turners operated lathes, machines whereby the work rotates on its axis at the optimum cutting speed of the particular metal, while the cutting tool moves in a horizontal plane only. They cut internal and external threads, bored out the centre and face-finished the surfaces of cylindrical work pieces. The gangs of men who assembled the component parts of a steam locomotive were the fitter/erectors in the main. Other trades included welders, electricians, smiths and boilermen, but the majority on the loco side were known generally as either fitters or machinists. Building carriages and wagons also required mechanical engineers for underframe, bogie and wheel work. Carriage tradesmen such as bodymakers, carpenters, trimmers, polishers and coach finishers built the carriage body and doors as well as the interior doors, panelling, upholstery and did the fitting out. Wagon builders and frame builders worked in 13 and 21 wagon shops. Loco, carriage and wagon all had separate gangs of painters (or signwriters), fitters, machinists, carpenters, sawyers, and riveters etc. There were separate gangs of carpenters, electricians, plumbers and gas fitters for workshop and building installations.

Each profession invariably became known by a more basic term according to the types of work performed: a 'rubber', 'flatter', 'shingler', 'fettler', 'straightener', 'pressman', 'clothier', 'saw doctor', 'dings separator', 'knocker up', 'holder up', 'hooker on', or any one of half a hundred other mysterious titles. The labour was divided up into gangs usually consisting of men of the same grade, such as labourers, skilled or semi-skilled. Sometimes they had assistants (apprentices) attached to the gang. Individual gangs were known by the surname of their chargeman. I have heard it said that some chargemen were not very agreeable to those of lower station, such as the apprentices and labourers in their charge. Alan Lambourn said that some chargemen had been known to clip an apprentice round the ear. A good worker was sometimes overlooked when promotion was being considered because the foreman didn't want to lose his output. Another unfair practice was that of promoting a union agitator in the certain knowledge that this would temper his militant ways.

SHOP OFFICE 'BOY'

Harry Bartlett started work as office boy at the beginning of 1943 in 20 Shop. This was one of the workshops concerned with carriage repairs in the north-east of the site. Harry, who lived in nearby Northern Road, was mainly occupied with collecting and distributing the post between shop offices in this part of the works and the carriage and wagon main offices. Post for other parts of the works was deposited into canvas bags at the C&W offices too. I have condensed the following from his written recollections:

My first call, the stamp shop, was a black hole of noise, smoke and soot interspersed with bright lights from the furnaces and required time for the eyes to adjust. From there it was a short walk to 16 (Wheel) Shop and up a steep flight of stairs. Mr Hillier, the head foreman, would often be stood at the top outside his office, surveying the workers. Next stop was 17 (Road Wagon) Shop where, unique among the shop offices, all the clerks were female. The last call before the offices was to 5 (Electrical) Shop where train lighting and dynamos were set up and tested and coach batteries were assembled, repaired and charged. I had to complete this round three times in the morning and twice in the afternoon.

I made friends with two other office boys who had post rounds nearby: Laurence Gilby and John Ealy. We would arrange to finish at the main offices at the same time so we could spend time together. Between 15 and 21 Shops there were two overground air-raid shelters of concrete construction and covered with earth. The two entrances each led to a tunnel with bench seats on either side. Our game was to go individually from door to door in total darkness. On occasions we tried to persuade office girls from the stores department to accompany us through, but without success: they had more sense. Sometimes, if there was no one else about, we would ride up and down the yard behind 21 Shop, on a platelayers' trolley. These were small flat wagons propelled by two people pumping a lever up and down to drive cams on the axles.

One of the recognised but unofficial duties of the office juniors was to collect privilege (railway travel) tickets for men in the workshop, from the works' booking office. This was a cheap way for workers to get away to the coast or to see relatives in wartime, now that Trip was cancelled for the duration. Working long hours as they now did and with the booking office only opening for short periods each day, the men would leave their stamped and authorized forms, together with the money, at the shop office. Harry goes on to record:

> It was like a rugby scrum at the booking office windows when they did open and it was easy to get into a muddle working out how much change to give each applicant but we were tipped well for it. Another useful sideline was going out into the town to buy men cigarettes. Office boys had free reign at the entrances and even the watchmen sometimes required our services. At Christmas it was a recognised custom for the office boy to go round and wish all the men in the shop a happy Christmas, while shaking a collection box under their noses. This brought in quite a lot of extra to supplement my low wages. In January 1945 I taught the new boy Eric Sanders the ropes and left to start my training in 15 Shop.

APPRENTICESHIP TRAINING

Many boys in the town wanted to be engine drivers and their fathers would point out that they would not like the shift work. There were only limited opportunities to work on the footplate, so most of those young men would settle for work in the factory and would, they hoped, be eligible for the loco side. By the 1950s some boys were more interested in aircraft than trains and would apply first to Vickers Armstrong, where there was an apprentice training school.

Jack Fleetwood started 'inside' when he reached fifteen years of age. As with all new starters, he presented himself at the office just inside the main tunnel entrance and was taken to the designated shop office by another recently appointed junior. (On the carriage side, Harry Bartlett remembers being taken over to 14 Shop by a Mr Richens, the registrar from the carriage and wagon staff section who dealt with the new recruits.) Until he could start his apprenticeship at the age of sixteen, Jack spent the year in the R Shop 'scraggery'. Here there were about thirty juniors working basic lathes under two chargemen. The automatic machinery was set up by turners acting as tool setters but the production was done by the youngsters who also fed the lengths of bar into the lathes. The scraggery was one of the few production areas certified to allow boys to work: another was N (bolt) Shop. Jack said that 'Swindon got through a lot of bolts.' It had been policy never to re-use them if they had been used on locomotives and had been drilled to take split pins, but if they were in good condition, they did start re-using them after the war. 'Nuts and bolts could be bought in cheaply enough, and that's what most firms did. Not us, though, because while the low paid were producing them, we could make them just as cheap.'

One of the smaller lads working in the scraggery might be sent to B Shed where the dismantling and erection of tenders took place. Alan Lambourn remembers being given a lighted candle, which was pressed into a large nut to form a base, then lowered into a tender tank:

> I had to crawl to the narrow front end and fasten nuts and washers on to bolts that were pushed through from the outside. You disturbed a lot of rust in there and if you sneezed and blew out the candle, you were in trouble. I remember too, finding small dead fish in the bottom of the tender tank. They once lived in the lineside water tanks that supplied the columns.

Typically, Alan got most of his loco side fitting experience on machine tool maintenance. In George Marchment's gang they would strip down Tool Room machinery, replace worn parts and rebuild them. Later he moved on to the R Shop safety-valve fitting section, which involved mainly bench fitting with Tommy Marchment's (George's brother) gang. Tom was also chargeman of the men on the boiler and vessel testing section.

Jack Fleetwood's father was classed as semi-skilled and therefore could only manage to secure a semi-skilled position for his boy. He could not afford to pay for a premium apprenticeship, even though the £110 fee was spread over the whole term. Nor could he afford to keep him while Jack repaid the costs of learning a trade. Because he worked 'inside' himself, on internal transport, Mr Fleetwood was given a choice of work for his son when he reached sixteen years of age. He could choose between rough painting of wagons and buildings, moulding or machining. Jack enquired which job paid the most and was told that the moulder got an extra shilling a week on the rate. He therefore started in the brass foundry on Georgie White's gang; this was on 16 July 1937.

The majority of the men in the shops were what was known as journeymen: they had successfully completed a recognised apprenticeship in one of the engineering or building trades. Only the eldest son of a skilled man in the service of the GWR might obtain a course of training with the costs met by the company. I have heard it said that when a boy was born his name could be registered at the works for an apprenticeship place when the time came. The training started on or just after the sixteenth birthday and lasted a full five years. A commitment to attend night school at The College, formerly the North Wilts Technical Schools, on two or more evenings a week was also required. Additional engineering workshops had been built behind The College, in Byron Street, by 1930. This was to cater for new courses in electrical engineering, welding, foundry work and blacksmithing. Pupils from the works were also taught signwriting and plumbing in the new annexe.

Fitting and turning apprenticeships in the carriage works amounted to a total of three years on various types of lathes, and two doing such things as bench fitting or factory maintenance work. On the loco side the first two years were again spent operating chuck turning machine tools and vertical borers etc., then eighteen months each on fitting and loco erecting. Alan Lambourn said: 'Despite still learning we were nevertheless expected to produce. This together with the low wages made us cheap labour.'

The labour requirements of the railway factory could not be forecast five years ahead, so it was in the company's interest to have an ongoing surplus of apprentices coming out of their time. Those dismissed at the end of their training were said to be 'going on an improver'. If they later returned with a good report, as many did, the company would usually take them back and gain an experienced hand. It is often said these days that these men wanted to return to the factory, but old Swindonians with long memories say it was more likely they wanted to return to the place of their roots, where no other work for which they were qualified was available. After the war the situation changed completely and apprentices were usually offered work 'inside' at the end of their time.

Dave Viveash started his apprenticeship as fitter, turner and erector in March 1956. As usual his first stop was R (machine) Shop. He did not go straight into the scraggery like Jack Fleetwood and most others; he worked on Reggie Emmon's gang using specially adapted Ward No. 7 combination turret lathes. They turned the smaller firebox crown stays and, when more experienced, put the threads on them using a thread chasing cutting tool, which was easily chipped if not kept sharp. Dave's first week's pay was about £3 10s. Even at this date R Shop still used some overhead countershafting to drive machine tools. It is said that one or more of the machines used here were salvaged from ships, possibly German, after the First World War. In the 1950s the last hour on Friday afternoon throughout the workshops became a time for winding down for the week; production stopped, benches were cleaned and machinery was lubricated. An issue of oil and cleaning materials as well as hand soap could be drawn from the stores for this purpose.

FOREMEN

At Swindon, foremen were in charge of a workshop or of one type of tradesmen if, as was often the case, the shop employed various types of skilled workers. Promotion was usually from within the shop: the usual route was to chargeman, then piecework inspector, then foreman. This privileged position meant a responsibility for anywhere between twenty and one hundred men, occasionally more, and in areas with higher concentrations of men there would be under-foremen too. The more men under his control the higher a foreman's status was considered to be. Before the war the fear of being unemployed was enough to keep the men in check, but if that was not enough, the foreman, it is said, could summarily dismiss a worker who came to his attention. On the other hand a foreman who became too familiar with his men risked being considered a soft touch and would lose the fear of authority that was sometimes misinterpreted as respect.

The majority of photographs recording the works' activity were taken by professionals before the 1930s, at a time when the works' foremen wore bowler hats. That is therefore how they are remembered nowadays. But by the 1940s, the younger foremen especially were more likely to be seen in the more fashionable trilby. The larger shops had more than one foreman on the payroll. Swindon's A Shop, the largest workshop in the works, had four chief foremen, one for each of the main sections: erecting, machines, boilers and wheels. All these types of work overlapped with other locomotive workshops so these foremen were not confined to this one shop. It sounds a bit top heavy, but it should be remembered that these foremen, between them, oversaw around 1400 men who were producing the company's most valuable asset. To co-ordinate each of the A Shop sections there was an assistant chief and a chief foreman in overall charge. Stan Millard succeeded Mr Plaister as chief A and B Erecting Shops foreman in 1934 when he was only in his thirties himself. He remained there until he died, in office, in 1954. The funeral service was held at the Wesleyan Chapel in Fleet Street, possibly the last time the building was used for this purpose.

Mr Millard was succeeded by Ernest Simpkins who came over from G Shop. Jim Owen, the other long-serving A Shop foreman and one-time president of the Foreman's Association, retired as assistant chief in the early 1960s. Mr Millard had been a member of, and contributor to, the Swindon Engineering Society, as were all the more ambitious and capable engineers at Swindon. On the carriage side there were chief foremen for bodymakers, finishers, fitters, painters, trimmers, wagon builders and the sawmill workers. The most senior foremen had, in earlier times, been referred to as 'superintendent', but by the 1930s this title was used more for the senior divisional and outdoor engineers. When the term 'chief' was used by the men, they were likely to be referring to the chief mechanical engineer.

When he was works manager, Mr Collett brought a fitter in as chief foreman to take charge of the boiler shops. Normally, of course, someone from within their own ranks would be promoted, so this was a controversial decision. The reason for this was 'to bring precision into boilermaking'. In 1914 or thereabouts when this situation came about, the resentment felt by the men towards their new boss was of little concern to management. When the foreman in question retired in 1937, Mr Collett was still in a position to decide who would replace him. However attitudes had changed in the intervening period, and a more even-handed approach was taken over grievances and work practices. The possibility that morale might affect production could no longer be ignored. The replacement this time was a boilerman by trade.

CONDITIONS

Despite the state of the economy in the 1930s and the uncertainty of secure employment, improvements for the men were successfully negotiated. The previous fifty-four hour, six-day week was reduced to forty-seven or forty-eight hours by starting at 8 a.m. instead of 6 a.m., to be worked over no more than six turns. When Jack Fleetwood first started 'inside', there were no proper (tea) breaks, although this meant that for those who could get away with it, no time was deducted while consuming some refreshment. Like many others, Jack took in a tea can, some sugar and a tin of condensed milk and took his chances. Doug remembers cocoa being more popular than tea in the 1930s. He said: 'If you got caught having a drink in the boiler shop, you were sent home for three days.' In Jack's experience:

> Some foremen were more sympathetic. If Taffy Thomas, the foreman in the iron foundry, came across anyone having a drink or a crafty draw, he usually said, 'that's alright lads,' as he lit his own pipe. Then you had the situation of the foundry foreman nervously looking out for the loco works manager while the rest of us still had to watch our backs for the junior foreman, Charlie Webb. Mr Webb was a 'works man' and did not negotiate over the rules. When you were working and you sensed someone approaching, you kept your head down. If Taffy's shiny shoes came into view, you often found a sweet on the bench after he had gone. Only if people from Paddington were being escorted around did the CME himself appear, labourers having previously put in some overtime to get the shop tidy. I occasionally spotted Mr Hawksworth when he was in charge but I never saw the reclusive Mr Collett. Mr Cook, the loco works manager, came through sometimes and always spoke: he was more down-to-earth.

I am surprised how few workers I have spoken with ever saw the chief mechanical engineer.

Nights at Swindon were worked on a rota. There was a small group of workshops that had a permanent night shift while others never had the need to work round the clock. Of course in some shops the scale and urgency of the work fluctuated, and at busy times working at night was necessary. A few men preferred nights, in which case they could take on extra from those who disliked late working. When Jack became junior foreman, he continued to give away his nights and was told his enhanced pay included a night allowance, so he had to do his share. Of working at night he remembered:

> During the war, when you went in at night there was often a freight train waiting in the 'up loop' at Rodbourne Lane, usually with a 28XX class locomotive simmering at the front. When you came out in the morning it was often still there. Even with the odd spell of nights, the factory men did not envy the shifts worked by the men at the running sheds and on the footplate. The first thing you did when you arrived at night was to put your sandwiches in a tin box to stop the rats getting them. Because of the reduced light in wartime, we would sprinkle white powder on to newly cast surfaces to identify rough spots, and until an alternative was found, we used household flour to which the rodents were attracted.

One of the early concessions gained through the Joint Works Committee was that men in the 'hot shops' – areas where iron and steel were worked when hot – could have access to cold drinks. The dehydration from sweating caused fatigue, they argued, and affected production. A solution was made from oatmeal which was thought to reduce sweating. Jack said: 'It seemed to be beyond the wit of man to stop the oatmeal being spilt and attracting rats and mice, so was short-lived.' GWR land and premises came within the Rats and Mice Act of 1919 and if infested, the company was required to take all necessary steps to exterminate the pests. Swindon men have told me that the only steps taken were a reliance on cats, before poison was used in the 1950s. There were, for many years, two cats in the iron foundry, but cats had always refused to stay in the brass foundry, so Jack and his mates caught rats in humane traps. They then tried to gas them but this was a slow process as they seemed to like coal gas and would push their noses up the pipe. The company handbook offered no suggestion as to methods of eradication, only that 'if necessary the CME department should seek the assistance of the Divisional Engineer'.

The taking of snuff or chewing tobacco was very popular in the workshops. The old boys who took snuff turned their white moustaches brown. Until the end of 1939, smoking was strictly prohibited as a fire precaution. Jack said he never knew of serious gambling 'inside' or out in the town, but his workshop, like some of the others, had a bookie's runner who took bets and placed them, on the men's behalf, in the dinner hour. He said: 'When Walters the bookmakers up the lane (in Rodbourne Road) had a lot to pay out, old Albert, the proprietor, would often ask the men to accept their winnings in tea or sugar.' The football pools collector was another traditional part of life in the factory. You had to keep in with the pools man in Jack's part of the works. Then if you had a win he would forget to tell the taxman. The pools man for the loco wages office in 1954 was still collecting from some of those same people in their homes in 2007, said George Petfield.

The Factory and Workshop Act of 1901 was a parliamentary enactment designed to ensure that manufacturing could be achieved without risk to health and without the exploitation of women and young persons under the age of eighteen. A factory was defined, for the purposes of the Act, as 'any workshop where power other than just manual labour was in use'. A workshop was defined as 'a place where only manual labour was exercised by way of trade or for other purposes of gain', the latter applying more to sheds and warehouses of the chief goods managers' department. The whole of the company's workshops, whether they belonged to the engineers', the signal or the CME departments, were thus classified as factories or workshops, even if only one person was employed in them.

Works managers and divisional superintendents in charge of workshop personnel were responsible for seeing that measures were taken to prevent personal injury to those under their control. A current rule book and general appendix giving clear safety instructions was issued to each person, and an abstract of the Factory and Workshop Act, the Workman's Compensation Act and the Notice of Accident Act 1906 were displayed in every shop that qualified as a factory. The company officials were required to make periodic inspections of workshops under their control to ensure machinery and appliances were maintained in a safe condition and used only for their intended purpose. Men suffering from a disability were not to be employed in positions they could not cope with because of the potential for accidents or strain injuries. Ambulance (first aid) cabinets were supplied to all depots and workshops and they were to be regularly inspected and stocked by a competent person. All of the workforce were encouraged to learn first aid and were supplied with basic instruction booklets.

The Act required that a supply of clean water for drinking and washing was laid on where twenty-five or more men were employed. In reality, many men in the shops spoke of limited access to fresh water during the shift, particularly before the war, unless they were in direct contact with furnaces and forges. Peter Reade remembers being given a drink designed to stop sweating when he first went into the smiths' shop in 1939, but soon after, he said, 'That was stopped. Yes, we had access to drinking water, but as a hammer driver I only drank it in hot weather.' To obtain hot water for washing hands and face, some men said they had to drop a piece of hot metal into a bucket of water. District factory inspectors had, on behalf of the Home Office, full powers to examine premises that came under the Act at any time and see that safety and health requirements were being enforced.

In some welding work, breathing in fumes made men feel ill and fatigued. Mick Ponting, who started 'inside' in 1948 as an apprentice coppersmith, remembers that the men who welded galvanised iron such as the ends of carriage body frames were entitled to a pint of milk each day. Mick never actually saw anyone have the milk, which was thought to stop the nausea caused by the fumes before proper facemasks became available.

Every factory area on the Great Western that employed young persons under the age of sixteen had to obtain a certificate of fitness. The loco and carriage works managers would hire a certifying surgeon who would inspect the site and, if it was acceptable, issue the certificate. For this, certain standards regarding temperature, ventilation, sanitation and illumination had to be met. Since 1939 a programme of changing from gas to electric lighting had been undertaken to comply with the Factory and Workshop Act. All the company's electric lighting installation and maintenance had been the responsibility of the CME since 1924. Conditions at the works, in many cases, appear to have fallen short of the requirements of the Act, as many production areas were off limits to boys under sixteen years of age. Boys did work in some of the carriage shops: the large fitting and machine shop was one. Conditions to keep the men healthy and safe were not so clearly defined, concentrating more on the procedures once accidents had occurred. Every accident that resulted in an absence from work of three days or more was recorded in the general register and notice sent to the district inspector of factories.

The department would have to provide records of regular treatment to seal walls, floors and ceilings, and of lime washing. For 3d the men could take a brush and a bucket of whitewash from the medical centre and treat walls at home: 'It made the dark corners lighter, if nothing else,' said Jack. 'At work the ventilators in our shop were, for the majority of the war, covered with blackout sheets, making conditions very unpleasant at times. This was not picked up by any factory inspector.' I asked Vic Tucker what the AM Shop was like to work in during the war. His first thoughts were: 'The blackout was in place day and night so it was not only half dark during the day, it could get hot too. If somebody had been allowed to go round and open the windows and roof lights and close them at night, it would have solved the problem. Towards the end of the war the blackout precautions were removed.'

During the war workers received extra clothing coupons if their work was particularly dirty. The office boys, who visited the various carriage repair shops, thought they should get the same consideration as they were required to wear smart clothes, which soon got dirty. They elected Harry Bartlett, one of their own, to go and put their case to Mr Richens, the staff assistant to the C&W works manager. He listened to what Harry had to say and then told him to get out. Walter Sheppard, a clerk in 18 Shop Office, heard about what was taken to be a rejection, and took up the case. Walter was secretary of the local branch of the Railway Clerks' Association. From 1944 the office boys also got extra clothing coupons, and this lasted until the end of rationing.

WOMEN IN THE SHOPS

In peacetime, women conciliation and wages staff were employed in the CME department as office cleaners, charwomen, gatekeepers, carriage cleaners, linen sewers and machinists. At Swindon they were also employed as stores assistants and laundresses. Women's pay for manual work was about half what the unskilled workshop man took home, and 'girls' were paid less again. However, the published wage tables for females that I have seen do not state whether they are for full- or part-time hours. Office cleaners' hours, for instance, are known to have varied considerably. It is also worth remembering that a man's working conditions were likely to be a lot tougher too.

Women ('ladies' worked in the offices) first entered the Swindon workshops in any numbers in 1916 and 1917, replacing men who went to war. They worked with a range of fabrics and produced wood finishes for carriage interiors and furniture. In retrospect it seems that the utilisation of female labour was never fully exploited in the carriage works, presumably because of prejudices and traditional ways of thinking. Before 1939 there were three polishing sections, one of which was staffed by women and overseen by forewoman Miss Fagin. After 1945 only women worked in 10A (Polishing) Shop, although there were male polishers working nearby. They produced fine finishes on mahogany and walnut surfaces by French polishing, staining and lacquering. The other areas of the shop floor that women worked in were the trimming shops and the sewing room, where, as well as carriage upholstery, they made aprons, canvas bags, tablecloths, towels, window straps, flags, blinds, axlebox pads, cushions, pillows, slips and so on. A purpose-made women's rest room and mess room were provided in 1939 for employees of the sewing room and the polishing shop, sited at the eastern end of London Street.

Maureen Eveness started as an apprentice French polisher in 10A Shop in 1954. She left school at Easter having just turned fifteen years of age. Her older sister Margaret worked in the offices of the stores department, and is mentioned in Chapter 10. Maureen would ride in from her home in Cheney Manor Road and leave her bicycle in the racks on the ground floor below the polishing shop. She explains her working environment:

> A labourer named Reg who lived in Whitworth Road looked after the checkboard and made sure all the checks were on the right hooks. All the internal doors (usually eight or nine), handrails, panels and wood fittings from the same coach came to us as one batch. The old finishes and polish were removed by 'pickling'. All the girls on that section had to wear rubber gloves as the chemical stripper would burn your hands. After that the surfaces were scraped, sanded and cleaned before they arrived at our section for treatment. All the work was now done with the surfaces horizontal, starting with a coat of colour which we mixed from a powder and brushed on. Each type of wood required a different shade of colour. When that was dry the first coat of a proprietary polish was applied. For this we used a pad made of wadding wrapped in old cotton material we had brought in from home. The chargehands checked the tone and sheen at each stage. For inspection, all the work including the heavy doors had to be positioned to catch the natural light. Once passed, two of us would carefully turn the doors over to treat the other side. Each coating took a day to dry so we would work on the other carriage fittings in between. Three of four further coats of French polish, which was shellac dissolved in spirit, were put on to build up to the required finish.
>
> Other girls in our shop were June Allan from Gorse Hill, Edith Eggleton from Whiteman Street, Diane Inkpen from Bassett, Sandra Weaver from Hook, Pam Dowswell from Whitworth Road, Eva Prentiss from Broadway, Margaret Pearce and Jean Brooks. Violet Newton was one of the two chargehands; the other woman's name I can't now recall.

As elsewhere in the works, females in positions of authority were of a different generation to the girls in their charge. Therefore, as was the way of things in those days, these supervisory staff rigidly applied the rules. In the polishing shop, for instance, talking was only allowed in the course of one's work. 'You had to ask to go off to the toilet,' Maureen recalled. 'The answer usually included the order, "Don't have a cigarette".'

French polishing was very labour-intensive and therefore expensive, and less and less was being done during Maureen's time. The Western Region wanted new modern materials such as laminated plastics and Formica, which were not only considered more stylish but were also cheaper, more durable, and easier to keep clean. As new coaches with modern interiors were introduced, the remaining work went to the men's polishing section. More and more females found themselves cleaning glass, chromium plate and felt instead of the craft they were trained for, but this kept them employed a while longer. The polishing shop was closed down in 1958 and Maureen and her colleagues were made redundant. Only Miss Woodruffe, the forewoman, was retained: she was given a position in the offices until retirement. The unions had an agreement that where men did the same work as woman, the latter would be first out if dismissals were to take place. A similar situation existed after the last war, except that then it was to make way for men returning from war service. It was accepted by everyone that the male breadwinner was more dependent on long-term employment.

Princess Elizabeth visited Swindon works on the afternoon of 15 November 1950 after performing some civic duties in the morning. As had happened when her grandfather visited in 1924, the longest-serving staff were presented to the royal guest on a tour around selected workshops. The princess was naturally taken around the areas of the carriage shops where the work of the female manual workers could be seen. Those who met Her Royal Highness included Miss B. J. Baden, forewoman in charge of the sewing room, who had worked 'inside' for an impressive forty-six years; Miss M. Webb, the linen sewers' chargewoman, who had completed thirty-one years; Miss R. M. Woodroffe of the polishing shop, twenty-nine years; and Miss I. Newton, French polisher, twenty-six years' service. The works had provided a welfare section for women (and men) by the 1930s; the rest of the company did not get a women's welfare officer until 1941.

Forming a helical spring on a Greenwood & Batley spring coiling machine. (BRW)

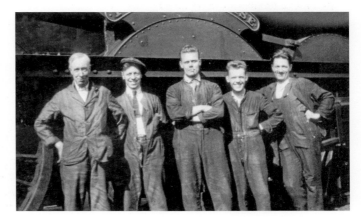

Chargeman W. Hanks, fitters and enginemen during trials with Star Class 4-6-0 *Princess Louise* following overhaul. The date must have been sometime before 1950 as the locomotive was withdrawn in 1951. The ageing 'Stars' were being withdrawn from the 1930s onwards although some were rebuilt as 'Castles' in the 'twenties' and 'thirties'. (R. Clarke)

BRITISH TRANSPORT COMMISSION

BRITISH RAILWAYS

APPRENTICESHIP AGREEMENT

This Agreement made the **Twentyfifth** day of
October 19 **54** BETWEEN **Harold Gordon JOHNSON,**
WORKS MANAGER, CARRIAGE & WAGON WORKS, SWINDON,
on behalf of the BRITISH TRANSPORT COMMISSION (hereinafter called
" the Commission ") of 222, Marylebone Road, St. Marylebone in the County
of London of the first part, and **William Henry Percy RICHENS,**

_____ of **165, Whitworth Road, Swindon,**

in the County of **Wiltshire**_____ (hereinafter called " the Guardian ")
of the second part, and __ **Dennis Arnold John RICHENS,**

_____ of **165, Whitworth Road, Swindon,**

_____ in the County of **Wiltshire,**
(hereinafter called " the Apprentice ") of the third part.

WHEREAS—

1. The Apprentice has completed a period of probation from the
Thirtieth day of **August** 19 **54** to the
Twentysecond day of **October** 19 **54** and has
attained the age of 15 years.

2. The Commission are willing to accept the Apprentice to be taught
and instructed in the craft of **Wood Wagon Building.**

3. The Guardian having enquired into the nature of the business
conducted by the Commission desires that the Apprentice shall learn the
craft of **Wood Wagon Building**_____in the service of the
Commission.

Now it is hereby AGREED as follows :—

(1) The Apprentice, of his own free will and with the consent of the
Guardian, hereby binds himself as Apprentice to the Commission in the craft
of **Wood Wagon Building**_____on the conditions
hereinafter appearing.

The front page of an apprenticeship agreement relating to Dennis Richens of the Carriage & Wagon Works. It lays out the commitments expected of, not only the apprentice, but also his guardian as surety for his son. Before the war the probationary period prior to the five year training was one month and unpaid: I'm sure Dennis's three month probation period was not now without pay. Typically his 'time' was to start shortly after the sixteenth birthday. The agreement was witnessed and signed by the Carriage & Works' Manager; Dennis's father and by a clerk in the C&W staff section.

After completing his time in 1959, Dennis worked as a carpenter in 12 Shop. Here he would have made and repaired furniture and platform barrows etc. for the Western Region.

Photography was banned in the works but surviving unofficial snapshots, whilst interesting nowadays, are not particularly rare. Here someone has captured Arthur Myers, a 'carriage side' foreman, at the workplace. Mr Myers retired in 1949 after fifty-one years 'inside'. (R. Myers)

The control board in Foreman Millard's office showing the progress of locomotives being stripped and re-erected in the A Shop circuit. (BRW)

The linen sewers in 9A Shop worked on a range of fabrics and leather products mainly for carriage interiors. (GWR)

8

Offices of the CME Department

The Great Western knew there was little publicity value in the work done by the clerks, typists and secretaries, so finding information nowadays, official or otherwise, is very limited. Apart from fragments in the staff magazines, the only other source that I know of is the 1957 booklet *Electronic Accounting*. It was produced for the introduction of the first computer and other electronic machinery that would gradually take over all forms of accounts and statistical compilation for the Western Region. It also gives a short history of accounting at Swindon and is fully illustrated. My copy had been presented to the works' cashier of the 1940s and 50s, Mr Eynon. I have never seen another, which perhaps bears out what I say at the start. I suspect that once further new technology overtook these first machines, and it wasn't long, the books were no longer of any interest and discarded. Most of this chapter is, therefore, based on personal recollections, from the 1940s and 50s. This will, I hope, be of particular interest to the growing number of people who study local social and family history.

The chief accountants' department at Swindon was divided up into costing, departmental and new work, final accounts, rolling stock records, statistics, stores and wages. This was the breakdown in 1952, and no doubt it had changed little since the amalgamation of the loco and carriage/wagon accounts in the 1930s. Most of the accounts sections were now centralised in the CME's building which was, and still is, situated in the 'angle', an area between the Paddington-Bristol main line and the Gloucester line. This three- and four-storey building had evolved as further office space was anticipated, up until the 1920s, in line with the expansion of the rest of the works. Over the period of this book some offices moved as the work and methods changed. Some were renamed, amalgamated or became obsolete. Most offices had numbers but were better known for the type of work they carried out.

A second floor had been added to the original part of the office block to accommodate a drawing office in 1904. It was divided into six sections: carriage and wagon; locomotive; general; survey; mechanical; electrical; together with the chief draughtsman's office and a clerks' office. The extension to the print house above B Shop, where drawings were copied, was completed in 1951. The plan for this extension also shows another area next to it where the draughtsmen who dealt with cranes, surveys and plant machinery were moved, although not until 1958 or 1959. The print room and new DO annexe were reached by an overhead walkway from the main building. The estimating office, where costs could be calculated from engineering drawings, was at the far end of the locomotive section, and the drawing office stores was a little way away on the other side of B Shed.

The chief draughtsmen from the 1930s onward were Mr Smith, Mr Mattingley and, in the 1950s, Mr Scholes. Each of the DO sections was headed by an assistant to the chief draughtsman. 'Old Charlie Dunford was in charge of the clerks when I first started,' (in 1944) said George Petfield.

The carriage and wagon offices formed the façade of the large fitting and machine (No 15) shop just to the north-west of the station. This building was probably the most striking of any works buildings seen by passengers from the junction station. As you looked at it, some of the general stores offices were on the right, with the CME stores offices above; on the left were the managers' offices, the time office, the drawing office and the registrars' office. Above them were the progress office, accounts and chief clerks' offices, and, until 1952, the wages office. After the latter had moved out it became the cost office, with George Ruddle in charge. The C&W office block also had staff and record sections, a correspondence office, special loads office, drawing stores and in 1930 the timber storekeeper and his staff moved into an office here, according to the *GWR Magazine*. Mr Evans was the carriage and wagon works manager until he retired in 1946. Upon nationalisation Mr Johnson became C&WW manager and Mr Colton was his assistant; Mr Ford had been C&W chief clerk from 1931 to 1948.

Mr Kelynack was the chief accountant to the CME in the 1930s: Frank Bailey and Harold Gardner were his assistants. In 1941 Mr Gardner took over as head of CME and stores accounts. The new 'chief' was a member of the town council and had been mayor of Swindon. He was also the last honorary treasurer of the GWR Medical Fund, taking over from his former boss Mr Kelynack in 1946. Along with others from the factory, Mr Gardner lectured at the college some days and evenings. He had been on the staff at The College's commercial and literary department since the 1920s and many of his students were employed by the GWR. Following nationalisation, direct control of the CME, and stores accounts and statistics were transferred to Paddington under the control of Mr Dashwood, chief accountant to the general manager. Mr Gardner was then appointed assistant to the accountant (rolling stock and stores) Western Region, but remained the most senior clerk at Swindon; his assistant was Cliff Sanders. Although he was fifty-five years of age in 1955, Mr Gardner worked on for about another ten years. (I remember seeing him on his early evening visits to the Cross Keys in Wood Street throughout the 1970s.) In the mid-1950s, publicity from the Western Region claimed that there were 600 clerks at Swindon, working on accounts and statistical duties, out of a total workforce of 10,000.

By the late 1930s representations were being made on behalf of female staff with a view to setting up a pension scheme. Many of those who joined the company during the First World War were now realising that having such as scheme would be advantageous. The directors agreed to this in 1938, for female clerks. At this time, the GWR as a whole employed 1,831 females who would be eligible.

The retirements section of the staff magazines showed that many of the accounts people in the department left with forty-five years of service: a few managed nearly fifty years, as they were allowed to work beyond the age of sixty. Because works and office staff could be retained during the war, some clocked up even more than that. A Mr J. Street managed fifty-seven years by the time he was released in 1946, nearly all of it in the east time office. There was no upper age limit at which senior officers had to retire, and this applied to departmental heads as well. They would not, however, be able to hang on to office as long as their bosses in the 1930s, Mr Collett and Mr Auld. Mr Collett, the chief mechanical engineer, reluctantly retired at the age of seventy, not because of pressure from the board, but because his assistant Mr Auld, also seventy, would not stay on any longer and support his cause.

The whole of the CME department accounts was based at the Swindon works, and it was said that only one in three clerks dealt with factory work. The three largest accounts offices were 21, 22 and 26. They would have up to fifty staff working in each at any one time. The clerk in charge of these larger offices was senior in status to his equivalent in those with less staff, and was graded a 'special C'. Some offices had a raised area at one end where the clerk in charge and his assistant had their desks; anyone of a lower station who needed to speak to them did so by respectfully standing at the lower level. This often had the effect, intentional or not, of making the messenger feel intimidated. The offices in the CME building were centrally heated and had large iron radiators. They had large windows to capture the maximum natural light, and high ceilings. Each window frame held two sets of sash windows to minimise noise and fumes from the nearby workshops. The majority of men smoked a pipe or cigarettes; unlike in the workshops, there had been no smoking ban prior to 1939. Barbara Carter said:

> A lot of women in the offices smoked as well. I didn't because my father suffered with asthma and I thought I might get it if I smoked. The double sets of windows were very effective at keeping out the noise and the fumes as long as they stayed closed. One of the girls in my office made herself very unpopular by keeping opening them.

Each section had a telephone and outside lines were available via the exchange. By the 1950s every double desk had a phone and some people were able to dial straight out to the General Post Office network. Clocks were made by Smiths and were connected to an electrical circuit driven by a master clock in No 8 office. Mechanical clocks were checked and wound by a fellow known as 'clocky'. He would go round the works on a bike and also helped with any repairs, cleaning and adjustments. All offices kept selections of reference books and books of conversion tables. Personnel could obtain 'rough books' from the stores, which had hard covers and were impressed with the company initials. The blotter doubled as a homemade directory of names and extension numbers and would include those who could help when there was a problem. A shrewd clerk soon worked out who to ask for and who to avoid when contacting other departments. The office furniture was all getting on a bit by the 1950s, which was not usual in those days. A works' carpenter told his daughter-in-law, who was a clerk in the offices, that when he had to replace some of the oilskin pads built into desks, there were small creepy-crawlies underneath.

Within either the loco or carriage sides, office people generally had more opportunity to move around than the shop workers. Consequently they all seemed to know one another, at least by name. Some bad feeling towards the clerks, who had remained loyal to the company during the General Strike of 1926, persisted through the 1930s, but fizzled out after 1939. There was no need of a night shift in the offices and only occasionally did a clerk work in a workshop at night. The company knew that the efficiency of the clerk was significantly reduced at night by progressive fatigue.

Academics could undertake further education in accounting work on weekday evenings at night school, or day release if they showed particular promise. They would attend the old North Wilts Technical Schools, which, by the 1930s, was officially known as The College. The majority of students attending engineering and commercial department classes were employed in the works in those days. According to the annual report on the work of The College for the session of 1931/32, the decrease in enrolment of the junior evening institutes (courses) was due to a low birth rate during 1914–18: no mention is made of the severe economic depression that must have had an effect on people thinking of taking up extended studies. Up until the 1930s, the most successful students had been able to go on and study at the London School of Economics. They would attend a department exclusively for railway staff, one evening a week after work and a day for the annual examination. The most senior clerks at Swindon works, Messrs Dening, Minchin, Gardner and Sanders among others, had gained the Brunel medal earlier in their careers for consistently high marks each year during their studies at the LSE.

From 1929 the Churchward Testimonial Fund awarded a number of book prizes each year to the best students in the department, to encourage education in engineering and commerce. The trustees of the fund, Messrs Hawksworth, Auld and Kelynack, considered the results obtained throughout the year. Most of the awards came to Swindon because they provided much of the CME department training. The money came from a fund set up at the suggestion of Mr Churchward himself. The great engineer made the first payment from money collected and presented to him at his retirement at the end of 1921.

Barbara Carter's family, like most in Swindon, had several members who spent all their working lives in the railway. Her grandfather, Richard Dening, retired in 1931 as chief foreman of the carriage fitters in 15, 15A, 18 and 19D Shops and as president of the Foreman's Association. Her father Henry (known at work as Harry) became clerk in charge of 22 Office, and Barbara's two aunts Freda and Irene started in the works accounts in 1913 and 1915 respectively. They too achieved academic distinction for their work 'inside'. Barbara thought they may have gone in to train as shorthand typists. At the time, there were few females on that sort of work 'inside' or anywhere else on the GWR. Like their older brother, Freda and Irene won the Brunel medal, for shorthand and advanced bookkeeping respectively. Barbara thought they were the only females to get these awards, and it was the only time three Brunel medallists came from the same family. They were awarded in 1920, 1921 and 1922. Freda retired early, in 1952, aged 55, by which time she was in overall charge of the loco side typists. She wanted more time to care for her elderly parents at the family home in Hythe Road. Irene Dening (born 1900) held a senior position in the stores accounts from at least as early as 1932. She worked her full term and was personal assistant to the stores superintendent when she retired.

By the mid-1930s, with more applicants than positions available, it had become more difficult to secure employment as a clerk in the works. Candidates had to pass a medical as well as an educational examination, although those in possession of a matriculation certificate or its equivalent were exempt from the latter. Barbara Carter (nee Dening) began her working life in 40 Office in 1940. She was given a favourable final report from her school, the Elms at Faringdon, and in common with most school leavers, took the Schools Certificate examinations before the end of her final term. This she passed to credit standard in the required subjects enabling her to get a start in the offices of the CME department. She said:

> I decided to continue my studies at The College after work to advance my career. This was my choice, as the company did not insist on it. We worked twelve-hour shifts, but I left work early on night-school evenings so as to be there from 6 p.m. to 9 p.m. It was a long day, often working in artificial light due to the blackout. To try to counteract the dingy lighting the office was painted brilliant white and gained the nickname 'White City'. I did manage to get away early on Thursdays to attend the Wesleyan Guild, my weekly social evening out.

For the first six months Barbara was using an advanced Muldivo machine, calculating timber measurement and prices. 'There were eight ladies to a section here, including the section head.' Her first net wage in 1940 was 5s 8d and she still has that first, very austere, payslip.

Barbara's friends and colleagues included the daughter of senior wages clerk Fred Hook, whose name she could not recall; Marjorie Parsons, whose mother conducted the

Swindon Ladies Choir; and Doreen Pullen. Doreen was an impersonator in her spare time; she travelled round locally, with a concert party, entertaining the troops. Another girl, Ivy Davis, ran a sort of magazine club in the office. Barbara said:

> Each of us bought a different women's magazine which, after we had read it, was passed on to Ivy who redistributed them among the contributors. Another co-operative scheme enabled me and some of my colleagues to buy saving certificates which the government were promoting during the war. Twenty of us got together and all paid in a shilling a week; a certificate was purchased and every twenty weeks each person received one. Reg Cook used to come and have his tea in 40 Office. He was in charge of the storehouse where all the old documents were kept. Reg always looked scruffy, probably because the old papers got very dusty. To supplement his low pay, Reg would get you scarce items on the black market.

No 40 Office was really two long offices on the first floor of the CME building in the northern aspect above the cash office money make-up sections and the wire rope shop. Half of it was taken up with accounting machinery; the other half had girls working at long desks. Across the corridor was a stores office laid out very similarly but looking out across the tracks towards the general stores building. Some older staff still called these machine sections by the old name, Addressograph offices, although that type of machine was now only one of a range used. No 40 Office had glass screens separating the desks from the machinery. Around the walls of the office were fitted cabinets containing the punchcards and, in common with all offices, cupboards of stationary and ledgers. Percy Richards was office chief of the CME machine sections and Muriel Whale was section chief over the sorter and tabulator machine operators. I think it is likely that Mr Richards was also responsible for the stores machine room too. Barbara told me:

> Mr Richards rode an upright bicycle down from Old Town every day and this inspired me to do the same in an effort to avoid being late so often. Some evenings and weekends he served as a major in the Home Guard. Because I was the quickest typist in the office, he would get me to do all the Home Guard paperwork.

After being there a few years, Barbara was required to go and issue coal tickets to retired workmen every other Tuesday afternoon. This was done from an office in the former mess rooms near the tunnel entrance. The job appears to have been given to clerks from any office regardless, as Enid Hogden in the cash office and others remember going there on occasions. Later, Barbara was moved across the corridor to the stores accounts. Miss Foulds was the most senior person in their machine room, and Barbara was the senior operator over the twelve or fifteen females on key-punching machines. These girls typed the information from cost statements, into the machine, which then converted it and stamped it into punchcards as combinations of holes. Because of the strict division of staff in the two departments, there was some resentment at the appointment of an outsider as section head.

Barbara's father, Henry Dening, started his working life in a workshop office, probably on the loco side, about 1907. By the time he was twenty, he had gained his advanced bookkeeping qualifications, which took him three years. Later, Barbara told him jokingly that she would beat that, which she did, but then admitted the course was condensed due to the wartime conditions. Mr Dening also taught at night-school to help make ends meet, but he must have progressed quickly because Barbara remembers him telling her that his salary had reached £400 per annum. This is thought to have been in the early 1930s when a grade 1 clerk with five years' experience received no more than £350. Mr Dening, a

Methodist, took charge of 22 Accounts some time in the 1930s. We get some idea of the conduct observed in his office by something he told his daughter. He said that he only had to look up from his desk and any talking stopped. She remembers the story because he went on to say that, 'Wearing my spectacles for short sightedness, I couldn't actually see a thing when I looked up, but nobody seemed to have worked that out.'

Just after the war, Mr Dening suddenly lost his voice and could only whisper faintly. Because of this, he was given a single office, still on the first floor next to those of the chief clerk and his assistant. He communicated by writing notes, to which sometimes a reply would be written back, something he found very amusing. Harry Dening died while at work in 1947, and after a period under the deputy, Mr Minchin, Frank Dance took over as clerk in charge of 22 Office (Mr Dance also looked after the finances of St. Mark's Church as parish treasurer). During his time as 'acting clerk in charge', Mr Minchin had to ask Barbara if he could borrow her late father's notebooks so he could properly manage the office. 'He obviously felt uncomfortable about asking,' she said.

Each office had an office junior, sometimes more than one, usually a 'girl' or 'boy' (names given to those who were between school or further education and becoming a junior clerk at eighteen years of age). Achieving the latter was still dependent on a good conduct report and passing the examination. There were plenty of jobs available for female school leavers in the town, particularly after the war. Yvonne Hodey (née Jones) said:

I could have gone into the departmental stores Morse's or McIlroy's, or factories such as Wills's and Compton's but I applied at the works, passed the medical exam in January 1953 and started work 'inside' the following month. I was an office junior with a single desk at the back of '21 Accounts CME. The office seemed vast with about forty or fifty male and female staff; very daunting at first. I was positioned in a cubby hole out of sight but within earshot of the clerk in charge, Mr Rendall, and his assistant, Mr Nash. I made the tea, ran messages and collected or delivered post to Mr Chesterman in the correspondence office. This was in the days when you called your elders Mr or Miss . . . and never by their Christian name, unless invited to do so. Once judged to be trustworthy, another regular job for the junior was to take money to the bank, sometimes quite large sums. I would collect a large canvas bag of money from the clerk in charge of central wages, Mr Roberts, or from the assistant chief accountant, Mr Sanders. On one occasion I was stopped by a policeman who told me I should not be out walking with all that money. This was money paid in for concessionary bus and rail tickets at the works booking office, which had been bagged up for transportation at the cash office. Making the tea was fun. It was a major operation, done in very little space under the staircase on the ground floor with girls from different offices. Carrying large trays of teas for the whole office up and down the stairs was tricky to say the least. Then we had to wash up and do a repeat performance in the afternoon.

What staff do I remember in 21 Office during my time? There was Mr West, Mr Harris, Mr Youll, Don Curtis, Miss Wykeham-Martin, Winnie Stroud and Dorothy Wirdnam. Office girls from elsewhere were Cecilia Brown, Janet Knighton and Jennifer Allen who was in 22 Office. Most people had close relatives 'inside' but I only had a cousin, Maureen Stokes, who worked in the stores managers' office (see Chapter 11) since grandfather Stevenson retired before the war.

After nine months, Yvonne became a junior clerk and was moved to what she remembers as the 'Powers-Samas Department'. This was the machinery part of 40 Office, CME Accounts and in 1953 'Pop' Richards was still in charge. It was just down the corridor from 21 Office on the first floor. After a short training period, Yvonne operated punchcard machines. She was put on to a pay rate starting at 25 shillings net.

George Petfield left school and started his working life in the offices of the CME Department in 1944. He had been interviewed by Don Rendall:

> I found out later that Mr Rendall was in charge of No 1 Office and was the third most senior clerk in the department (later, in the 1960s, Mr Rendall got the top job: works accountant). It was all very informal; when I asked when I was to start I was told, 'Start tomorrow.'

Mr Rendall put George on departmental accounts, calculating the costs of work being done by or for other departments. More specifically he had to determine the costs of certain outstation work. George worked in 22 Accounts, where his bosses were Harry Dening and his assistant Tom Minchin. Tom was a Methodist preacher in his spare time. He was also an accomplished orator and, along with the head of department, Mr Gardner, had won awards for public speaking at the GWR Music Festival.

George's salary was £98 per year when he started in 1944, leaving him below the figure at which he would start paying tax. For this he also had to work an hour's compulsory overtime per day under special wartime arrangements. The start of the day for office workers was 8 a.m. instead of the pre-war time of 9 a.m. After the war they changed again to 8.30 a.m. George still had to be on the 7.25 a.m. train from Wootton Bassett, only now he could have a look for any new locomotives that had arrived in the reception sidings overnight. A bell sounded in the offices at the start and finish of the shifts. He remembers:

> Dinnertime was 12.23 to 1.35 p.m. and that never altered. After 1954, I remember the roar of the up Bristolian express would remind us to get things up together before going home. The afternoon shift finished at 5.22 p.m. It was then a mad dash out through the tunnel and along to the station to be on the 'all stations to Temple Meads via Badminton' train in exactly ten minutes.

On Friday, overtime started at 5.45 p.m. Duties then included meeting at the cash office at 8.30 and proceeding to the pay point to pay the night workers at 9.00 p.m. Overtime in the CME accounts was worked more towards the end of the financial year, when the books were brought up to date for inspection by the auditors. If necessary office staff were expected to stay behind to catch up, although they were rarely kept back more than half an hour because after that overtime could be claimed. The accounts were scrutinised by auditors based at Swindon and annually by public auditors appointed by the shareholders.

After six months of employment, George was entitled to concessionary or privileged rail travel. This was a generous 25 per cent of the standard fare. When he went off to do his national service in July 1945, George lost this for the forces rate of 66 per cent. With regard to the privileged rate, George remembers that 7s 6d got you a Swindon to Paddington standard return in the late 1940s and early 1950s. Following his time in the RAF working on pay accounts, George returned to the works, and his chair was about four feet from the one he had vacated two and a half years earlier. He would now be dealing with personal accounts. His section handled claims against outside firms and individuals for damage or fraud. Back in 1944/45, a lot of the men in the office should have retired upon reaching sixty, but for the war. So when George returned in 1948, his office seemed to be full of newcomers. Men and women clerks returning from the war might talk about the lighter side of their experiences, but others never mentioned it at all. There was a lot of anti-German feeling at that time. When interviewed for promotion, the clerk Harold Turner was asked what he was studying at night school. When he replied, 'German, so as to make new friends,' the answer ensured he remained in his present position.

A few familiar faces from 1944/45 were still there or dispersed throughout the department, such as Frank Davis, Cliff Sanders, Syd Carnsew, John Partridge, Guy Hemming, Grace Clack and Isaac Carter, formerly the works cashier. Inevitably, romances were formed in such a close-knit group: Pam Sheppard, for instance, was there at that time and later married David Coombes from the loco wages section. 'I don't remember seeing Winnie Chowles, the most senior woman in accounts, when I returned. She may have retired in the meantime,' said George. Charlie Selman was still in 22 Office dealing with cost accounts for docks and waterways. He often spent time away in South Wales and retired about 1950. His brother George was a section chief in 21 Office and had served the town as mayor. Quite a number in the offices had come up from the absorbed railway companies of South Wales, and alterations to the internal layout had been made to accommodate them. George Eynon had come from the Barry Railway and was employed in the GW Savings Bank for a while; Frank Davis had been with the Brecon & Merthyr Railway. Others had been transferred to 'outstations', which in this case meant CME offices elsewhere on the system. Mr Gardner, the chief accountant or office assistant to the CME, to give him his proper title, came into the works as early as 1907. Archie Jefferies, George's first section chief, had started in 1912, but most of the senior staff at the time had joined the company in the following ten years.

George Petfield travelled in on the workmen's train and one morning it suddenly came to a halt in the cutting; looking out of the window they could see a bull walking towards them. The animal ambled passed the train, allowing it to proceed without too much delay. But the 28XX with coal empties for South Wales had to follow the bull all the way to Bassett at walking pace. This was one of several stories remembered by locals who used the workmen's train services.

Jack Hartley had started his training to become a clerk at the junction station and transfer goods yard, and then asked to move into the works to get more experience. He told me:

I went into the correspondence office on the first floor of the CME's building in 1951 or 52. This was one of several sections manned by the M&EE's personal staff. Harold Coleman was head of the office at that time; it was amalgamated with the carriage correspondence office shortly after I arrived. Sid Brown became chief clerk in charge of the C&W side. Correspondence clerks dealt with all the incoming letters and sent them on to the appropriate person if necessary; typists produced replies and the appropriate 'technical' people signed them. The incoming letters were then stored in 5-foot high floor-standing wooden cupboards with sliding doors in the main corridor outside our office. When matters were settled the accompanying correspondence was removed to the storehouse to make way for more.

(A corridor ran down the middle of the first floor of the east wing where the offices of the mechanical and electrical engineer were situated. Jack only had dealings with two: staff sections and records. The majority of the other offices here were for senior M&EE staff. Previously, of course, these were the offices occupied by the GWR CMEs, Mr Collett then Mr Hawksworth.)

I worked for a time on the electrical section dealing with wayleaves: the annual rent and rates collected from firms running electrical cables and telephone lines across our land. Our outgoing correspondence was sent on to the electrical assistant to the M&EE to be signed. There were two distinct groups of personal staff working for the M&EE: clerks and technical staff who were all former 'time served' tradesmen. It was we clerks that seemed to do all the work while they [the technicians or engineers] took the credit and were paid more, and a growing resentment built up. A Mr B was a case in point: he had a technical position but was just a staff administrator and he looked down on us. We had a meeting and decided to write to the general manager at Paddington. This resulted in a works' study investigation. The clerical side wanted to be regarded as equal, and eventually we were. Clerks were now in charge of clerks and on the same pay rates as our counterparts.

Promotion got me moved to the carriage and wagon section of the office, and I had four females working for me. Mary Covey is the only name I can now recall (probably the prettiest). They filed all the internal and external letters away with others of similar subject matter. The records office also handled correspondence and our work overlapped with them. About a dozen people worked here compiling crane, stationary boiler, machinery and publication records using a card system. The person in charge was a technical man whose name I can't now remember, but Maurice Dunscombe who lived in Drove Road took over and his assistant was Bob Johnson or Johnston. William (Maurice) Dunscombe had moved upstairs from the works (shop floor) to become a cost clerk/estimator in the loco cost office before becoming head of records.

By 1960 Jack was in the CM&EE (the word 'chief' had been reinstated in the title) administrative (general) section. Here he had two jobs: one was processing applications for permits for visitors to the works. A piece appeared in the *Swindon Railway News* in April 1960 which focused on the two key planners of works tours: Bert Stratford, the senior watchman and guide, and Jack Hartley. Part of the article stated: "At a time when theatres, cinemas and soccer clubs were playing to diminishing audiences, the drawing power of Swindon works increases. 26,080 visitors arrived last year. Many came by rail and this means valuable revenue estimated at £7,500 annually."

The other part of Jack's work at this time was handling the clerical side of reports in connection with claims against the Western Region. These were usually for damage to goods in transit: anything from farm machinery coming loose from its fastenings in open wagons to wooden packing crates breaking apart and their contents being damaged. The latter would require the works timber storekeeper to get involved. His timber inspectors would investigate to determine whether the packaging and type of wood used was sufficient to withstand the expected wear and tear of the journey. The M&EE's personal staff included two general claims inspectors whose work involved assessment of damage by rail movement. In the late 1950s they were Charlie Eynon and a chap named House, possibly Bill. One or other would be dispatched to wherever on the region the goods in question were held.

Most Swindon girls leaving school did not want to work in any of the local factories if they could avoid it. Even factory offices were frowned upon by them and their mothers. The railway works, however, was different, and a position in the CME department was *the* place of choice. The brightest girls from Commonweal, Euclid Street and later, Headlands grammar schools went 'inside', and some school leavers went on to study bookkeeping at The College's commercial department while waiting to go in. Having a father in accounts helped, but there was still the entrance test and a medical before acceptance. All medical examinations for CME staff were carried out at Park House on the corner of the GWR estate.

The impression given by girls looking for office work that nowhere compared to the works is a recurring one. Even after the war, when several other large firms came to the town, it persisted. From what Noreen Harris (and others) told me, it appears that generally these other employers put women on repetitive work requiring little mental skill:

In the early 1950s I came to Swindon to find work as I had relatives in north Wilts. I took lodgings with a Mrs Kent in Plymouth Street because Plymouth was where I came from. First of all I worked at Plessey's, then Vickers Armstrong. Six months at each doing clerical work, but it was boring and I was educated beyond what I was doing. I had heard good reports about the railway works, so I applied there. With the general schools certificate I was moved up the waiting list to go into the motive power department. When I did start in 1952, Mr Pellow was the MP superintendent. The office I was in dealt with personnel records, and I was on the footplate section. We compiled information on firemen and engine cleaners' promotion and progress. There were six to a section, and I remember Eric Lane, John Cavello, Vera Carter and Nancy Titcombe from those early days. Nancy had been a knocker-upper during the war and Vera, who worked on the conciliation staff section, was a town councillor.

Junior females, not males, had to take turns at making the tea for the office. This was done in the messengers' room in the central offices, accessed via the 'posh entrance' at the front of the building. While in the MPD I had my 21st birthday and (as was a tradition) I received a large brass key which was made in the workshops. The hairstyle was short like Audrey Hepburn's in those days, and if we girls were going out that evening we would be able to wash our hair in the basins in the cloakroom, apply some gel and return to our desks without it being noticed. Sometimes I was asked to go and issue coal sales tickets to staff at the tunnel entrance. Down there they had underfloor heating ducts and on more than one occasion a rat had got in and died and the smell was awful. I always walked through the middle of the tunnel because rats sometimes ran along the water channels either side.

Another clerk and I were sometimes asked if we wanted to go into town with a collection tin for the Widows and Orphan Fund. Presumably this wasn't a very popular task because they offered us another day off in lieu as an incentive, and of course we always said yes. The Saturday morning shift was stopped while I was in this department, so I started working for Mr Bartlett, the landlord at the Glue Pot, where I was now lodging. He paid me 10 shillings a week for working in the bar some evenings or at weekends.

Females worked in most clerical areas but not in shop offices, nor did their duties include visiting workshops in those days. They monopolised the typists' and machine sections of the CME office building and their prospects for promotion, especially in the machine rooms, were better than anywhere else in accounts. The company acknowledged that female operators were faster and better when using accounting machinery than men. Women and girls first came into the offices in any numbers, during the 14–18 war, and this valuable source of labour was continued thereafter. Upon getting married, female staff were required to resign, although this did not apply in wartime and presumably after 1945; when Barbara Dening left to be married in 1950, it was her husband, not the company, who wanted her to stay at home full time. Noreen Harris remembers being given a first-class travel pass to use when going on her honeymoon. When it was known that a person in the office or shop was to be married, it was usual to have a collection and presentation of a gift to wish them well. Barbara told me:

When the person leaving arrived in the morning, they might well find that colleagues had come in early and decorated their desk. A poem and some words offering marital advice would be prominent among the embellishment. They were allowed to leave a few minutes early the evening before the 'big day', to a cacophony of banging noises. Staff in other offices heard the din, so as the victim passed them they joined in.

A young Henry Dening at the start of his career in an unknown workshop office. (B. Carter)

This office view shows the earlier style of sloping desks. Nearly that had been remade into flat desks by the 1940s. D Shop carpenters did this and any refurbishment of furniture and cabinets etc. (GWR)

Some of the loco side typists' section attending the wedding of a colleague at Christ Church in 1930. Sixth from the left is section head Freda Dening. (B. Carter)

This 1948 view shows the larger east wing of the Drawing Office where locomotive, carriage and wagon work was undertaken. Sometime later the C&W sections moved into the north wing. (Author's collection)

9

Other Work

MANAGEMENT

Information about the day-to-day work and remuneration of the senior managers was never recorded outside the railway and by the time researchers took an interest these people, being that much older, had usually passed on. Consequently research is limited to surviving internal documents and the occasional observations of ex-employees.

The chief mechanical engineer was the head of department. He was responsible for all the mechanical and electrical work within the company and, by the 1930s, reported directly to the general manager, Mr (later Sir) James Milne. Once a year the CME would submit his recommendations for what he considered the department should build in the year ahead to the general manager and the board. His proposals were arrived at by close consultation with his most senior staff, who are listed below. Most of the company's manufacturing was carried out by the CME department and was almost all centralized at Swindon, the signal works at Reading being the main exception during the period of this study. Costly new work required the approval of the board and the general manager at the appropriate committee meeting. Apart from those workers normally associated with the department's workshops and offices, the CME was responsible for all running shed grades, enginemen, carriage and wagon maintenance staff and cleaners. The company docks were managed jointly by the chief docks manager at Cardiff, the chief civil engineer at Paddington, and the CME at Swindon.

C. B. Collett succeeded G. J. Churchward and remained head of the department until 1941. It was the board of directors who had decided upon the choice of the new CME in the years leading up to the change in 1922, just as they did for all heads of departments. Of course they also took into account the views of the general manager and the outgoing CME. This appointment, it is said, was greeted with hushed amazement because the locomotive works' manager Mr Stanier showed more potential. However Mr Collett had remained one step ahead in seniority because of his age and this, historians agree, was another example of the bad system of promotion adhered to during those times. Whatever the true feelings were at the time, I believe the 'Collett or Stanier' debate has only persisted because of Mr Stanier's great achievements after he became CME on the London, Midland and Scottish Railway in the 1930s.

The principal assistant to the CME was next in line of seniority. All senior staff had assistants who were expected to succeed them upon retirement. The company nearly always adopted the controversial system of promoting staff at all levels by seniority regardless of capability. The principal assistant would share the running of the department, sign documents and deputise for the CME when necessary, chair meetings, and have influence over new designs and modifications.

The locomotive running superintendent and outdoor assistant to the CME was next in line: he was usually chosen from the most senior and experienced of the divisional superintendents. The responsibility for making the most efficient use of the company's locomotives and rolling stock was a very important one. Locomotives were the most important asset, yet they needed constant attention, which was expensive. If the fleet was not kept in the best state of readiness, the company reputation would suffer and the business could collapse altogether. Churchward summed up the role of the running department inspectors by saying, 'They are my eyes and ears,' with regard to the evaluation of locomotives and rolling stock performance. The running superintendent would coordinate the inspectors' reports and work with the CME and a designated draughtsman to improve efficiency and influence new designs. Whether stock was withdrawn, repaired or rebuilt was also decided upon in the same way.

The CME's assistants, together with the chief draughtsman and chief clerk, were the heads of the offices staffed by those known as the CME's personal staff. The CME's chief clerk oversaw offices, sometimes referred to as sections, dealing with correspondence, staff and machinery records, and until the 1950s, the loco and the carriage and wagon operations were separate.

The locomotive works' manager was considered to be of higher status than his counterpart on the carriage and wagon side. He had five assistants to manage the various parts of factory or outstation work. The two works managers were ultimately responsible for all matters relating to production within the department. From Mr Collett's time onwards, it was the works managers who were expected to deal with labour disputes. It was the works managers, Mr Cook and Mr Evans, who headed the company side of the Joint Works Committee from its earliest times during the war. Some managers were very resourceful, and designed aids to improve ways of working. One was C. T. Cuss, assistant to the loco works manager Mr Hannington until he retired in 1936. Cook called him 'very ingenious': Cuss was instrumental in bringing glass-lined tanks for the bulk conveyance of milk to the company. He also invented several fire-fighting aids in his role as works chief fire officer.

The loco works manager's office was in the south-east corner of the managers' office building behind R Shop. He and his assistants used the ground floor while the loco wage offices occupied the first floor. Selbourne Smith got the job of loco works manager in 1956 at the age of 47. His route to the top was fairly typical of those with exceptional ability. He had distinguished himself as an apprentice on the loco side and gone on to further education at The College. He then went into the test house and then on to the drawing office. Promotion took him through a number of locomotive positions at divisional level before he became assistant loco works manager at Swindon in 1948.

Because of the policy of promoting from within the department, the younger a man was when he was promoted, the further he would go. A good example of this is the well-known story concerning the popular and capable Mr Stanier. He accepted the top job on the LM&SR because he was only slightly younger than his boss Mr Collett, and would therefore be too old to succeed him at Swindon when the time came.

In 1930, F. C. Hall was assistant running superintendent; later he became loco running superintendent and outdoor assistant to the CME, then principal assistant in 1941. At that time K. J. Cook was works assistant, becoming principal assistant to the CME when Frederick Hall retired in 1947. When Mr Hawksworth retired as CME at the beginning of 1950, Mr Cook became head of department. Jack Dymond had become an eminent engineer in the works by the 1940s, having transferred from the Taff Vale Railway upon its amalgamation. In 1957 he made a very unconventional move from assistant to the mechanical engineer to taking control of the supplies and contracts department. The Western had always placed great importance on an efficient stores department, now called the S&C department, but had never installed an engineer quite this senior to run it before. After nationalisation, management staff would move right across British Railways to take up higher posts.

The position of chief foreman was the highest position attainable by a tradesman, although this had not always been the case. Until the 1920s, apprentices in the loco works who had shown particular academic distinction would spend time in the drawing office early in their careers and could go all the way to the top. All the most senior men in the DO in the 1940s and 50s were ex-Swindon apprentices, as indeed was the CME himself, Mr Hawksworth. By the 1930s engineering apprentices who excelled might still be offered a three-year studentship, a small number of which the directors offered free each year. The object was to raise the general standard of technical training among those who might be capable of higher positions in engineering. However, a career in management would now require a BSc in engineering or its equivalent.

After the war, university graduates with technical engineering training could now take up junior management positions in the department. Their training included working alongside gangs in the workshops, and prolonged periods away at college. Some suitably qualified men were now coming in from outside firms or from other regions of British Railways. Senior staff, who had always expected to have to move around within their own company were now moving throughout the mainland UK. No doubt this was justified as giving them wide-ranging experience. The new BR administration, the Railway Executive, split up the CME department after Hawksworth retired. The word 'chief' was dropped from the title because the carriage and wagon section as well as outdoor machinery were no longer under the control of that person. Mr Cook was to be known as mechanical and electrical engineer, while and Mr Pellow, who had been loco running superintendent and outdoor assistant under Mr Hawksworth, was now motive power superintendent to Mr Cook.

Mr Randle, who had been works assistant to the CME, took up the new post of carriage and wagon engineer. The new head of the C&W department was to be considered equal to his counterpart on the locomotive side. He was installed in an office near the mechanical engineer in the east wing. The post of C&W manager, responsible for the production side of the works, remained, with H. G. Johnson taking over from C. T. Roberts in 1948. Mr Creighton was made electrical assistant to the M&EE: another new post due to the reorganisation. Jack Hartley, a clerk on the personal staff of the M&EE, said:

> Just as the former head of department's position had much of its responsibility stripped away, so we, as his personal staff, felt aggrieved at being, in theory at least, equal only to our counterparts on the C&W side: always the poor relation.

In 1951 it was all-change again. The 'chief', Mr Cook, who had been at Swindon all his working life, moved to Doncaster on the Eastern Region and was replaced by Mr Smeddle. Ethal Panting was Mr Smeddle's personal secretary: she did all the typing for her boss, including a good deal of his private correspondence, said Jack. Tommy Turner was chief clerk to the M&EE and he dealt with all correspondence and matters relating directly to Mr Smeddle. They shared No 101 Office, which was next door to their boss. Carriage and wagon engineer Randle moved away and was replaced by C. T. Roberts, and the loco works manager post went to a Mr Finlayson, who came down from Scotland.

INTERNAL TRANSPORT

A considerable amount of the work done by the internal transport was moving materials and components between workshops during the different stages of manufacture. There was also all the supplies to be delivered around the site from the various stores and the central laundry. They would move incoming goods such as timber and other raw materials, plant and machinery, from wagons. They also moved machine tools into position, ready to be bedded in by the bricklayers (see Chapter 6). It is recorded that a total 1,145 tons of items were transported around the works each day in the 1950s. The work also included taking coke to the mechanics' reading rooms in Gorse Hill and Rodbourne Road, and to the luggage office under the Junction station. Gordon Turner joined the factory transport in 1947 as a labourer. His first work was unloading scrap metal at the foundry which was destined for its furnaces. In the early days, horse manure from the stables at the transfer goods depot, about a mile east of the works, was collected and taken to a brick-built bin outside the foundry. Every so often works transport men went 'outstation', digging and loading red sand at the company's own quarries in Kidderminster. This was also for use in the foundry.

The transport garage was next to the F (smiths') Shop on the loco side. Of the 1950s, Gordon remembers:

> There were thirty drivers and twenty to twenty-five labourers. We had thirty-four tractors of various types (they were supplied by the Mercury Truck and Tractor Co. and had been since at least 1938), six petrol/electric mobile cranes, four rigid lorries, four forklift trucks and a large and small loading shovel. Another tractor was kept on the carriage side just for moving batteries between the battery house and the sidings where they were fitted on to coaches.

There were other vehicles available to the internal transport staff to cover different shapes and sizes of loads. You did not need a license to drive vehicles 'inside', but you had to be over twenty-one years old. Handcarts, sometimes called bogies, and mechanical petrol trolleys with trailers were used for smaller loads. Tractors usually hauled 1-ton trailers, but larger loads up to 20 tons, such as locomotive cylinder blocks and frames, could be carried on specially constructed trailers. Bulky loads were also moved in railway wagons and shunted between shops by tractor or locomotive; before the 1950s horses were also used to some extent. Some tractors were fitted with towing plates front and back, and shunted wagons and coaches in and out of 21 and 19 Shops respectively. Gordon remembers the names of factory transport men: Harry Stiles, Percy Smart, Derek Johnson and Clem Manning. Gordon's brothers also worked on the transport: Stan joined in 1950 and Ivan in about 1954. Teddy Rowe was the internal transport foreman in the 1940s and 50s, and when Reggie Hinton took over from him.

After nationalisation there was a growing realisation that the storage of raw materials and finished components by thoughtful utilisation of the storage space available could keep costs down. An investigation over several months by the works study people concluded by making several observations: one was that moving internal consignments by railway wagon was slow and costly compared with the use of the latest industrial transport vehicles. They found that, as well as congestion, wagons were not being used to capacity and far more reliance should be placed on internal road vehicles. The accessibility of stocks and keeping handling to a minimum would also, said the investigators, increase productivity. This, you might think, was common sense, and tends to imply that the old Great Western system of handling materials had never been studied with the intention of saving costs.

Based on the findings of the study, a range of vehicles for handling materials was brought in. Fork lift trucks for stacking, withdrawing and moving loads over short distances and larger fork lift carriers for stacking and transporting long lengths of timber and wagon solebars in the carriage works, were introduced. This work had formerly been done by various stationary and travelling cranes and moved by railway wagons. Four standard sizes of wooden pallets were introduced, along with purpose-built four-wheeled trailers to stack them while being towed by a Fordson tractor.

For moving loaded pallets one at a time, hand-operated trucks were brought in. They worked by jacking up the two forks a few inches from the ground to lift a pallet and manoeuvre it. The various types of powered aids were adapted in different ways to suit the requirements of each workshop. For instance, the handling of swarf in the A Machine Shop was much reduced by palleting it; in the grease works, a fork lift with a boom attachment enabled two oil or grease drums to be carried at one time; similarly in 16 (carriage wheel) Shop, special attachments enabled a fork lift to move two wheelsets at a time.

THE WATCHMEN

Outsiders coming on to works' land uninvited were usually just young men trying to spot locomotives. However, crossing the busy lines could be very dangerous, and the authorities naturally took a dim view of it. In those days people took responsibility for their own actions and expected to face the consequences without sympathy. So it was probably not the potential for injuries that concerned the company as much as the adverse publicity, with perhaps even an inquest, and the questions that would have to be answered at all levels. Much of the railway works was surrounded by high brick walls, but there were places where iron railings formed the boundary and these could be breached, especially with the help of a mate or a wooden box. Young children were very conspicuous on company land, but some corners of the railway yards were quite remote.

The duties of the watchmen were of two main types: 1) patrolling the shops and yards between 6 p.m. and 7 a.m. on weekdays and throughout weekends and public holidays; and 2) to act as gatekeepers at the works entrances. The premises were divided up into a number of areas to be patrolled; each watchman was responsible for one round each turn of duty. He was to apprehend trespassers and look out for fires; each round took about an hour and had a number of 'stations' which had to be visited. To prove that the watchman had covered the rounds as required, each station had a fixed key which, when inserted into a clock he carried round his neck, recorded the exact times he was there. When he first became a loco watchman, Mick Fisher was warned not to put shop lights on at night. There had been occasions when a manager had seen workshops that didn't have a night shift lit up from his home overlooking New Swindon. The following day questions were asked. Jack Fleetwood said: 'I remember two distinct types of men employed to maintain security around the works. Some were overcome with a sense of self-importance in the uniform, while others were quite agreeable.'

Another duty of the watchmen was to act as guides on works tours, although this was not exclusively their job. Watchman Bert Stratford used to talk about an incident that happened when he was accompanying a group around, probably on a Wednesday open day. As often happened once visitors got into the erecting shop, some wandered off to try to spot a locomotive or take a picture, and the guides usually turned a blind eye. On one occasion Mr Hawksworth came out of an upstairs office, shouted at the offenders, and told the guides what he thought in no uncertain terms.

At the entrances, the watchmen had to be seen in order to deter intruders and check suspicious-looking activity. Workers leaving before their normal finishing times were required to present a 'pass out' to the man on the gate, who would endorse it with exact times of leaving and re-entering. Goods and the accompanying paperwork arriving at or departing from the works were initially dealt with by the watchmen, who also received the Royal Mail from the postman. In addition to the watchmen on the gates, others were stationed at some railway crossings, which gave access to the works via the railway lines. For instance, there was a wooden foot crossing between the west end of platform 5 and the works. It was used by footplate crews walking between the Junction station and the running sheds.

George Petfield told me a story about an unofficial visitor at the running shed in the late 1940s. When approached by watchman Frank Cottrell, the engine spotter decided to make a run for it through the works, and was pursued by Frank for some considerable distance. The intruder easily kept ahead of the short, burly watchman, but was caught after others joined the chase. In court the villain was fined, and when asked if he had anything to say, said: 'I should like to apologise for the distress I caused to the short fat man who chased me.' The other watchmen who were present with Mr Cottrell ensured the apology passed into works' folklore.

THE GWR LAUNDRY

The company's central laundering had been done in the trimming shop basement alongside Sheppard Street from 1893. In 1938 a much larger building was brought into use. The laundry's workforce was almost entirely female and presumably always had been, as the *GWR Magazine* reported in 1931 that a Mrs Robinson, one of the laundresses, had worked there for thirty-four years. The only man was the foreman, who probably also carried out maintenance on the machinery. Wicker boxes filled with used laundry came in from the company's hotels, refreshment rooms, sleeping cars and camping coaches. Towels made up the biggest proportion of items dealt with. Linen, blankets, doyleys, dusters and antimacassars were also laundered and starched, then sent back. Thirty-six laundresses were employed before the old laundry closed, when there were five washing machines, four hydro-extractors (driers) and three large ironing machines. The new building was sited close to the station, in Whitehouse Road, for easier delivery and dispatch of consignments. The washing, drying and ironing machinery was of course increased and in addition, there was now a dry cleaning machine and a proper sewing machine section for repairs. Fifty staff worked in the new laundry, including a resident engineer in charge of the machinery and water-softening plant.

THE WORKS' FIRE BRIGADE

The brigade consisted of a chief officer, a second officer and twelve firemen who were available for immediate call. There were six men working full-time in the station during the day: they maintained fire appliances and equipment, practised fire drills and were ready to fight fires. A further two sets of men lived nearby and either could be 'assembled' at the fire station very quickly. In accordance with the Factory and Workshop Act, auxiliary fire points were situated around the factory where pumps and extinguishers were available. Before the war all firemen had to live in the GWR estate across the road from the fire station, and they were on a bell code system between the station and their homes. After the war new recruits did not have to live in the railway estate and some existing firemen were able to move further away. The part-time firemen worked in the shops, offices and yards. In wartime their number was increased to twenty-four. The part-timers were normally on-call every other week and would average about two call-outs in that week.

William Harber became a part-time fireman in the 1930s, and he and William Bown were the first-aiders for the fire station. Both men lived in the railway estate alongside the works, of course, so when Mr Harber's son Bert wanted to join in 1939, it was a formality to get him on to 'the strength'. Bert said:

> There were several fathers and sons in our brigade. You got *6s 6d* a week for being on-call, which paid the rent, and there was always the chance of more if you had to turn out. We went straight from work and did half-hour training four evenings a week and an hour, sometimes two, on Sunday mornings.

The station was divided into the appliance bays, a store, an office, a watchroom and, nearest the main lines, a workshop. Its position in the corner of Bristol Street was quite remote from many of the works' buildings most at risk of fire. Ian Sawyer told me that if there had been a fire in No 2 Sawmill next door to the station yard, they would have had to put ladders up against the dividing wall and direct heavy hoses over the top. This sawmill and the carriage building and painting shops next door were fitted with sprinklers which, when activated, set off alarms on the watchroom panel. Getting the fire engine and men to these buildings via the approved routes was very roundabout.

If a fire-call went out, the chief was called first then the on-call 'A' or 'B' list, usually about five men. Not all calls to the station watchroom were fire calls. A list of the various tradesmen on call was displayed in the fire station. If, for instance, a plumber was required during the night because of a burst pipe or a crew was needed to take out a broken-down train, one of the on-call firemen was sent off on a bicycle to knock them up. It wasn't until the 1940s that a motor vehicle was available to bring on-call staff into the works. If a person was killed under a train locally, by accident or suicide, the brigade would have to retrieve the body. In the 1930s the 'first call' fire vehicle was a 1912 Dennis Bros fire engine. A motor ambulance complete with trained staff was also available to be turned out for a fire call if required or for other medical emergencies. The ambulance was required a lot more often than the fire engine.

In 1942 the first motorized fire pump was superseded by another Dennis engine of the latest type. The earlier vehicle last saw action when the largest of the works' gasholders was hit during an air raid in 1942. After that it was only used for pumping water from flooded drains. This fine looking vehicle is now in the Steam Museum collection, still in the livery of when it was the first-call vehicle. There was also a foam trailer pump kept in the appliance bays to deal with electrical and oil fires. Two early horse-drawn steam pumps, probably built by Merryweather, were kept in the station, even though they had been obsolete for many years. They eventually went for scrap during the 39–45 war.

Alan Lambourn remembers seeing Mr Seeley, the fire officer, coming to work from his house in Church Place in the early 1950s: 'He always wore a very smart dark blue suit and was one of the "old school" who still favoured a bowler at that time.' Mr Sealey retired in about 1954 and Sid Smith took over. Sid had been a full-time fireman for more than twenty-five years apart from war service with the Royal Engineers. He also had a son, Harold, in the service. After nationalisation, if not before, all the Western Region fire extinguishers were serviced in the fire station workshop. When the Severn tunnel was closed for maintenance the opportunity was taken to replace the extinguishers fitted to its walls and bring the old ones in for servicing. The 50-foot tower in the station yard was for hanging up the hoses after use, allowing proper drainage so they could be rolled up and stored dry. The works brigade could, in theory, be called on to assist the borough brigade to fight a fire in the town. The only problem there was that the two brigades used different couplings: the works used screw fittings and the borough 'instantaneous' fittings.

For more on the works fire service, see the companion book *In and Around Swindon Works*.

THE GASWORKS

The company made their own gas at the northern edge of the works site, in the largest privately owned plant of its kind in the world. Up until the late 1920s, power for the works had been provided by sixteen gas engines, coupled direct to electric generators working at 250 volts. It was said that the factory gasworks produced more gas than the Gorse Hill works, which supplied the rest of the town. The plant was rebuilt after the First World War using vertical retorts, whereby gas coal was descended through red-hot retorts and converted to coke; the resultant vapours and gases rose and were then drawn off. Each day the gasworks would carbonise 240 tons of coal, giving approximately three million cubic feet of gas. These figures were given in company publicity in 1924 and were the same as those given in 1950, so I would say they are very approximate. Bert Harber, who worked as an office boy here in 1937, said:

> There were three clerks: a chief and two. I had to take paperwork to other offices and deliver messages to people who could not be contacted by phone – the usual duties of the 'boy'. I also wrote out coal tickets for the staff and assisted with the labelling of coal wagons before they returned to the collieries. Copying letters for the clerks was tricky: you had to place a damp tissue over them and put the two under a press.

Men in the gasworks were either engine or boilerhouse workers or gas or retort workers. They worked round the clock in three shifts. Throughout the works use was made of temporary labour available in the 1930s because of unemployment. Bert remembers the winter of 1937 when railway wagons couldn't deliver coal to the gasworks on account of the severe weather. Thirty men arrived from the labour exchange to shovel coal from the stockpile. Colin Bown was in the gasworks during the severe weather in early 1947: 'The coal stocks froze solid so a bulldozer was brought in from Hills (a local excavating and haulage firm). Railings along Iffley Road had to be taken down to get it in,' he said.

Mr Ackroyd was the manager in 1937 and Mr Jefferies was foreman; Mr Wilcox was chief clerk and Ernie Wordsell was the timekeeper. Another person remembered by Bert was Leonard Lucas, who was a full-time painter. Len, together with his mate, painted lovely country scenes around the internal walls of the meter house. A piece in the staff magazine in 1948 by R. J. Blackmore tells us that other walls were brightened up around the site too, such as in the Governor House. Len started work here in about 1931, repairing gas light fittings including seals and glass shades, sent in from all over the GWR. This type of work decreased as electric lighting gradually replaced gas, and so Len took on the gasworks painting work. This led to him painting the well-known murals.

'The workforce did not seem to mix with other railway workers or visit the rest of the works as I remember,' said Bert. This was not the experience of John Jefferies, who began his apprenticeship here in 1957. He was the last apprentice taken on and based in the gasworks. John spent much of his time in the factory or outstation assisting gas fitters. Within the gasworks they would maintain and repair gas- and coal-fired boilers, and John remembers testing samples of tar as well. Tar is a by-product when coal is carbonized or gasified into coal gas. They would heat it and put it in a hydrometer to test its density. 'Calcium carbide was also produced in the gasworks and used in large carbide and hand carbide lamps. As the apprentice I was taught to clean and adjust these lamps so they gave off a brilliant white light,' said John.

A scheme to modernise the gasworks was worked out in 1957, but the region decided the costs were too high. Gas started to be received from the South Western Gas Board in May 1958, and t he old GWR gasworks closed completely in early 1959, although the gas holders were retained. The gas fitters were moved to a corner of D Shop and the ordinary fitters to the G (maintenance) Shop; all then came under the supervision of Mr Gibbs, the maintenance fitters' foreman.

BRANCH PUMP HOUSE AND BACK CUTTING

A much less well-known source of employment for works staff was the branch pump house, as titled on a plan of 1925. This was a brick building in Rodbourne, just north of the works. It contained two steam-driven engines for pumping used and return water between the 'lagoon', sometimes called the 'back cutting' (see the book *In and Around Swindon Works* for how and why the works recycled water). The lagoon was not part of the nearby disused Wilts & Berks Canal, but may have been connected to it, because the railway did get into trouble on occasions for letting oil and impurities contaminate the canal. The local authority was probably mindful that people, especially children, swam in it. There was a break between the two halves of the lagoon where oil was skimmed off and reclaimed. According to some locals, this involved a man with a punt.

It is thought that there was a resident workman employed for the pump house. There was certainly a telephone to the works exchange. Kevin Weaver told me that his father Jim worked there, and remembers him saying that he worked a twelve-hour day, so maybe Jim was there during the war. It is possible he was one of the stokers sent out each day from the nearby GWR gasworks. His duties must have included firing a boiler as it is unlikely to have been supplied with mains steam, and presumably keeping the water filters clear. A 12-inch main was installed to replace the 8-inch one in 1938. This ran between the pumps and the running shed water tank. A more recent plan of the site states that electric pumping plant was installed in 1957 and was working by the following year.

WAGON WRITING (OR SIGNWRITING)

Ron Harper started his working life in the wagon works as an office boy in 13 Shop. His father worked as a labourer in the AE Shop bosh and they lived in Harding Street. After six months, Ron was moved out on to the shop to heat rivets for wagon-frame building. During the six months he spent here, Ron was asked to choose what he wanted to do when he reached sixteen. The choices were wagon building, blacksmithing or painting, and Ron chose to become a semi-skilled wagon writer, painting instructions and lettering on to wagons and containers coming out of the works after building or repairs.

Ernie Stowe did the rewriting or over-painting and Ron would go over and watch him while still employed on rivet hotting, so as to get an idea of what to expect. On the appointed date he was instructed to report to Bill Richen's gang in the south-west corner of 21B Shop. Others in the gang were Ken White, Chargeman Bert Barnett, Fred Gwillam, Dick Sturgeon, Den Carter, George Hobbs, Albert Brown, Len Blackwell, George Luckman, Fred Watson, Bob Jefferies and Phil Sargeant. Ron thought Phil was the most accomplished wagon writer. The foremen were Reg Sheppard and Ralph Stowe (no relation to Ernie). There was no training given: Ron learned by 'watching, copying and trial and error'. They used sable chisel, sable point and stipple brushes, a mahlstick to steady the hand, a palette, chalk lines and bags of pounce for surfaces where the paint might run. The work included painting the 1-by-2-foot CME panel on the end of the wagon. On it they had to paint the wagon number and specification, the date it arrived and the date it was expected to return to traffic. Other things that might be written on certain wagons were tare weight, telegraphic code and logos on private vehicles such as Birds Eye and Fyffe's Bananas. Wagon writers might also have to add 'Empty to' followed by the goods yard from which the truck originated. The long-wheelbase wagons such as 'crocodiles' and 'macaws' were 'written' in 21A Shop, known to the men as 'the extension' (they were normally parked just south of 21A in sidings reserved for special load wagons and known as 23 Shop). Tarpaulin sheets used to cover open wagons were written using stencils they had made. In the container shop the bodies that were to be chained on to flatbed wagons were labelled too. Ron told me:

> A typical day for me once I had found my feet was to meet at the annexe in 21 Shop, which we shared with the wagon roofing gang, and collect our paints and equipment. Six of us would work on the thirty-odd, mainly mineral wagons on No 1 road, which had to be finished before the 10 a.m. break, to get our piecework. Next we would go on to No 2 road to work on covered and open wooden wagons. There could be just as much work here but, as before, it depended on whether it was 'new writes' or 'rewrites': the latter involved painting over existing figures and letters. After dinner, if the weather was dry, two of us would go over to the transfer goods yard and put tare weights on wagons that had just been on the weighbridge. Or else we might be sent up to the sidings at pressed steel to write on weather sheets covering car bodies waiting to go out; for this we used a scaffold.

An official staff photo including, in the centre of the front row, the two Works' managers: Mr Evans and Mr Hannington; the assistant to the CME: Mr Hawksworth; the principal assistant to the CME: Mr Auld. I have yet to identify any of the other men: I don't think they are divisional or the CME's personal staff.

It was unusual to record management and lower grades together: presumably the latter had achieved some distinction in their working lives. The date is likely to be sometime between 1932 and 1937. (GWR)

Bert Stratford the chief 'loco side' watchman is on the right. The man on the left may be assistant chief watchman Mr Cooper. As a watchman, Bert would often accompany groups of outsiders around the works in the 1950s and '60s. He is still well remembered by visitors and workers because of his friendly manner and probably his upright and lofty stature.

Bert lived in Wanborough and would cycle in to work. Before the war he was in the Boiler Shop and when war came he was called up and spent four years in the RAF. Being invalided out with a back injury, Bert could not return to his manual work so the works took him back as a watchman. When Bill Leader retired in the 1950s he was promoted, becoming the senior watchman on the 'loco side'. The office where he was based was to the right of the tunnel entrance. Bill Poolman was his opposite number on the 'carriage side'. (Dave Stratford collection)

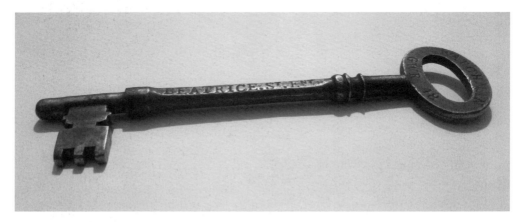

A watchman's key for the Beatrice Street entrance which was just north of the five Whitehouse bridges and next to the Central Laundry. By the 1930s all the external door locks on buildings and gates were standardized and designated staff carried a master key. The Works' Fire Brigade also held a full set including master keys.

The Blending Room in the Oil and Grease Works: below the floor were huge storage tanks. (BRW)

The Works' fire brigade in 1950 with the Avon Cup and diploma. Left to right: Jimmy Little, Bert Harber, Ron Adams, Ray Sealy, Arthur O'Farrell, Jessie Collett, H. Cripps. (B. Harber)

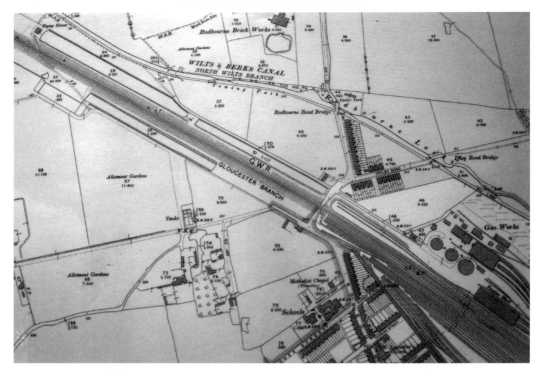

An early map showing the Gloucester line embankment at north Swindon and the Wilts and Berks Canal which was disused by the 1930s. At the top left can be seen the Branch Pumps' House with the 'back cutting' running parallel with the railway. Part of the works can be seen at the bottom right, including the Gas Works which had been extended towards Iffley Road by the 1930s. The pump house was ½ to ¾ of a mile beyond the works' perimeter. Whether this was classed as 'outstation' work for the attending person I do not know. If it was he would be paid for the time it took him to walk to and from his normal base in the works. (Swindon Central Library, local studies section)

Mr. C. Crump.

Mr Charles Crump OBE retired in 1931 from the post of Locomotive Running Superintendent and Outdoor Assistant. A man who reached this high office would, if he was young enough, almost certainly go on to become Chief Mechanical Engineer. (GWR)

10

Outdoor and Factory Maintenance

The CME department installed, maintained and if necessary, dismantled all mechanical equipment used by the railway company unless there were special arrangements agreed with the manufacturers. Various tradesmen were sent out to work on site or within the works. In both cases their base was the workshop at Swindon or other works, where spares and repair facilities were available. These men were responsible for the working parts; the water supplies, if any, were dealt with by men from the platelayers shop. Stocks of replacement parts were bought in to be held by the various warehouses of the stores department. Some Swindon men spent part of their working time away from the workshop, and some spent all their time 'out'. The D Shop carpenters' and bricklayers' checkboard continually displayed outstation checks for some personnel who were, for the purposes of administration, based there. Mechanical equipment at the company's depots, goods yards, at the lineside and at the docks was usually built by outside firms and delivered in pieces. Equipment such as cranes and lifting appliances, turntables, water tanks and columns were erected by men from Swindon and/or from the relevant division, sometimes with the help of contractors on behalf of the makers.

Of the five assistants to the loco works' manager, three were responsible for outstation and outdoor machinery. From 1929 onwards there was a lot of activity at the South Wales docks in preparation for the handling of the new 20-ton steel coal wagons. Although this involved men from Swindon, especially supervisory staff, the docks department had their own mechanical engineers. Gangs of men based mainly in L2 (tanks) and PL (platelayers) shops would go out to maintain the water troughs, and with them would go the tool and mess vans. The galvanised steel-plate troughs were 6 inches deep, 18 inches wide and, in sections, anything up to 1,838 feet long. They were bolted down the middle of the 'four foot' (track) at strategic points along the main routes. With full line occupation and temporary speed restrictions on the other running lines, the 10-foot sections of troughs were removed, repaired and replaced. Permanent way gangs also took the opportunity to work on the track at this time, thus minimising the disruption to train services. Trough maintenance was done mainly at night and could take up to a week before locomotives were again lowering their scoops to fill their tanks. Meanwhile, locomotives on non-stop trains would have to make unscheduled stops at stations to fill up at a water column.

The Severn tunnel ran through severely waterlogged ground and millions of tons of water were left to seep into it daily. This stopped the pressure building up around it, but then that water had to be raised. Pumping stations were situated on both sides of the estuary: two at Sudbrooke on the Welsh side and another known as Sea Wall on the English side. Electrical and mechanical gangs from Swindon would go outstation to do maintenance and repairs to the boilers, the old Cornish beam engines, pumps and ventilating fans. As most of the work had to be done on-site, they could be there for weeks at a time. The permanent staff there included Mr Stephens, the works manager, based at Sudbrooke, and the maintenance foreman who, from 1954, was Mr Bull: both ex-Swindon men. A lot of time was spent underground replacing the suction and delivery valves and bucket plungers, which varied in size between 26and 37 inches. Worn parts would be inspected and if possible the seating surfaces were turned and scraped. Otherwise they were scrapped, depending on the extent of the corrosion and pitting caused by silt and salt water. From the late 1950s, the Cornish engines were replaced by electrified pumps, and again Swindon provided the manpower. Swindon draughtsmen Terry French and Brian Stephens, son of the pumping stations works manager, had produced the drawings for the new pumps.

A 13-mile pipeline brought the all the fresh water needed at the Swindon works from boreholes at Kemble. The CME department maintained the pipeline and would put right any landslips due to leakage. Kemble water was found to be nearest supply containing the reduced levels of chemical salts required to minimise the fur-up of boilers. For the efficient use of steam boilers, it was essential that the water supply was 'clean' and 'soft', which meant free of impurities and chemicals, particularly lime. Men went out daily to the electric and steam pumping station, which was just north of Kemble railway station. They would check and, if necessary, replace crankshaft, crosshead and connecting rod bearings. At the bottom of the wells, the bucket plungers and valves in particular would often need attention like those of the Severn tunnel pumps. The cylinders, barrels and snuffing boxes of various types of these and other steam pumps were brought back to G Shop, Swindon, for turning back to true. New seatings and valves were fitted to suction and delivery valves. When necessary the cast-iron pump barrels were 'brought in' and set up on a boring mill and bored out to accept the replacement gunmetal liner, which was turned to suit the diameter of the plunger fitted. Swindon shed sent a pannier tank loco to Kemble once a month so that steam could be supplied to the original pumps while their boilers were shut off for maintenance.

Boiler work and tests throughout the company were the responsibility of CME department boilersmiths and inspectors. Apart from the administration, the majority of this work was carried out by each division and not by men sent out from Swindon. The works here had a central boiler station supplying mains steam and as a consequence it had few separate stationary boilers. All the routine maintenance on boilers was carried out by the men who fired them. When cold, they would be washed out, usually once a week on the Saturday. Periodic examinations were carried out by a boiler inspector or a competent boilersmith depending on the type and working pressure. The inspectors also tested locomotive boilers in the P1 Shop. Brian Carter was a highly regarded inspector of boilers; 'the best they ever had', Jim Lowe said. C. J. Robson was another one based at Swindon from 1947 until 1958, when he became chief inspector. Stationary steam engines like the ones that powered the rolling mills were worked by a 'driver' while the repairs and maintenance was done by loco fitters.

Bert Harber told me that during the war, electricians from E Shop worked outstation on new cranes being built at various South Wales docks. Two or three men, and sometimes himself as the apprentice, worked from 6 a.m. until 8 p.m. under licence to Stothard and Pitt. They came home every other Saturday morning and returned again on Monday morning. The other weekends they came back just overnight for a bath and change of clothes.

Men often went out just to evaluate mechanical equipment before a programme of work was authorised. In summer, men worked outstation, removing the steam heating hoses from carriage stock. These hoses were then sent to Swindon for testing and repair or replacement by the 'steam gang'. This gang dealt with all the steam heating apparatus used on rolling stock. G Shop maintenance men periodically inspected the hydraulic capstans used in shunting yards; they found that the trunion valves regularly needed replacing. New ones were turned in G Shop and fitted on site. Certain staff based in the drawing office regularly went out to depots to evaluate complaints about locomotives and rolling stock. These people were the 'experimental gang' and would, when requested by the running department, travel on the footplate or in the train, to investigate and if necessary redesign the offending parts. Fitters from A Shop went out on the footplate of ex-works locomotives to make any adjustments while the engine was in steam. They included the men who had refitted the pipework, to make sure it was steamtight; they knew which connections had left-hand threads and which were right-hand.

A new section was formed in the Swindon DO in about 1950, and known officially as Research and Development. It was made up of staff from the experimental section and, as usual, this name persisted unofficially. They investigated the performance limitations of locomotives and running characteristics of rolling stock, and how to improve them. Sam Ell was the engineer in charge of this section and Herbert Titchener (Titch) was his assistant. Sam had been on the experimental section most of his working life, and by the late 1940s was put in charge of the new R&D section, reporting direct to the CME. When the new grading system came in, Ell and his team became technical assistants, and are perhaps best remembered for redesigning the draughting of express locomotives so effectively. Train timings and motive power requirements were also worked out by TAs, according to gradients and loads. They moved into the office above the new telephone exchange building in the mid-1950s. Technical assistant Ken Ellis told me about a discussion he had with Ell in 1956, concerning a delay in taking him on. When Ken mentioned his letter of application, Sam Ell took him to his office and said, 'How am I supposed to keep track of such things?' Ken said it was floor to ceiling with plans, letters and paperwork: 'You could hardly move in there.'

Other work of the technical assistants in Sam Ell's section included measuring the performance of locomotives on the stationary test plant in A Shop. Here the driving wheels rested on rollers which allowed them to be driven up to 80 mph. Data obtained at various speeds included horsepower and water and fuel consumption. 'The tests are principally concerned with thermal efficiency at constant rates of evaporation and combustion.' The TAs also recorded data out on the road under controlled conditions using the WR dynamometer car. This 48-foot vehicle was equipped with scientific instruments for measuring the drawbar horsepower of the locomotive, water consumption, smokebox gas analysis and the effects of wind resistance. Some indicator instruments were positioned around the sides and front of the locomotive itself. Some of the technicians would be seated on the frames behind wooden screens, relaying the results back to the dynamometer car.

The TAs also went out with the track testing car, along with others from the works including labourers. It was impossible to develop smooth-riding carriage bogies if the track was not in good condition. This vehicle, No 139, in use since 1932, was coupled to the rear of a special train. A Hallade recorder electrically detected rapid lateral movements as it passed over rough-riding sections of track, and white water was deposited. The permanent way gangs would then know to attend to the marked lengths of track. British Railways used seventeen of these sophisticated Hallade recorders, and all were serviced annually at Swindon.

As well as financial allowances, the company conceded that men working away from their bench or machine could not be doing the job they were employed to do all of their working time. If they had to travel, including walking, to get to the place of work, from where they booked on, an allowance was made for this. 'Outstation' men were also paid a meal allowance when they were away from the home station during a booked mealtime. Where applicable, men negotiated through their sectional council an issue of protective clothing for inclement weather. In the rules and regulations, it is stated that 'Any pay due to any employee leaving the service will not be paid until the uniform and all articles belonging to the company and supplied to him, shall have been delivered up or satisfactorily accounted for.' In the 1930s and thereafter the working roster had to allow a minimum of twelve hours between shifts for a person working from their home station, and in all other cases, nine hours minimum.

MECHANICAL MAINTENANCE WORKSHOP

Maintenance staff worked all round the factory site as well as outstation, and could be on call seven days a week. G Shop was the mechanical maintenance workshop, the base for men maintaining and repairing all the overhead lifting appliances, cranes and pumps in the works. Keeping the eight Stirling boilers that generated the steam for engines, steam hammers and heating in good order was their responsibility too, as was the plant necessary for the central supply and distribution of electric, hydraulic and pneumatic power and the oxygen and acetylene mains supplies to the shops that required it. All the heavy machinery inside the works was cared for by G Shop men, as were internal transport vehicles and outstation mechanical equipment that could not be dealt with on-site. O Shop maintenance fitters overhauled and repaired the smaller machine tools in W (loco frames and cylinders), L2 (tanks and plate work) and K (coppersmiths) Shops, while men from the boiler shop dealt with machinery in the P1 (boiler mounting and testing) Shop.

Hydraulic cylinders were bored on Kearns or the larger Shanks boring mills in G Shop. Hydraulic rams were machined on the Tangye lathe: a machine that had the capacity to take work up to 50 feet in length. To allow it to be installed, an internal wall of the workshop had to be knocked through. The 9-inch diameter rams were used to open and close dock gates. Some rams were over 44 feet long, and these were of two sections joined by 2-foot long dowels. The bored-out ends were heated and the dowels screwed in as the ram expanded. The dowel would be held tight as the ram cooled and shrank around it. Capstan turntables used in goods yards for turning wagons were dismantled and brought to the works maintenance shop too. The usual type was the Armstrong turnover, and most weighed 1 ton 30 cwt. Setting a capstan bed plate up on a vertical table of a boring mill was a specialised job. Capstan rams were also machined on a boring mill using a special fixture. Bricklayers from this shop had a cabin in the rolling mills, from where they regularly had to replace the firebricks in the furnaces. This was just some of the many varied types of work of the mechanical maintenance workshop.

John Brettell moved from A Shop to G Shop in 1949. It was still known as the millwrights' shop by some of the older hands. Bill Brown was head foreman in those days, having taken over from Mr Marshman in the 1930s. Mr Simpkins took over from Mr Brown, then, by 1954 Harry Philpott had become G Shop and wire rope shop foreman. It was not unknown for Mr Philpott to turn up in the workshop in the middle of the night if he was preoccupied with some work-related matter. There are those who say he was just checking up on what the night workers were, or were not, doing. John's first job was as a fitter in the shop; later, he was an outstation fitter, after which he became a crane tester. John told me:

> Les Humphries and I would go all over the Western Region to supervise the regular loading tests that had to be carried out. My next move was to grade 2 workshop inspector before becoming assistant engineer (cranes) in the drawing office. All the electrical, boiler and crane inspectors

now came under me: a combined total of ten or twelve at Swindon and others throughout the WR. I, in turn, was answerable to the assistant mechanical and electrical engineer for outdoor machinery. Each division would send in a report when they required work to be carried out. I would meet the engineers involved and submit a report to the M&EE, detailing the conclusions reached and how best to apply the department's plant and resources and which depots should take on the work. The chief never once questioned or changed my proposals.

E Shop was the electrical maintenance and installations workshop for the factory and outstation. Like G Shop, they too had sections in other shops. Any outstation electrical work that could not be done on-site was brought to E Shop, Swindon works. Electricians dealt with such things as machine tool motors, automatic train control (ATC) equipment, lighting circuits, electric pumping stations, substations and later, electric crane gear and permanent way machinery. Carriage lighting was the exception; this was done in 5 Shop. Bert Harber became an apprentice in E Shop in 1938:

> There was no set programme of training: I gained experience with each gang in turn as determined by the foreman. There were about sixty men based in E Shop then; the two foremen were Mr Sutcliffe and Mr Hugo. There were seven gangs and my first was that of chargeman George Dan; there were also seven of us apprentices [for this information Bert referred to a list of personnel he made at the time]. In 1942 we moved from our main base in a corner of O Shop to take over a part of D Shop over by the running sheds. I was immediately called up upon completing my time, and when I returned in 1947, the foremen who had stayed on past their normal retirement age had been replaced by Mr Money and Mr Hewitt.

The electricians had an ongoing programme of servicing machinery with the fitters, and this included working while production stopped for the annual holiday. For four years running in the 1950s, each one of the 100-ton overhead cranes in A Shop was overhauled in turn. Bert remembers the work started at 5.20 p.m. on Friday, as the day shift left for the two-week shutdown. He said: 'We removed all the electrical gear as well as the motors and control gear, then we stripped it down. The day before the end of the holiday, everything had to be back together ready for the testers to move in and do the load tests.'

Permanent way work had become more mechanised by the 1950s, and a corner of B Shed nicknamed 'the cage' became the track maintenance section for the Western Region. Ballast cleaners, tamping machines, track-laying machines and excavators were overhauled here, but repairs could usually be done on-site.

John Jefferies from Albion Street started an apprenticeship in the Western Region gasworks in 1957. While waiting to reach the age of sixteen he had been rivet hotting to 'Nobby' Clark in 21 Shop. John's father Henry (Harry) Jefferies worked in B Shop as a chargehand labourer. Although he was based in the gasworks, John's work would take him all round the factory and beyond. He remembers:

> On one occasion after working on a dual-fuel [oil and gas] furnace in the rolling mills, the gasworks' foreman Mr Ellison arrived to see it tested. A small leak caused a fine jet of oil to squirt over his light-coloured and recently pressed smock. That was about 1959. Another time I was called out to an emergency in the Mechanics' Institute with a couple of gasfitters [probably chargehand Jack Hedges and Ian Ricks]. A coke-fired boiler had reached a very high pressure and the [weighted type] safety valve wouldn't lift. We had one option before clearing the building and waiting for the explosion: I hit the valve as hard as I could with a large hammer. There was an almighty noise of escaping steam and the pressure slowly came down.

Replacing oil gas lead seals on dining cars and their supply equipment took men from the gasworks all over the region. Upon completion the system was tested to 150 lbs but worked at about 100 lbs p.s.i. For this and other outstation work, John usually went out with gas fitter Ernie Webb and sometimes fitter's mate Bill Tyler as well. One of the last jobs gasworks apprentice John Jefferies was involved with was renewing gas pipes and some gas fires at Old Town station about 1960. John was made redundant upon completion of his time in 1961.

TRAVELLING STEAM CRANES

I have met several Swindon railwaymen who were fascinated by steam cranes just as others were, and still are, by steam locomotives. The Swindon factory looked after the maintenance and repair of all the travelling cranes, following which they were load tested using flatbed wagons filled with cast-iron weights and fitted with lifting slings. There were various types of cranes in use around the works and running shed yards. Cranes awaiting attention were held on sidings that curved around the east side of the CME offices alongside the Gloucester line. These sidings had pits, so that work could be carried out there, as well as in part of B Shop, which was manned by G Shop personnel. In the 1950s this was chargeman Ralph Angold's section. The locomotive department's crane drivers carried out their own routine maintenance back at their home depots. Swindon had about three 6-ton and one 12-ton travelling cranes for use around the works. They also had two large travelling cranes, which were kept in G Shop yard.

Work done by cranes around the Swindon factory included loading and unloading timber in the yards around the sawmills, and moving assembled trackwork in and around X Shop. If a 4-6-0 locomotive had overrun the turntable and the bogie had dropped over the pit, it was one of the big cranes (45- or 36-ton capacity) that lifted the front end so it could be driven slowly back and rerailed. A lot of the time cranes were standing idle during the week, but were sent out in goods and breakdown trains at weekends to do engineering work. Harold Couling was the G Shop chargeman responsible for allocating the labourers to their work routine. George Petfield remembers him from the early 1950s: 'He could drive anything,' he said. Other crane drivers remembered from the 1940s and 50s were Jack Norris, Claude Prince, Bill Ireson, Eddie Jones, Bob Waite, Norman Smith, Sam Jones, Dick Selwood and Les Smart, who later went into A Shop and drove one of the 100-ton overhead cranes.

Cranes on their own wheels, lifting loads, could be unstable, especially without the careful use of extension girders or outriggers to stabilize them. Dick Selwood had to jump clear when the ground gave way while he was working on the construction of the new points and crossings shop in the mid-1950s. During working hours, the outdoor assistant to the CME, Joe Clarke, would often see the breakdown train away. He would always say, 'No more than 10 per cent overload, mind,' which meant, be mindful that with the jib lowered, the lifting capacity was much reduced. But often there was no choice, said John Brettell. 'The large cranes were often lifting more than they should because of the need to lower the jib further to reach an adjacent load. The dangers of crane work were perhaps offset by the opportunity to earn good money through overtime, as crews could expect to be away for long periods. On the rare occasions that George, in the wages office, was questioned by his boss as to why a man was receiving so much more than his normal money, it was usually due to a timesheet submitted by a crane driver or his mate.

Steam cranes, together with their match trucks, formed part of the breakdown train, the rest of which was made up of mess/sleeping and tool vans and a guard's van. The largest engine depot in each division would have a 45-ton and a 36-ton crane, to go out with the breakdown train. Swindon, although not the largest depot in its division, also had two 'big uns': for many years they were No 2, a 36-tonner, and No 19, a 45-tonner, both built by Ransome and Rapier of Ipswich. The 45-ton crane was one of four ordered by the Railway Executive for the GWR and delivered in 1941. During the passage of a royal train, the depots along its route kept a crane in steam, together with breakdown vans and gangs, as well as prepared locomotives standing by. Crews liked these 'Deepdene' specials, the code word for the royal trains, because they got overtime for usually doing next to nothing.

The Swindon breakdown cranes were based in the works, not in the running shed as was usual. These, together with the Bath Road depot (Bristol) cranes, often made those at Swindon surplus to divisional requirements. Therefore they would sometimes be dispatched to assist cranes elsewhere: to where the engineering department was installing a pre-fabricated girder bridge, perhaps. Then the position of the 'foreigner' on-site had to be such that if called away, it was not boxed in. The Swindon crew would be made up of the supervisor, who was a G Shop foreman, the crane driver and four or five groundsmen. The latter were general assistants who went whenever the crane went out and were paid a little more than the labourers' rate. During the week, if not required to go out, groundsmen worked in G Shop as fitters' mates.

A full crew went out with the breakdown train, even for routine work, in case they were called away to a derailment. All work carried out on the permanent way, including the installation of bridge girders and viaduct maintenance, came under the control of the civil engineer's department. Although other departments had their own cranes and crews, it was the CME department that passed all crane drivers as qualified to operate them. If bridge girders or other large loads were to be lifted, a depot's two large cranes would need to go out in tandem. As the superstructures of working steam cranes were slewed out by anything up to 90 degrees, they needed the occupancy of adjacent running lines too. Some ex-railwaymen remember that a breakdown train, usually with a 36-ton crane, regularly left Swindon at 2.00 a.m. to work at the engineering depot at Taunton, arriving back around teatime. During the war, the cross-channel guns that were aimed at the Germans in occupied France had to have their 16-inch barrels replaced. Swindon's big cranes were sent down to Dover to help remove and replace the barrels, which were then brought back to the works for relining.

Other travelling cranes such as hand (manual), hydraulic and electrically powered types also came into the works for repairs, but the smaller types were likely to be maintained at the home depots. Swindon had built their own cranes, but the GWR came to rely more and more on specialist builders such as Stothard & Pitt, Ransome & Rapier, Cowans Sheldon and Smith Rodley, especially for the larger types.

The boiler house at Seawall Pumping Station on the English side of the Severn Tunnel. Although there were resident engineers here to maintain the machinery, Swindon gangs came out for repairs and new work. (*GWR Magazine*)

The cylinder floor at Sudbrooke Pumping Station on the Welsh side of the River Severn, showing parts of the Cornish beam engines. (*GWR Magazine*)

Technical Assistants Ron Lucas (left) and Martin Lloyd at their desks, sometime in the late 1950s. This was the Research & Development drawing office above the 1952 automatic telephone exchange. The photographer thought the man in the background, doing the work of three men, was probably Ernie Nutty. (Ken Ellis)

Crane men at what was known as 'the triangle' on 22 July 1962. Those identified are, left to right: unknown, Vic Corbett, unknown, Sam Jones, Fred Archer and Jack Bates. (R. Grainger)

Retirement presentation for Fred Selby: maintenance chargeman in G Shop, 1953 or '54. In the front, left to right are: John Brettel, Foreman Bert Price, Harry Philpott, Bill Simpkins (chief foreman), Fred Selby and Charlie People (chargeman painters). 'Of the senior G Shop staff at that time, only Jack Tyler (Inspector) is missing', said John Brettell. (*Swindon Advertiser*)

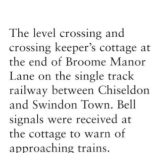

The level crossing and crossing keeper's cottage at the end of Broome Manor Lane on the single track railway between Chiseldon and Swindon Town. Bell signals were received at the cottage to warn of approaching trains.

G.W. Gas Works' staff maintained and repaired the gas plumbing here and presumably other trades from The Works looked after the other mains' services and building repairs.

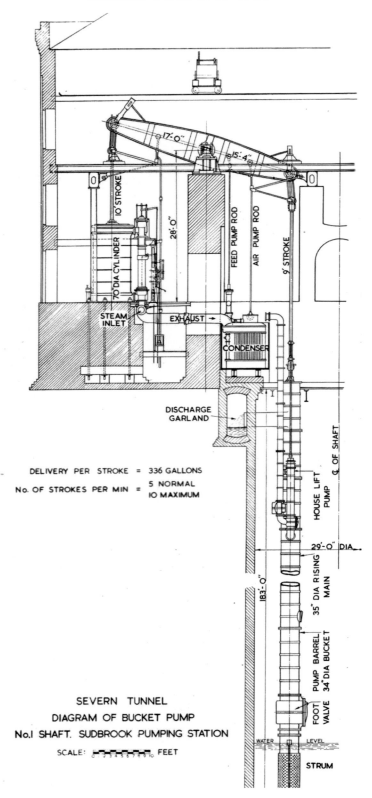

DELIVERY PER STROKE = 336 GALLONS

No. OF STROKES PER MIN = 5 NORMAL
                        10 MAXIMUM

SEVERN TUNNEL

DIAGRAM OF BUCKET PUMP

No.I SHAFT. SUDBROOK PUMPING STATION

SCALE: ⬛⬛⬛⬛⬛ FEET

11

The Stores Department

The stores department was the distribution centre for the whole GWR, and later the BR Western Region. In the early 1930s, it was divided up for administration purposes into superintendent's offices; accounts' sections including a machine room; the correspondence section; carriage and wagon stores offices; carriage and wagon storehouses (later called warehouses); general and traffic stores; loco stores office; loco storehouses; and timber stores. The latter consisted of three large sheds and a receiving yard at Rodbourne Lane. Most incoming timber was stacked in open sheds or on open ground for seasoning. The role of the stores department was the purchase, storage and distribution of materials for use by other departments within the company. Only the company's coal was purchased by another department: the CME department. Of course the CME department, being largely made up of manufacturing facilities, also had stores attached to the larger workshops, but these were not part of the stores department. Some time in the 1950s, the name was officially changed to the supplies and contracts department, but most people continued to call it by the original name.

Swindon works was the largest single purchaser from the stores, and according to the BRW staff magazine, 90,000 items of stock were held here; I presume this means types of items. Various stores were also held throughout the railway system if keeping them at a particular site or sites would be advantageous. For instance, a docks material and spare parts store was sited at Cardiff docks, which were best situated to distribute items to the major docks within the company. Similarly stores for maintenance and repair of road transport vehicles were held in a building near the main depot at Slough. Raw materials too, bound for the workshops of the CME department, the signal works or the civil engineers, were strategically held. It was not until as late as 1936 that the stores had a fully comprehensive catalogue of items handled, all fully coded and described.

Mr Cookson was the superintendent of the department; his assistant and successor was Mr Boxall. Mr Webb, Mr Dashwood and Mr Willis were the assistants to the superintendent, next in line of seniority. They were responsible for either purchases and inspection; storage and distribution; or accounts, sales and staff. After the war the responsibilities changed; from the works telephone directory, it can be seen that they were then divided into iron and steel purchases and sales; and general stores purchases and supplies. The third assistant to the superintendent position had gone, and I wonder who dealt with all the timber transactions. The other senior stores posts were the storekeepers, the chief clerk and the inspector of materials. The value of receipts (or purchases) from contractors or from the company's own workshops rose steadily as the economy slowly recovered from the recession. The money reclaimed from sales to the various departments also rose in line with receipts, although it should be borne in mind that both sets of figures would include rises in the cost of raw materials when compared year by year. (During the early 1930s, however, these prices remained almost static.) The value of stock in hand, that kept on-site at any one time, also increased in a general upward direction through the 1930s.

STORES' ACCOUNTS

Before stores were received, contracts had to be drawn up, orders placed and accounts kept, and this was done in the stores offices in the CME building. 'Goods inwards' were purchased from contractors and occasionally from other departments and sold on within the company, the receiving department being debited with the cost. The stores' accounts section of the chief accountant's department did the purchasing and handled the paperwork of goods coming in, known by the staff as 'progressing'. By 1936 material movements started to be processed by electro-mechanical means from information on the requisition cards. When materials were moved between the stores and the CME or other departments, it was accompanied by a requisition card. The card contained the details of the order: the weight, the quantity, the coded charge and the signature of the storekeeper or foreman. The respective accounts sections then evaluated the requisitions in turn. The information was then transferred to punched cards for compiling statistics and record keeping.

The stores were not in the business to make money when buying and selling. However, there was quite a difference in their favour between receipts and issues. In other words, they did sell certain commodities on to other departments for more than they had paid. Mr Gardner, the assistant chief accountant in the CME department, said in a paper read to the Swindon Engineering Society in 1929:

All articles manufactured in the CME's Department workshops went into Stores at a price fixed by the CME's accounts staff and were charged back again at the same figure when drawn out for use, unless in the interim the price had been revised. I understand the Stores Department cleared their expenses by adding a percentage to the cost of raw material which was purchased from firms and issued to the CME Department.

The fact that Mr Gardner was a bit vague about stores accounting emphasizes the division between the two departments, even though it was his department that compiled their figures and statistics.

GOODS INWARDS

Wood screws, glass, hand lamps, door locks and keys, and engineman's steel (Grimsby) boxes were among the goods inwards. Some train lighting and other electrical equipment was also brought in. The works' water-softening plant and oxygen plant were built and subsequently enlarged by specialist companies. One of the biggest areas of expenditure was stationery and office expendables, and although much of it was marked with the company initials, the factory relied on specialist suppliers.

Cranes, pumps, scales and pressure gauges were brought in, while the works usually looked after any calibration and repair. A policy of continuous renewal ensured such things did not become outdated. Contractors for the manufacturers were responsible for repairs, testing and regulation of the balancing machinery of the locomotive weightable, the wagon weightable and all weighing machines in the works (all such equipment used for buying and selling commodities had to be 'verified and stamped' by an 'inspector of weights and measures'). Air compressors for operating tools, used by the engineering department to break up foundations, were bought in and then partially maintained by the CME department. Any defective tools or hosepipes used with compressed air, if they could not be repaired on site, were either sent back to the makers or to Swindon, depending on prior arrangement. Micrometers, vernier calipers and other measuring instruments were all made outside and checked periodically using slip gauges (gauge blocks) from specialised makers. The works tool room did make steel rules and other measuring tools; this was all done on the section that repaired clocks and watches (see below). Custom-made optical alignment gauges, used on locomotive frames in the erecting shop, were purchased from the German company Zeiss in the early 1930s. Machine tools used in the factory came predominantly from makers in the Midlands and northern England, but many of the cutting tools and hand tools were homemade.

WAREHOUSES

The 230 staff in the loco stores handled items ranging from copper boiler plates, heavy iron and steel sections, raw materials in the form of steel blooms, billets and bars for the rolling mills and stamp shops, base metals for the foundry, loco wheel centres for turning and other semi-manufactured components, right down to bolts and nuts. They also kept such things as paint, permanent way materials, gas and electrical fittings, and crane and turntable parts. Another 176 people worked in the C&W stores. Besides every component for current rolling-stock building programmes, they held road vehicle parts, oil and grease and platelayers' materials.

The works' telephone directory shows that by the early 1950s, the stores at Swindon were divided between locomotive, carriage and wagon, timber and general stores: each had a storekeeper and an assistant in overall charge and, as with the larger workshops, each store had an office run by a senior clerk. Except the timber stores, each was further divided up into numerous warehouses. The storekeeper was responsible for the orderly storage and handling of stock, as well as supplying the works, depots, outlying stores and, in the case of general stores, stations throughout the company. He had to strike a balance between supplying items without holding up production, and holding only sufficient quantities to minimise loss of capital interest and the risks of deterioration and obsolescence. Storage and distribution of coal at the three local coal wharves also came under the control of the stores department.

GENERAL STORES

The general stores was a branch of the stores department also based at Swindon (for more information, see the companion book *In and Around Swindon Works*). Its function was to supply consumables, cleaning, clean laundry and other (household) supplies to the company premises and to vehicles of the traffic department. One of the items most commonly handled were brushes of all kinds, and inspector Ken Watts said the firm of Davis and Burrows was the supplier of choice. He remembers a consignment of superior brooms and brushes arriving on one occasion and a stores issuer taking it upon himself to store them on a high shelf. They were, he said, 'For cleaners of management offices only. He got into quite a lather over people taking them for other use on Saturdays when he wasn't there,' said Ken.

Travelling store vans were sent out to deliver every type of tool for the job: things such as brooms, lamps, shunting poles and clean laundry on a new-for-old basis. Engineering hand tools including woodworking tools were issued by the general stores on an exchange basis too. In the works hand tools were not the property of the individual but did generally stay with the one gang. Tools going 'outstation' were the responsibility of the foreman or trusted to the tradesman using them. A lot were issued to the engineering department for work away from workshops and depots. The vans were attached to passenger/parcels trains and each of the five vehicles supplied a different part of the system; with them went the attendants known as tallymen. In addition to the stores vans, a further fleet of vehicles was based at the general stores for the purpose of delivering consumable stores quarterly to something like 1,100 offices, stations and depots.

INSPECTING AND TESTING MATERIALS

Samples of ready-to-use materials and basic commodities purchased by the stores department were checked and randomly tested at various sites around the works to ensure they were up to the job. They also had their own inspection and test room at Swindon. The research laboratory, next to the fire station in Bristol Street, carried out a range of chemical, metallurgical and bacteriological testing work. Samples from the works' own brass, cast-iron and non-ferrous furnaces were analysed here too. Mr Dawe was the chief chemist for many years, having succeeded his boss Mr Davison in 1935. Some assistant chemists were employed just to analyse the water supplies. They visited water-softening plants from which the water for boilers was supplied in hard water areas. The chemists at Swindon also decided the rate charged by the company for carrying perishable goods, and it was they who would investigate if a claim was made regarding deterioration of such goods.

The materials and inspection section was attached to the stores department. Mr Phillips had succeeded Henry Arkell as chief inspector of purchased materials here in the late 1930s, and had a staff of about twenty-seven. They carried out physical tests on random samples and visual checks, which were done in the warehouses. Machines for testing tensile strength and elongation of iron and steel were used; others accelerated ageing or checked hardness. Steel, copper plates, wheels and timber were, on occasions, inspected by stores staff before they left the contractors' works. Physical tests on materials were also carried out on the loco side in the test house. This building was mainly concerned with the preparation, maintenance and testing of wrought iron, steel chain and hemp rope lifting tackle. They also checked over the hand-operated chain pulley blocks.

Shunting poles were brought in from contractors and a random one or two from each batch was inspected in the material stores. Bill Kent or his assistant Frank Smart did this after the war. The hickory shafts were tested by leverage: one end was inserted into a socket and, with a mid-point fulcrum, a man put his full weight on the other end. Used poles also came back in and if necessary the hooks were replaced or reshaped by inspectors. Linesmen's belts, for climbing telegraph poles, were tested using another home-made system of pulleys and weights.

MATERIALS INSPECTORS

After being wounded in Malaya in 1949, Ken Watts returned to civilian life, but found it difficult to get a job. Ken, of Avenue Road, Old Town, was failing the obligatory medical examinations and his fiancé, Hazel Newman, who worked in No 48 (mileage) Office, suggested he try the stores. For some reason the medical was not carried out there, and he was offered a start. This was 1950:

> My first job was marking metal items with a vibrating pen. Then I moved to a pattern store in the old medical fund swimming baths, one of a number of satellite buildings of the general stores. The pool area, now drained, was where patterns, moulds and templates were held. My job was to arrange to have them sent out to firms making items for the railway. There were several of each pattern and a master which didn't leave the premises; the inspectors used these to check castings etc., coming in.
>
> A first floor had been added to the old baths and that's where Eric King, the paint inspector, was based. He would coat various surfaces and leave them to weather, having carefully recorded when and what paint was used; send samples to the works' laboratory; and send supplies intended for marine use down to Weymouth where they would be painted on to surfaces and submerged to test durability.
>
> When Mr Phillips retired in 1949, Mr Tyler became chief inspector of materials. In time his assistant Jack Tudman succeeded him and Bill Morris became his assistant. Bill later went to the timber stores, and I remember him telling me they ordered wood for the Southern Region too. The clothing/uniform store in M warehouse kept samples of every type of railway uniform material, which were sent out to manufacturers as a guide to work from. Tom Mapson, the clothing inspector, would visit suppliers such as Compton Sons and Webb, a local factory next to the works in Sheppard St, set up many years earlier to supply uniforms to the GWR. The contact at Compton's was on the works internal telephone exchange. The cut and finish of uniform material was inspected and Tom or his assistant Gordon Hancock would check samples of weave from each batch by counting the thread per inch.
>
> Other materials' inspectors I remember are Norman Raven and Ray Harris, who played in goal for Chippenham Town in his spare time. The assistant inspectors included Bill Larkin, Archie Wilson and Bill Iles, who dealt with the lamps among other things.

THE STORES OFFICES

Noreen Harris didn't want to transfer to Paddington when the motive power department where she worked, moved. Instead she transferred to the general stores office as a clerk dealing with purchasing and stock control:

> Some of the contacts I had made with outside suppliers while working at Plessey's and Vickers, now came in handy when doing similar work here. The office was very hot in summer and draughty at other times. On the ground floor of the general stores there were three coke-fired ovens that were part of the original 1896 building and were listed. When the building was demolished a hundred years later they were broken up too. Mr Curno was in overall charge and all letters and documents had to go to him to be signed. Reg Cripps was in charge of the GS warehouse floors and his assistant was Arthur Hunt. Two of us were sent on a course to Windsor in connection with our work. The film *Psycho* (1960) was on at the pictures there so we went to see it.

Both Maureen Stokes and Margaret Eveness started their working lives in the loco stores office in 1950. This was one of a group of offices on the first floor of the CME building that formed a sub-section of the stores department. The clerks and typists here handled all the incoming and outgoing paperwork relating to ordering, receiving and dispatching of materials stored in the loco works' warehouses. This included raw materials and sub-contracted work such as electrical fittings and material; paint; and non-ferrous metals, iron and steel for loco building and overhaul. Components sold back to the stores from the CME workshops and movements of stock to outstations all made work for clerical staff. Alongside them were secretaries and typists of the stores superintendent who dealt with correspondence and the organisation of the department.

The materials inspectors' office was another section within the stores offices, and Maureen and Margaret both spent time here later in the 1950s. Materials inspectors checked samples and recorded the results from batches of items that were brought in to the general stores. The resulting paperwork was dealt with by the clerks of this office.

Maureen Stokes was fifteen years old when she went into the stores offices as office girl. She lived in Guppy Street, just behind Rodbourne Lane:

> A lot of workers going to and from the factory passed our house every day; little did I think I'd soon be one of them. After work I went to night school at The College and did English, shorthand and typing courses with the intention of becoming a shorthand typist. This was achieved, although some of my time was still spent doing clerical work. Head of section in loco stores was Jack Basham at that time, and I remember Carol Paulley and Doreen West who started as office girls in those early days. Later I worked in the material inspectors' office, which was mainly connected with general stores.

Maureen's typewriter was a model called the All British Bar-Lock of Nottingham, a type designed for business use and made about 1930. When she left the railway in late 1959, Maureen was allowed to keep her typewriter as they were all being replaced by electric equivalents. At the time of writing she still has it, and still meets up with several ex-colleagues including Carol Paulley, Mary Barnes who had started in the carriage and wagon stores office, and Audrey Clarke whose working life began in the stores correspondence office. Like Maureen, both had moved around within the offices of this department.

Unlike Maureen, Margaret Eveness completed her further education before going into the works. She enrolled on a day commercial course at the secondary technical school on the Goddard's estate. This was a two-year course starting in 1947. From the Education Committee handbook for that year it can be seen that the syllabus included the main school subjects of arithmetic, geography, physical exercise and French together with commerce, shorthand typing, craftwork and handwriting. Homework would, no doubt, have been an important part of the course as well. Margaret told me:

> I came from a typical Swindon family, most of who worked on the railway and married into other railway families. Grandfather Albert Eveness was a top-link engine driver and a big ASLEF (union) man from Rodbourne Green. My father was colour blind so they wouldn't take him on; my sister Maureen was a French polisher and my brother was apprenticed to fitting, turning and erecting. We had been bombed out of our house in Ipswich Street in 1940 and had to be moved to Beech Avenue, so I moved from Ferndale to Pinehurst School. I was 18 when I went 'inside', but still had to do the duties of office girl along with Jeanette Absolom from Westcott Place. As well as running errands I had to collect supplies from the canteen for tea breaks. Mr Plyer, a tall thin man, was in charge and Mr Hobbs was the storekeeper. I used to come in through the Beatrice Street entrance and so had quite a walk to the main offices. After a few months I was moved to the material inspectors' office where we all sat in rows at high desks. Eric King and Ray Harris were the inspectors here. After a year you had to move again to either a typists' pool or the machine room. They offered me the latter and I went to have a look, but didn't fancy it. When a job came up in Garrards' accounts, I left and went there.

In the late 1950s, Ken Bowles's outstation section of the loco stores office was spending a lot of time dealing with requests from Western Region diesel depots for locomotive parts. Roger Wise from Lowestoft Street was a junior clerk on this section at the start of the diesel era proper. He told me:

> The office would receive a phone call for a part for a diesel that had failed (very common in the early days). After ringing us and setting the wheels in motion, so to speak, the depot would be required to send in an 'Urgent Vehicle Standing' requisition to the stores accounts' office. Meanwhile I would look up the part number in the appropriate catalogue or manual; there were dozens of makers' manuals in the office. On a works bicycle, I would go to the diesel stores in 'A' Warehouse and the collect a part(s) from the stores issuer. As a junior I was also, usually, the one who took the part to the station, where it was handed over to an engine driver whose train stopped at Swindon. It had been pre-arranged that it would be picked up by an engine crew from that particular depot. Charlie Matthews at Cardiff Canton was one man among several I remember dealing with, concerning UVS requests. As the depots became more familiar with diesel loco faults, they kept their own ranges of spare parts.

SCRAP

As already mentioned, the stores also dealt with the company's scrap. Residual materials were sent back to Swindon where the department received it and reclassified it as either saleable, salvageable or for disposal. During the war the CME department arranged for as much waste material as possible to be processed for reuse, on the premises. Some metals, for instance, could be melted down and recast and sometimes rolled in the rolling mills. Wood shavings and sawdust were burned for heating, but this may not have involved the stores. According to the *GWR Magazine*, 'Striking economies in the use of materials have been effective by a variety of special means including modern methods of reclamation and the painstaking salvage of bomb damaged and worn equipment for repair and reuse.' It also fell to the stores during this period to find suitable substitutes for scarce items.

In 1937 there had been difficulties in obtaining supplies on account of a government rearmament programme and general trade requirements. Therefore the works recycled more of the scrap that they would normally have sold. The following year the supplies situation had improved, but market conditions for the disposal of scrap materials became less favourable. The company waited for values to increase but with the introduction of controlled prices in 1939, they did not. Presumably they then decided to cut their losses and sell the stockpiled scrap, and despite the lower price, the annual figures for material sales didn't look too bad. No doubt the accounts people at Paddington were not fooled.

The Western realised the value of railway enthusiasts and invested in such things as Swindon works excursions and open days. Another way in which they encouraged interest was by selling nameplates from withdrawn locomotives to the general public. It was common knowledge among men who stood on the stations and watched trains that a letter to the 'Stores Superintendent, Swindon, Wilts' could secure a nameplate for a sum that would just cover handling costs. The railway would dispatch the item requested, or offer an alternative, to the nearest station for collection.

One of the larger stores in the Carriage and Wagon Works. (*GWR Magazine*)

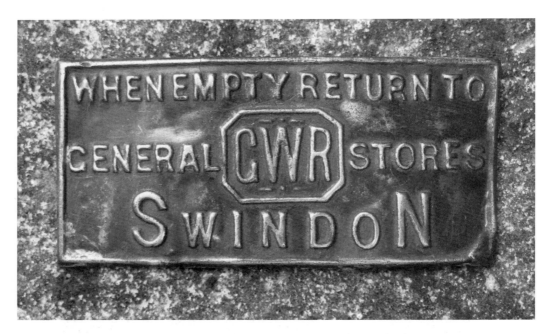

A small brass plate once soldered to an oil reservoir can, giving the standard instruction.

A tender register plate sold by The Stores Dept to a Mr Mython Hunt in 1950. The price asked was 2/6d (two shillings and sixpence) and this was based on the scrap price of the brass at that time. A surviving letter concerning the sale advises the purchaser that the two tender plates he had requested had been "broken up". From that and other research I deduce that, up to that time the Stores rarely had requests to buy anything other than surplus engine nameplates.

Tender number 1054 was attached to four different 'Dean Goods' locomotives between 1930 and 1940 when it was found to still be in serviceable condition. By this time many of the 'Dean Goods' locos had been withdrawn or 'called up' and sent to France so 1054 was attached to a new 2251 class 'Collett Goods' until withdrawn in 1950.

This is the Stores Accounts' Office on the second floor of the CME building in the 1940s. According to the 1935 Works' telephone directory those with their own telephone here were: E.J. Burrington - clerk in charge; E.A. Blackman - section head of Invoice Accounts, later to be succeeded by W. Scott; G.W. Worthy - head of Ledger Accounts which included paybills and stores sold; F.C. Tomes - head of Mechanised Accounts; B.E. Turner - Pricing Accounts. Irene Dening, seen on the left of the third row, was already quite senior but, assuming this was her normal place of work, it would appear, not yet senior enough to have her own telephone. (B. Carter)

Maureen Stokes photographed next to her desk which has been decorated up by her colleagues for her twenty-first birthday. As was traditional, she also received a large brass key made 'inside', with her name engraved upon it. This was 1956, during a period when Maureen was working in the Clothing Office. (Maureen Marvell)

Mr Faith was appointed 'assistant to the stores superintendent' in 1940. At that time there were three men of this title each responsible for a different branch of The Stores' activity (see text). These posts should not be confused with 'assistant stores superintendent' who was second in line to the head of department and one position higher than that which Mr Faith now held.

Charles Frederick Faith must have shown particular promise soon after joining The Stores Dept in 1901. He did so well at night school that a day release course at the London School of Economics studying Accounting and Business Methods, followed. This was successfully completed in 1908 to class 1 standard: one of only about three on this railway that year. After demobilisation in 1919 with the rank of captain, Mr Faith returned to the GWR and was seconded to the London division as a storekeeper. He was now the head of the electrical stores for the London area. Secondment was usually reserved for staff that had been singled out for higher station. In 1924 he was brought back to its headquarters and promotion came again in 1932. He was now storekeeper in overall charge of the Carriage and Wagon stores.

Mr Faith lived in Westlecot Road and was a member of the nearby Bowls Club. About the time he retired in the late 1940s he moved to a house in Marlborough Road where he lived until his death in 1958.

12

National Emergency

Both sides of the works were 'taking on' again in 1939 after a bad 1938. K. J. Cook, who was locomotive works' manager at the time, wrote in his book *Swindon Steam 1921–1951,* 'When war broke out our locomotive and rolling stock position was well under control.' The 'chief' naturally wanted to retain all the facilities of the department for railway purposes and so Swindon managed to avoid taking on munitions work at first. They got on with adapting the railway for the expected conditions ahead. Air-raid precautions were undertaken, such as building shelters; fitting anti-glare screens to locomotives; fitting air-braking apparatus to the 2301 Class (Dean Goods) locomotives, which were expected to go to France with the British Expeditionary Force; and converting carriages for use in ambulance, casualty evacuation and fire-fighting train sets. All were fitted with steel brackets, six to a solebar, which caused quite a bit of speculation in the carriage works until it was revealed they were for lifting the vehicles in and out of ships' holds. Passenger coaches had to be made invisible from above at night. To this end blinds and metal lampshades were soon being turned out from Swindon in their thousands. Eventually, in the face of growing outside pressure, Swindon fell in with the other railway factories that were making armaments, bombs and ammunition.

The CME department relied heavily on suppliers of raw materials, and early in the war it became increasingly difficult to get sufficient to cover existing contracts. Materials were being diverted elsewhere for armament production. A Ministry of Supply Order was sent out to manufacturers stating that they must collect their own redundant and residual materials for salvage. On the GWR, salvage vans travelled the system collecting textiles, rags, sacking, paper and metals. It was then sorted and sent on internally or externally by the stores department. Iron, steel and non-ferrous metals were still dispatched to the usual contractors, but Swindon was reusing a much higher proportion than before for its own needs. The *GWR Magazine* reported that incoming supplies of quarto and foolscap paper were severely disrupted from the middle of 1939.

Males called up for war service were drawn from shop and office indiscriminately, depending only on age. The first to be conscripted were men up to the age of twenty-five: those whose work could theoretically be absorbed by the remaining workforce. They included apprentices, labourers, clerks, vehicle drivers, shunters and, later, anyone whose work could be done by females. Young single women were also called up, and a few of those already in the company's employment from before the war were drafted into the Women's Auxiliary Air Force (WAAF), the Auxiliary Territorial Service (ATS), or the Civil Defence services. Presumably their railway work was done by hastily trained older people brought in. Colleagues of those departing temporarily would often buy gifts and have a presentation to wish them well, particularly in the offices.

Works men on active service made up a sizable proportion of the Royal Electrical and Mechanical Engineers (REME). Their particular skills would, wherever possible, be utilised in their new deployment. Some men, not surprisingly, felt a strong moral dilemma between doing their duty and potentially having to kill someone. Others felt it clashed with their religious beliefs, but either way George Petfield remembers these types usually went off to war and conducted themselves very well. There were pacifists among Swindon clerks sent off to work at the Ministry of Munitions at the relocated GWR audit section in Aldermaston, and again George heard they had worked commendably. There had always been a bond between railwaymen, and it was stronger than ever during wartime. Jack Fisher, a rough painter in the erecting shop before being called up, couldn't let his family know where he was for months on end. Occasionally however, his army unit passed through Swindon and he would throw a note tied to a weight, on to the platform. His messages always reached his home in Ipswich Street, but he never found out who delivered them.

As time went on, the dilemma for the government was that although the criteria for retaining many skilled and trained railway staff within the reserved occupations had to be amended to allow more men to join the forces, the importance of maintaining an efficient railway system at home was being acknowledged by senior planners. Petrol was rationed to everybody except the military, so the railways were carrying more goods than ever. It was hardly surprising then that, together with millions of journeys being made by service personnel, the authorities wanted to discourage unnecessary passenger journeys. The problems faced by railway factories trying to meet government requirements for rolling stock and munitions work with a depleted workforce were immense.

There was now no holiday shutdown in July so this, together with so many workers being called up initially, put a stop to most planned maintenance. The works outings too were cancelled for the duration, but railwaymen and women were still getting away. Peter Reade got three free passes a year and unlimited quarter-fares on the company's trains. With some of his workmates from the loco smiths' shop, who now included women, he would often go up to the West End and see a show. Staff approaching retirement had been asked to stay on while some skilled men were loaned to outside firms. Others arrived at the works for the first time and a post was set up outside the junction station to direct incoming war workers to their lodgings. Later in the war, some skilled men were doing menial work with the forces, while their places on the railway were filled by outsiders with no experience, known as 'dilutees'. Men taken away from the department could apply for a 'class B' release, and those back home with influence would, in some cases, write to the authorities on their behalf. After the Normandy invasion, however, the War Office also needed railway workers to keep the continental railways working, and an early release became very difficult to obtain.

Numbers of workers were involved with the Local Defence Volunteers, later called the Home Guard. These men would have to turn up for work the next morning having been patrolling the works and the railway yards half the night, fire-watching and looking out for enemy agents. In 1943 on account of its growing strength and importance, the GWR Home Guard Company was detached from the 5th Battalion and became the 13th Battalion commanded by Lt-Col. Dyer, a member of the CME's personal staff. By May of that year, 640 GWR men guarded Swindon works and the surrounding railway premises. This number rose significantly over the following year, and there were a lot of railwaymen in other Home Guard units too.

Jack Fleetwood thought the Luftwaffe had scored a direct hit on the brass foundry one day. Every so often a large brass cylinder was sent to Swindon to be scrapped; they came from Sudbrooke pumping station, where they were normally submerged in water causing them to become badly pitted and corroded. The deterioration could cause water to get into the hollow chambers, and Jack remembers one going into a 2-ton reclamation furnace without the top having been cut off to drain out any water. The resulting explosion blew the top off the furnace. When the air cleared a bit, Jack could just make out two fellows standing next to the furnace where they had been working. There were bricks all over the floor and they were covered in dust, but unharmed.

The Germans would have known Swindon was an important railway centre from flying overhead, and aerial reconnaissance photographs were taken, but they almost certainly didn't know what else was being produced there for the war effort. At first they put all their efforts into attacking the means by which the British were attacking them: the shipbuilding yards; the ports; the aircraft factories; the aerodromes. The railway factories were, by comparison, considered less important. Later the enemy's targets were the big cities, particularly those with ports, and again the large manufacturing plant in Swindon was spared.

There were a few isolated attacks on the town by single enemy aircraft on their way back to their bases, either by strafing random targets or dropping their bombs from a high altitude. Official sources say the railway town as a whole suffered 158 bomb alerts: 104 bombs dropped; 48 people killed and 105 injured, of whom 33 were seriously hurt. Fifty houses were destroyed or had to be pulled down, and another 1,852 suffered damage to some extent. No works were hit or damaged, and the only urgent remedial work undertaken was the filling in of bomb craters in the yards and relaying of damaged trackwork. However, a lot of Swindon works staff and their families must have figured in these statistics.

The gasworks was attacked from the air by a lone raider in July 1942. This incident has been described several times in books, but some details from the Fire Station register add further to the story. On 27 July an air-raid message red was transmitted to all local emergency and ARP services by the civil defence control centre. They were acting upon information phoned in from roof spotters. The alert was received at 3 minutes past 6 a.m. at the works' Fire Station watchroom. The attendant would have then called the senior fire staff on-call followed by the 'A' list, those on call that week. For this type of emergency he would then have to contact the knocker-uppers to go out on bicycles to alert firemen who lived beyond the railway estate. Another caller at 6.48 a.m. told the attendant fireman of fires at No 5 gas holder due to machine-gun fire from the low-flying enemy aircraft. By 7.37 a.m., when the all-clear was given, '27 firemen were assembled' (changed and ready) at the station. The town brigade too, would have been asked to stand by.

Meanwhile the ambulance crew were busy too. They were called out at 6.15 a.m. to take a Mr Vance, a railwayman from Beatrice Street, to the GWR hospital; the reason given in the register is that he was knocked down by the ambulance. At 7.10 a.m. they were called to the east end of the stamping shop to take a Mr Dixon to the hospital with head and leg injuries caused by a bomb blast. The ambulance and first-aiders were out twice more that morning: once was for another victim of the bombs that fell on the northern end of the carriage works yards. The major fires expected when the gasworks was attacked did not happen, and the flames shooting out of holes in the gas holders were quickly extinguished by plugging them.

I have heard stories of men having to take cover under their machine tools or workbenches. Whether this was because the works' hooter, now only used as a warning of enemy planes overhead, had not been sounded, I don't know. Maurice Dunscombe, who worked in the AE shop, was fire-watching one night in the works yards when bombs started falling. He told his daughter: 'There were five of us in a coach having some refreshments. The explosions got louder and I counted six; the seventh, I felt sure, was ours. The others with me were all tabernacle people and were praying out loud. It worked, as no more bombs fell. I must have miscounted.'

After Shorts Brothers Ltd of Rochester was bombed in 1940, the company moved production to 24 Shop and two other sites just outside Swindon. Built in 1929/30 for carriage repairs and painting, the massive 24 Shop could hold up to 250 coaches. The work done here was considered low priority during wartime, so just two through roads were retained for carriage repairs. Another part of this shop produced shells and the rest was adapted for production of the tail sections of the new Stirling bomber. Much of what went on in here was, like other war work, kept quiet. Shorts were supposed to have been isolated within the railway works site and their workers were issued with ID cards.

A separate entrance was built for the new aircraft plant, which required large-scale civil engineering work to provide a ramped roadway across Ferndale recreation ground and up to 24 Shop yard. Heavy vehicles towing trailers with aircraft fuselages would soon be rolling down this road, and it gained the nickname the 'Burma Road'. In time some of the aircraft work was being done by workshops on the other side of the fence, while Great Western labour was being used in 24 Shop. One of the things people most remember about the displaced aircraft factory was the strong smell of dope that was sprayed on to the outside of the airframes. Even though they moved out in 1944/5, the new entrance continued to be known as 'Shorts' entrance' right up until the carriage works closed in the 1960s. Between the 'Burma Road' and Osborne Terrace entrances there was a prisoner of war camp put up on the green. Italian prisoners held here were put to work 'inside'.

A lot of carriage maintenance and building work was put off and the relevant shops were turned over to armaments production, but not all. In 1938 an order was placed for a further twenty diesel-mechanical railcars to work some of the passenger and parcel services on secondary routes. By this time diesel railcars accounted for 3 per cent of the daily passenger mileage on the GWR. AEC of Southall, who had built and maintained the first batch for the company, were now required to build military vehicles, so the new railcars were built in the carriage works. Swindon produced the undercarriages, bodies and some mechanical equipment while AEC still supplied the engines, gearboxes and transmissions. The passenger compartments (saloons) were fitted out, finished and painted by tradesmen in the same way as carriages. The standard automatic train control apparatus, electric lighting, batteries and dynamos were then fitted. The twenty railcars were outshopped between 1940 and 1942.

For some reason the CME department had been slow to start using female labour. Before 1942, women were taken on elsewhere as porters, van guards, carriage cleaners, ticket collectors and other positions usually filled by men. Many of the females, when they did start coming in, had relatives 'inside' and this helped them settle into the alien environment and break down any animosity towards them. At first they were put on light labouring and repetitive work, but they were soon doing semi-skilled machining and fitting. They proved to be equally good at light coppersmith and tinsmith work or as boilermakers' and blacksmiths' assistants. Following conscription for women at the end of 1941, they came into CME workshops in much greater numbers. They made up the labour shortage due to the combined effects of men being called up and the extra war work commitments. The general role of this new source of workshop labour was to supply and assist the skilled men and, with a few exceptions, they exceeded all expectations. Some went on to drive walking cranes and traversers and later, the cranes that ran up and down the length of some shops by overhead carriage.

The workforce gave generously to the Comforts Fund which the Staff Association had set up, with branches throughout the company. The phrase 'a penny a week' was used to promote a Comforts Fund paybill deduction. The fund paid for parcels containing such things as knitted clothing, cigarettes and a copy of the *GWR Magazine*, which were sent to workmates on active service or held as prisoners of war. In 1940 another scheme to help finance the war, the Spitfire Fund, was given a starting contribution of £500 by the company directors. They knew that, with the mood of patriotism so strong at that time, the company's employees would soon raise the £5,000 target; the theory being that the contributors were providing an extra fighting aircraft, which, at that time, was just about the only way of hitting back at the enemy. Stations, offices, works and depots were asked to set up their own National Savings groups. It was pointed out that there was no setting up or running costs and stationery (something the company was trying to cut back on) would be provided free. 'Lend to Defend' was the catchphrase, and Swindon GWR had seventy-six National Savings groups by the end of the war.

As a result of the extraordinary conditions brought about by this war, many traditions were discontinued, never to be reinstated. The foreman could no longer summarily dismiss a man, although in practice, the unions and shop committees had got this stopped in the 1920s; the dreaded discharges were a thing of the past and the smoking ban was lifted, with exceptions, probably as a concession for the introduction of the twelve-hour shifts. Promotions came along much quicker and even fashions seemed to be changing: most official photographs taken around the works are from the 1920s or before, when everybody seemed to wear ties and waistcoats, including the manual workers. Jack Fleetwood said that apart from supervisory, office staff and management, most of the men were wearing their shirts collars open by the early 1940s, although photographs tend to suggest this was only the younger ones. One-piece overalls were also becoming popular by then, said Jack.

Mr White was chief boiler shops foreman: he oversaw all the maintenance and new building of locomotive and stationary boilers at Swindon. He had been foreman in the AV (boiler section) prior to taking over from Mr Higgs in 1937. Under him were 1,343 workers such as boilersmiths, their assistants (including females), platers, riveters, apprentices, labourers, shop clerks and junior supervisory staff, spread across six workshops. Like many areas, not all boiler workers remained on railway work during this time. V Shop and the AV boiler sections in particular cut back on their normal work programmes to make way for armaments work for the various government war ministries. Initially plant and machinery were installed in V Shop to produce 2,000- and 4,000-lb bombs, the first of a new type still in the experimental stage in early 1941. The mild steel barrels were to be produced in the same way, but on a much smaller scale, as loco boiler barrels, rather than by casting the cases. Bulletproof steel plates for armoured cars and Hotchkiss naval guns were one of the largest types of outside war work undertaken. Each plate had to be tested, so a rifle range was set up outside the boiler shop. A semi-circular mounting platform for a 13.5-in calibre cross-channel gun was assembled in the AV boiler bays. A works photograph shows that it must have been all of 30 feet in diameter.

For the way the boiler shops adapted so well to these tasks while still fulfilling their commitment to essential railway work, Foreman White was awarded the British Empire Medal in 1945. No doubt, the successful application of female labour, with few of the anticipated integration problems, played a part in his recognition. He was also cited as playing a big part in perfecting new techniques for manufacturing bombs.

From 1943 the men were represented at the Joint Works Committee by elected members of the NUR, the craft unions and non-union men. The other half of the committee comprised supervisors and managers: Mr Cook, the loco works manager, was one of the wartime JWC. They met once a month to negotiate matters arising: it could be how best to use the resources to increase efficiency or reports that some groups of men were being unfairly treated; anything except standard rates of pay. Mr H. C. Horrell, a patternmaker, was the first JWC chairman; in the 1950s he had become secretary of what was then called just the Works Committee. By June 1944, the boilermaker Gilbert Luker had become chairman of this committee and as such, was invited to a large meeting in London addressed by Field Marshall Montgomery in the run-up to D-Day. The theme was the vital necessity of keeping supplies moving and the importance of railway staff in achieving this. In exceptional circumstances, the committee was invited to send a deputation to meet the general manager at Paddington. With the need for co-operation being in the national interest, the local meetings are remembered for the efficient way decisions were reached. There was an impression among some men that their negotiators became passive in the presence of 'the gaffers'.

Some batches of mixed traffic and light passenger locomotives were built during the war, but the '8750' 0-6-0 pannier tank engines were the only class of GW types produced throughout the whole five years. Not surprisingly, the 2884 heavy freight engines continued to be built well into the war. Not until the government wanted a common type of freight engine was production of Churchward's 1903 design stopped. Swindon then built eighty of the modern LMS 8Fs between 1943 and 1945. They had already converted some of this class to oil burning in 1941 for use in the Middle East.

Although the existing stock had to be patched up and sent back out, new wagons were built in large numbers throughout the war. Construction of new coaches was limited and then stopped altogether in 1942. Certain chemicals used in paint became scarce, so from 1942 express engines were painted in unlined green and all other types were painted black as they came through the works. The chocolate and cream coloured coaches were painted over in brown except for the stock of the *Cornish Riviera* and *Torbay Express*. Vans were painted a dark red; insulated vans were given a stone colour and open wagons were not painted at all.

The government introduced a number of schemes to improve the nutrition of the nation's workers. One was the expansion of industrial dining facilities. A contract catering company ran the works' dining facilities early in the war, but the workers soon started to complain. The standard of cooking in particular was brought to the attention of the Joint Works Committee. The situation did not improve, and perhaps out of frustration, management said, 'If you can do better, then get on with it,' so the men organised the catering themselves. A canteen sub-committee was formed and Gilbert Luker, as a prominent and respected member of that committee, was allowed to oversee the hiring of female staff and the ordering of supplies. Some premises were converted on the loco side early in 1942 and catering equipment was installed.

On the carriage side a completely new canteen building was erected between 15 and 21 Shops and was in use from 1943. A young Harry Bartlett would go there sometimes and have lunch for sixpence:

> On a couple of occasions we [two other office boys and himself] were lucky enough to see the BBC Workers' Playtime concerts. These were half-hour programmes broadcast every weekday from works canteens throughout the country. There was always a top-class comedian and singer from BBC radio performing.

The smaller existing facilities and mess rooms, which had served refreshments up until this time, were retained. Before the war there were no such facilities 'inside', and many of the staff within 15 minutes' walk, would go home 'middle day' for what was always 'a bit a dinner'.

Many of the staff could play musical instruments or sing and entertain in front of an audience, and turns were put on in the new dining halls on Wednesday dinnertimes. In the early days especially, people were worried about the way the war might go, and live entertainment raised morale and created a sense that they were all in it together. Enid Hogden sang in a choir and they toured the workshops, singing at dinnertime to lift people's spirits. By 1944, those in the works and elsewhere in heavy industry were allowed extra rations, such as tea, sugar and cheese. Jack's mother often told him that 'It is a sin to give away your sugar allowance; people are dying bringing that across the sea.'

The chief mechanical engineer, Mr Hawksworth, with the help of the running department and the drawing office, made some design improvements to the mixed-traffic Hall Class locomotives. This resulted in the building of the modified Halls, the first of which appeared nameless in 1944.

Looking ahead to the anticipated requirements after the war, the CME and locomotive committee wanted to build a new type of express locomotive, probably a Pacific (4-6-2), but the directors would not sanction it at that time. Latter-day researchers cannot agree whether the new 4-6-0, the 1000 Class, was a forerunner of something larger or a compromise. The first of these new mixed-traffic engines was outshopped in August 1945. It incorporated several features that were a departure from the Churchward/Collett designs, which were thought to need very little improvement even in 1945. Perhaps the biggest difference between the new engine and its predecessor was the use of two cylinders rather than four, to keep the cost of building down and make maintenance easier. The power was increased by giving them 6-foot-3-inch diameter driving wheels and increasing the boiler pressure, but with two cylinders the hammer blow on the track was increased and therefore maximum speed on all but the major (double red) routes was restricted. The rough riding that resulted made the 1000s unpopular with footplatemen until adjustments were made. Don Woodley, a Swindon engineman at the time told me:

When the prototype hit a locomotive jack that had been left between the rails at Knighton crossing, causing damage and wrecking one of the nameplates, it was considered a bad omen at the shed and in the works.

The proposed successor to the GWR express classes never came about after the war but, with hindsight, it is difficult to imagine anything better than the modified Castles and Kings that were relied upon instead. The 1000 Class were later to be named after counties through which the company operated.

A production line making 1,000lb high-explosive bomb cases in the old Points and Crossings' Shop. Peter Chalk worked on this 'bomb plant' before starting his apprenticeship. He remembers a gang of women worked lathes here, 'parting off' copper shell bands while others varnished the cases. (GWR)

The canteen on the 'carriage side' shortly after opening in 1943. There were no shortage of musicians and comedians among the staff, willing to do 'turns' here during the dinner breaks. (*GWR Magazine*)

Right: A female doing the job of 'hammer boy' in a photograph dated May 1942. Twenty year old Phyllis Bezer controls the hammer blows being delivered to an axle which Mr Davis the smith moves and turns to achieve the desired form. (GWR, courtesy of The Swindon Society)

Below: Cutting gear teeth on a turret ring for an armoured car: one of the first of the wartime contracts undertaken for the Ministry of Production. The mild steel rings were between four and five feet in diameter and had first been finished turned in the wheel shops.

Apprentice Maurice Parsons, who has removed his glasses for the photograph, watches over the gear cutting machine in O Shop, 1942. Like many of the machine tools engaged in war production, this gear cutting machine had been specially adapted in the works. (GWR)

Probably the most complex war work undertaken at Swindon was the '2-pounder multi pom-pom gun' for the navy. Some components were supplied by the Southern and the London & North Eastern Railways. (GWR)

From these programmes of events for the annual 'Holidays at Home', we can see that concerts, community singing and games were some of the entertainments organised for the town's folk. Church halls, parks and open spaces were utilised throughout the five week period; dance bands played at the Town Hall; 'cabaret fun for all the family' was staged at the Town Gardens and Edwards' funfair was installed in The Park. (Author's collection)

13

Post-War Developments

When peacetime returned there was little sign of improvement at first for the railway company: docks', transport and miners' strikes meant a fuel crisis and shortages of raw materials. This caused a twelve- to eighteen-month waiting time for the supply of new machine tools. No less than anywhere else, the CME department was struggling to catch up following the years of disruption to maintenance and new projects. Getting skilled labour demobilised and back into the factory was frustratingly slow. Therefore, staff who should have gone years before could still not be retired. Rationing continued, and in some cases was worse than it had been during the war. Bert Harber said that there was a general feeling that the depressed economy, cured by the war, would now return. On top of all this, at the beginning of 1947, came the worst winter in living memory.

The railways however, carried more people than ever before, and Swindon works had more work orders than it could cope with. Although with a further reduction in the working week, the department's aggregate production was not surprisingly down. The *GWR Magazine* tells us that for 1947, skilled labour numbers were still down and semi-skilled slightly up on the previous year. The works had been undertaking extensive re-conversion from large-scale wartime ordnance manufacture since early 1944. Fifty-eight coaches from ambulance trains returned from the Continent to be made ready for ordinary peacetime traffic; former restaurant cars were stripped at Swindon and reconditioned by contractors and military staff, and mobile firefighting vehicles were converted back to their former designs. The fuel crisis caused the company to undertake a regional scheme to power some of its locomotives by oil, hoping this might bring down the price of coal. The department converted some locomotives and tenders and Swindon men were involved in the design and installation of oil-storage plants at depots in South Wales, then in the South-West. The scheme was short-lived, as oil too became difficult to obtain. By 1949 the locomotives affected had been converted back.

As had happened following the First World War, ceremonies were held in workshops on Sundays for the men in their number who never returned. Managers, the mayor and church dignitaries conducted services and would unveil memorial tablets: colleagues and relatives made up the congregation. To perpetuate the spirit of comradeship, local railwaymen who had served in the Home Guard had a weekly get-together at the Staff Association club.

The chairman of the newly formed Railway Executive was bound to try to preserve morale on the eve of taking the British railway companies into public ownership. He said, 'Every one of us railway men and women is now working in the direct service of our country, and all that Britain means to us and to the world is something worth working for.'

It did little to alleviate the bewilderment and sense of loss felt by those who were fiercely loyal to the old Great Western. New staff coming in did not know any different of course, and outwardly little did seem to change. The people in the offices seemed less disturbed by the change of ownership. Barbara Carter remembers having to wear a badge with BR(W) and a number on it, 'but otherwise everything carried on as normal', she said. No sooner had the cynical mutterings of the die-hards started to subside than the new regime, the Railway Executive, or was it the British Transport Commission, nobody seemed quite sure, started to make their mark. One of the changes that would later become apparent was that senior posts would be filled more and more by outsiders, a practice alien to Swindon, which had thrived on a strong sense of loyalty and tradition. For instance, the top job went to Mr Smeddle in 1951, always an LNER man before 1948, but afterwards sent to the Southern Region then on to Swindon; while Mr Finlayson arrived from the Scottish Region to be loco works manager in 1952 before moving to the London Midland.

Men have told me that the quality of some materials coming in began to be inferior or not what they were used to, as they came from alternative suppliers. Jack Fleetwood remembers:

> The GW mixes we used to produce alloys in the foundry were light on tin. This did not adversely affect the castings and tin was expensive but no, the people at BR wanted the correct amount of tin. This in itself was okay but now it did not suit the runners and risers in our moulds. The size and shape of these channels, which let the molten metal in and the hot gases out, had been carefully worked out according to the original consistency. The altered mix with our moulds now produced inferior castings, but that was progress.

The need to replace ageing carriages and make good losses suffered during the war continued. The building programme proposed by the Western Region Executive in 1949 had to be cut back because of shortages of materials and limited workshop capacity. New wagons were also required in large numbers to modernise stock and reduce the heavy cost of repairs, but this too was frustrated, mainly by shortages of steel. Unskilled foreign workers were brought in, mainly Poles, Italians and Ukrainians, under the government's work-permit scheme in response to the shortage of labour. Jack reckoned that more immigrants came into the foundries than into other areas, and said: 'At first they worked hard. We had two West Indians who were good workers, but unfortunately one of them went mad and murdered his landlord, so we lost him.'

George Petfield in the wages office remembers allocating a new pay number to a Ukrainian with the surname Lenik: 'He was the first that I could remember and was given a start in the iron foundry about 1951.' The Western Region and possibly the GWR before that trained engineers at the works in Swindon from the developing countries of the Commonwealth. The government's London Overspill Scheme also brought some skilled and unskilled workers to the factory from the early 1950s. These newcomers described their new community as 'out in the country' and they never missed an opportunity to ridicule the rural accent. In return the locals 'inside' renamed Thursdays 'pie day' in their honour.

In 1949 the loco works manufactured seventy-five new locomotives and undertook heavy and light repairs of more than one thousand others in service. GW loco designs continued to be built under British Railways for a time, until new standard designs could be worked out for all operating requirements. Some small GW 0-6-0 tanks were built until as late as October 1956. Trials took place between locomotives from each of the four former railway companies and from these, a range of hybrid types was developed. The first of Swindon's BR designed locomotives, the 4-6-0 Class 4s, were completed in May 1951.

They then built batches of 2-6-0s, including some of pure LMS design. All were classified as mixed traffic types.

Comparative trials had taken place in 1949 and 50 between a Dean Goods (2579) and an LMS 2-6-0 (46413). They were tested in the works on the stationary test plant and under controlled conditions on the main line. A young Ken Ellis photographed the Dean engine at Steventon between trial trips and wrote on the back of the print: 'The only one of the class to be fully lined out.' In April or May of 1952, Ken's father accompanied him to Swindon to try to secure a position for him in the loco works. Mr Ellis senior had recently retired from the position of stationmaster at Steventon, to live in Whitworth Road, Swindon. With suitable qualifications, Ken was hoping to take up a five-year sandwich course in mechanical engineering. They saw an LMS 2-6-0 tender engine (43094) being evaluated on the testing plant in preparation for Swindon building batches of these class 2 engines, themselves. Ken got talking to one of the test engineers who said, 'Come and work for us.' Later he was told by someone in the staff office that there were no vacancies at the time, so Ken went and did his training at W. G. Bagnall at Stafford. During his time there he studied steaming characteristics of locomotives on the stationary test plant at Rugby. Years later Ken found out that the engineer who had invited him to come and work at Swindon was the highly respected Sam Ell.

Some of the LMS 2-6-0s numbered 465XX that Swindon subsequently built were sent to work on the Cambrian route in north-west Wales. The drivers started complaining that they didn't steam as well as the Dean goods engines they had replaced, although they did like the enclosed cabs. Sam Ell, technical assistant to the CME, was asked to investigate and he and his team came up with drawings for an improved front end. As the locomotives came through the works they were fitted with modified b oilers and smokeboxes, which solved the problem. A hybrid BR 2-6-0 was built at Darlington at about the same time, and some of them were sent to the Western Region. Former loco erector Jim Lowe assumes these engines were built with the modification because his notebooks only record them coming to Swindon for the fitting of the automatic train control apparatus. The draughting of the Manor Class 4-6-0 engines was also improved considerably, in 1952. Ken, who later came back to Swindon works, told me what Mr Ell said about it: 'The optimum measurements of the blastpipe and chimney are not mine, they are pure Dean.'

Richard Woodley, an authority on Western Region locomotives, told me that the cost of building engines in Swindon was far higher than elsewhere. This only came to light because various works were now sharing the building of batches of the same classes. The reason, he says, was due to shortages of skilled labour and a reluctance of some of the older hands to accept British Transport Commission changes designed to speed up production. Working to rule was usually sufficient to get the men what they wanted, so Swindon remained expensive to run. Richard said that although the loyalty and discipline of the old company had gone, the finished article was as good as, if not better than, the same product built at other railway works. The feeling among the men was that contracts were being diverted elsewhere, mainly to Derby on account of the influential ex-LMS (some at Swindon called this company 'ell-of-a-mess') officials on the BR board.

In 1957 a dispute over piecework caused the supply of components to the AE Shop to be held up and some partly rebuilt locomotives to be stuck there for extended periods. 5024 Carew Castle, for instance, went into the factory in April for a heavy general overhaul. As with any class of overhaul where the boiler was taken off, this engine should have been outside again, ready for trials, after no more than eighteen days, but 'fifty twenty-four' did not emerge until five months later. In 1956 Swindon completed the first heavy-freight class 9Fs. Freight engines were not normally named, but the last of these was called, appropriately, *Evening Star* (the very first successful locomotive used on the GWR was

North Star). This was the last steam locomotive built for British Railways, leaving Swindon works in 1960. According to Bob Grainger, a first-year apprentice on the loco side, 'The highest number allocated to one of this batch of engines was 92220, and that one left the erecting shop on the afternoon of 1 February to undergo trials.' Bob still has all his notebooks, which show engine movements around the works at this time. He wrote that this locomotive was painted unlined black (and nameless) and was back 'inside' the same day with axlebox problems.

In 1950 there were seven other major employers in the area, including four engineering firms. Over the next ten years the railway found it increasingly difficult to attract and retain skilled and unskilled workers with yet more firms coming in. The compulsory two-year conscription didn't help the railway factory labour situation either. The majority of young family men who arrived in the town in the 1950s were attracted by better conditions in the motor car and electrical component industries, where there were also plenty of vacancies. Typical of many railwaymen, Peter Reade was attracted by the thought of higher wages elsewhere and becoming worried by the rundown of his industry. 'Blacksmiths were no longer in demand, as forgings gave way to pressings in the manufacture of the new locomotives. However, the better money never really happened because of disputes in the car industry, and I regretted going,' said Peter. A letter in the *Swindon and District Review* in 1960 said that many local car workers were now on 'short time' and many others had been laid off through recession in the car industry. He or she also thought that the cars were poorly made and unreliable.

Despite massive post-war development and all the new employment opportunities that went with it, the railway works was still the town's biggest employer at the beginning of the 1960s. Thereafter, the railway industry locally was run down dramatically, with job losses to match.

Some young men, yet to have financial commitments, were not necessarily attracted by the firms offering the highest wages. The railways still held a deep fascination for many who wanted to work on them as an extension of their hobby. Bob Grainger was a trainspotter and photographer, but his introduction to a working life in the railway factory was not via the usual process. He did not live in the town but in Cirencester, not far from the chairman of the British Transport Commission, Sir Brian Robertson. Bob wanted to work with his beloved engines, so his mother asked someone who knew the chairman to see if he would help. After contacting the boy's headmaster, Sir Brian gave Bob a letter to take to Swindon, which of course, was enough to get him in. Unfortunately, he found himself in the iron foundry, then K Shop, offices, learning to become a clerk. After much form filling and explaining, Bob was transferred to become an apprentice fitter, turner and erector. 'All I remember about the coppersmiths' shop office was the senior clerk, Mr Phillips, getting me to write out coal and "slow combustion" tickets, which were nothing to do with the work of K Shop. My net pay then (January 1960) was £3.15s,' said Bob.

> We learn that all things have their day, and pass, as pass they must.
> The 'Castles' and their builders each in turn must 'bite the dust' . . .
>
> E. W. Chappell, 1955

Here the axle journals of a set of locomotive driving wheels were being reground. After this and balancing the wheels, which was also done on this machine, the wheelsets were ready to go off to the erectors. (BRW)

The relatively clean and modern Pattern Shop in the late 1940s. The patternmakers here worked with soft woods if the pattern was for occasional use or metal if the pattern was for regular use in the Iron or Brass Foundries. (BRW)

John 'Jack' Smithson working in the Coppersmiths' Shop, about 1950. (Brian Smithson)

K Shop was the coppersmiths' and sheet metal workers' shop, seen here on 17 March 1960. (R. Grainger)

This is the replacement X Shop where points and crossing trackwork sections were produced, on the north-east corner of the site. This building came about because of a need to produce flat-bottomed rails for British Railways. It was the last workshop to be built at the works and was used by the railway for just four years. (Ken Ellis)

14

Diesel Locomotives

THE GAS-TURBINES

Senior staff in the locomotive department realised that further development of conventional coal-fired steam locomotion after the war was limited. The company were desperate for a more powerful prime mover to meet its plans for post-war train services, a natural enough expectation in this, the dawn of the jet-engine age. The principle of gas-turbine locomotion is that air is drawn into a compressor then into a combustion chamber where it is heated sufficiently to force it through turbine blades at high pressure. The output achieved drives an electrical generator which powers traction motors: two in each of the two bogies. Some exhaust air is reused by mixing it with air drawn in at the start of the cycle, thus increasing efficiency.

When he was an assistant to the CME, A. W. (Jack) Dymond said in 1947: 'The steam locomotive, despite its cheaper building cost and longer life, seems to be approaching its demise, on account of its low efficiency and relatively poor overall availability.' This was during Mr Dymond's early association with the gas turbine locomotives. The advantages he noted were: 1) higher overall efficiency than steam locomotives; 2) less maintenance; 3) cleaner working conditions for staff at depots (it became increasingly difficult to attract men to work in steam sheds after the war). Although the diesel-electric also offered these advantages, the gas-turbine principle, when applied to a locomotive, would make it lighter and smaller than its rival of the same power. The other advantage that would have appealed to the Swindon and Paddington people was the driving cabs at each end of main-line diesels. This did away with the need for turning to face the direction of travel.

It was, of course, essential for the chief mechanical engineer to keep up to date with outside developments in railway engineering. O. S. Nock said that Mr Hawksworth had a great interest in the Swiss railways and in 1946 the CME travelled to Switzerland with Mr Dymond to see at first hand the then one and only gas-turbine locomotive. It had been ordered by the Swiss Federal Railways from Brown-Boveri of Baden, and delivered in 1941. One of the requirements of the GWR was that replacement locomotives should be able to haul the heaviest trains to times at least comparable to their own. After reviewing the Swiss engine, the CME got the go-ahead from the Locomotive Committee at Paddington and one was ordered, with certain changes to the specification, in October 1946. The company had also just ordered another gas turbine, to be built by Metropolitan Vickers in Manchester.

The Brown-Boveri arrived on the Western Region in early 1950 and, even though it was ordered first, the Metro-Vic was delivered in late 1951. These were the names by which the two locomotives soon became generally known. They were given the numbers 18000 and 18100 and both were fitted with the Great Western type automatic train control upon arrival at Swindon. Extensive trials followed using heavy trains and the WR dynamometer car. As well as conventional train recording apparatus, precision positive oil flow meters, volt meters and ammeters were among the instruments used for analytical testing with these and the later diesel hydraulics. Later observational trials on normal services would be carried out by staff of the running department and probably the drawing office too.

It was decided that the Swiss loco and the Metropolitan Vickers should have the same limited route availability as the King Class engines. Both visited Swindon works regularly because of failures, but overall the reliability of these locomotives was considered no worse than expected. According to the official publicity, this new form of traction was for experimental use only, to assess its potential. Jim Lowe was an apprentice on the loco side when they first arrived, and recalled that:

> You were firmly discouraged from getting close to them unless you were directly involved. Metro-Vic and Brown-Boveri would come into A Shop at the western end, on one of the three roads, usually No 1. They were then winched or shunted across to the east side of the traverser (Nos 2 and 3 roads were usually occupied here by bosh trolleys and loco wheels). The locomotive body was released from the two six-wheeled bogies and lifted clear. The bogies were then rolled back on to the traverser and taken to the diesel-electric shunters' gang at the bottom of the erecting shop opposite the new work. The locomotive body was lowered on to stands where the components and systems could then be inspected, either in the engine compartments, by removing body panels or by disconnecting and lifting out whole units.
>
> The turbines were occasionally split on the locomotives to decarbonise them, and erector Pete Brettel had knowledge of resetting the fixed and rotor blades before reassembly. I think this was mainly on 18000 as Metropolitan Vickers sent some of their own men for this work on 18100. Pete had previously worked on the steam turbines of P&O ships in the Merchant Navy.

The time spent under repair was not excessive considering that the mechanical fitter/erectors were working in an environment that was geared up for a totally different type of engineering. On account of costs, British Railways allowed only a minimum of spare parts to be held and no doubt this caused delays getting them back into traffic. Both these prime movers used excessive amounts of fuel, particularly the Metro-Vic engine. Brown-Boveri lasted until late 1959 on the Western Region and the more powerful Metro-Vic 18100 was to see only two years' service before going back to the makers in Manchester. By the mid-1950s things had moved on and the gas-turbine method of locomotion was no longer considered the best prospect for the future. The Western now, ten years on, chose to pursue diesel hydraulics as the alternative to steam for its main-line services.

DIESEL BUILDING

The biggest changes in the works' history took place in the late 1950s following the British Transport Commission decision to replace all steam locomotives with diesels within fifteen years. Swindon works had to be completely re-equipped to manufacture, test and repair diesel hydraulics, diesel railcars and diesel-mechanical shunting engines. They had some experience of producing and maintaining the mechanical parts of motive power worked by a four-stroke oil engine (diesel engine). In the 1930s the GWR had received its first diesel-electric shunter, which was built by Hawthorn, Leslie and Co. Ltd and given the number 2. In 1946 seven similar locomotives were ordered which would become Nos 15101 to 15107. These were built at Swindon with power units supplied by English Electric and Brush. The men in the works always referred to them as 'the 350 shunters', a reference to their horsepower. For shunting at various works around the GWR, they also brought in some Simplex four-wheeled petrol shunters. These 0-4-0 engines occasionally came into Swindon for overhaul, and because they belonged to the CME department and not the traffic department, they went into B Erecting Shop for some reason: later they were scrapped in the works. In the 1950s, private industrial short-wheelbase diesel shunters were also to be seen awaiting the works' attention. John Lowe remembers working on their wheels: 'Running in and out of sidings with tight curves put additional wear on the flanges, so we were regularly changing the tyres.'

Swindon was one of three works that were required to start building single and multiple-unit railcars, the cross-country and inter-city diesel sets which began appearing from Swindon in 1956. They were ideal for stopping trains on surburban services, as they had good acceleration and did not need to be turned between duties; the same qualities that had been incorporated in the large 2-6-2 Prairie tanks they were replacing. At the end of 1957 more diesel shunters were outshopped.

The main-line diesel-hydraulic locomotives of the Deutsche Bundesbahn and German Federal Railways appealed to the management of the Western Region because of their superior performance and low weight. They also considered that the hydraulic transmissions would be easier to understand by the existing workforce than the diesel-electric components. The hydraulic transmission dispensed with the generators and motors of the diesel-electric locomotive; the mechanical energy created by the hydraulic transmissions directly drove the axles via gear wheels and cardan shafts. Although they were less reliant on electrical components, there would still be a need for electrical fitters in the erecting shop. The dynastarters, for instance, acted as generators and provided current for auxiliary systems and to charge the batteries. The control system and numerous safety and warning devices were also electrically operated.

In 1957 and 1958 the first of the new main-line diesel-hydraulic locomotives were built here at a cost of £120,000 (of public money) each. These were the D800 class, which was based on the German V200 design and, like the D600s, would be named after British warships. Draughtsmen had the job of converting all the technical drawings supplied by the German company that designed them, Klauss-Maffei of Munich. It was not only the language that had to be translated: both imperial as well as metric measurements were required by the new builders. The engine-transmission units and other parts were first imported from Germany, and then made under license in this country, with German engineers coming to Swindon to give assistance in the early days. The Western Region alone decided upon diesel-hydraulics rather than the more popular concept of diesel-electric traction. Many took great pride in the new D800 with its impressive specification, something not seen since the introduction of the Kings in the late 1920s. Others would rather have waited for electrification, which they were told would eventually cover the whole country.

One of the problems faced by designers at Swindon was adapting the new British Railways automatic train control apparatus to work on the main-line diesels: the D800s, D600s and D6300s. On the Western, steam train continuous brakes were applied partially or completely by letting air into the vacuum pipe. With steam locomotives the vacuum pump was automatically isolated from the train brake pipe when the brakes were applied, by using a special valve. This ensured that the ATC and passenger communication cords remained effective. The diesels used exhausters instead of ejectors to create the vacuum and a similar valve would not now work. The research and development section of the drawing office led by Sam Ell came up with a device whereby the brakes could be applied by degrees via the deadman's control handle, without affecting the automatic warning and braking when approaching a distant signal in the 'on' position: the ATC.

The first alterations to accommodate the diesel-building programme were an extension to the carriage lifting shop for the building of the railcars and a testing area was also simultaneously built. A Shop was partially altered for the building and maintenance of the mainline batches of diesels and 200hp diesel shunters. There were new sections set up for the construction of bogies, wheelsets and final drive assemblies and repair of transmissions. A new X-ray testing house was built in 1958 because of an ever-greater reliance upon welded fabrications in the new types of locomotive construction. X-ray pictures would show whether welded seams were sound or if there were any cracks. Plans were being worked out by 1960 for an atomic hydrogen welding section which would require extensive alterations within the chain smiths' shop (part of F Shop). They included concrete floors, new welding plant, a pillar crane, fixed hoist structures, and asbestos screens.

The 'Barn', the large shop between the works turntable and A Shop, where tubes had been removed from steam boilers, was now being taken over, in sections, as a diesel engine test house. W Shop, the machine shop associated with the manufacture of loco cylinders and main frames, was being converted for repair and testing of diesel loco air compressors and exhausters. The amount of work done in the foundry had started to decline dramatically, so half the total area was to be used for adjustments and painting of the new locomotives, which would relieve the congestion in A Shop. This new section was to be set up under the direction of ex-G Shop foreman Mr Simpkins. The X Shop (points and crossings) had recently moved to a new building and the old shop became the ET Shop, to be fitted out for the repair and testing of motors, generators, dynostarters, control gear and other electrical equipment. Since October 1956, classes had been run in Emlyn Square to teach drivers and workshop staff the principles of the new motive power. Mr Clark, the first tutor, said the courses for fitters were the longest and most involved.

Alan Lambourn worked on D800 class engines in Peter Brettel's finishing off and trials gang in 1959. Here they took the finished locomotives outside to test and prime the two Maybach engines and Mekydro transmission units, cure leaks and bleed the injectors. Fitters on this gang at that time were Dick Gleed, John Bunce, John Dashfield, Arthur Cook, Bill Hobbs and Eric Turner. Two of them would also go out with the loco while it was tested on the mainline. To go 'on trial' with the engine you had been working on was always considered a privilege, and not just among newcomers such as apprentices. After the initial trials, the locomotive would work temporarily from Swindon shed where an A Shop fitter and sometimes an apprentice would keep an eye on it for twelve to eighteen days. New D800s would be put on the 10.47 a.m. to Paddington and work the 2.00 p.m. parcels back as far as Swindon. Then, assuming there were no outstanding problems, each new diesel entered traffic and was sent to the allocated depot. When the D800s returned to the works and had been named, the men called them the 'Maybach Warships' to differentiate them from what they called the 'Man Warships', the D600s. Bob Grainger, a fitter in the erecting shop, said that unlike steam, the main-line diesels were not brought back into the shop facing in any particular direction. Where the work in question could apply to either end, the terms 'Bristol end' and 'Paddington' or 'London end' were used by the men. When referring to the drawings, the 'A' or 'B' ends might need to be observed, 'B' being the boiler end.

The only electrical parts on a steam locomotive were the automatic train control apparatus, but the new diesel building programmes meant recruiting electrical fitters. As part of the government overspill scheme, the first of seventy or eighty extra 'sparks' arrived from London and the Midlands during the initial stages of diesel building from the mid-1950s. Some went straight over to the carriage side to work on the diesel multiple units. The Electrical Trades Union was quite militant, or well organised, depending on your point of view. Consequently, pay rates for electricians in industry were higher, making them expensive to employ. Tony Huzzey, a prominent union man 'inside', said:

> Danny Lee and George Hall were the ETU shop stewards at that time, with 'Nobby' Clark representing the electrical storemen. For other trades, Mervyn Hayward and Gordon Ing represented the coppersmiths and tinsmiths; Edgar Major, the boilersmiths; Bill Peacey, the vehicle builders; Jim Masters and Les Bates, the fitter/erectors in the Amalgamated Engineering Union (Bob Grainger remembered that 'you were in for a long sermon when "brother Jim" stood up at union meetings'). Terry Larkham was the National Union of Railwaymen steward in the stores, and internal transport man Gordon Turner was works' convenor for the Transport and General Workers' Union.

On the 'carriage side' George Scotford, Harold Seeley and Norman Piper represented the trimmers and upholsterers; Norman would later become grandfather to actress Billie Piper; Reg Clark was steward in the C&W stores; Les Bates and Reg Clark had, in turn, been full-time chairmen of the Works Committee; Jim Masters was on the AE Shop Committee and the Works Committee. Typical of many active in union affairs, Jim became a town councillor and went on to serve as mayor.

The gas-turbine locomotives ordered for the GWR in 1946. They were considered to be the best alternative to steam at that time. By the time they were delivered and had been evaluated however, the Germans were using diesel-hydraulics, and their V200 class now offered the best prospects according to Western Region management and senior engineers. (BRWR)

Diesel-mechanical shunter D2033: one of the early 204 horse-power shunting engines that were built in batches between 1958 and 1961. (BRWR)

A small brass plate from a bogie of one of the first D800 (Warship) Class diesels built at Swindon. (Author's collection)

The driver's desk and control cabinet in the cab of Warship D823. The date on the back of this photo is June 1960, some weeks before this locomotive entered traffic. (BRWR)

An Inter-City railcar underframe showing a driving bogie and final drive/reversing unit: photographed on the wagon weightable. (R. J. Blackmore collection, courtesy of Andrea Downing)

15

Other Aspects

GETTING TO 'THE FACTORY'

Before the war most Swindon railwaymen walked to work. There were fourteen entrances, which had manned gatehouses, around the 326-acre site. During normal working hours, the men were required to use whichever entrance was nearest to their workplace. All men working nights and shifts booked on and off at entrances with gatehouses, where their name was recorded in the register. If they wanted a pass-out they got it from the time office, which was staffed round the clock. George Petfield told me that the only gates manned and open all the time were the main tunnel in London Street; Webb's entrance further along in Station Road; Beatrice Street entrance (in Whitehouse Road); and the gasworks (also known as Bruce Street Bridge) entrance. All of these provided access for road vehicles. Beatrice Street was the main entrance on the eastern perimeter; the next one round was known as Osborne Terrace and then from 1940/1, Short's entrance, used exclusively by the aircraft workers, at least that's how it started out. Carriage, wagon, running shed and CME office people living in the east and north of the town used these gates or the foot gates along the old canal path. Jack Fleetwood told me: 'The routes to the factory were always covered in spit. They used to hose out the tunnel leading into the loco works every day. The state of the average workman's lungs was very bad.'

If you didn't know someone by name, then 'Hello, brother' was the usual acknowledgement before the war. Many of the older men touched their caps to the foreman if they passed him on the way to and from work, hoping to get a nod in return. In the 1930s, bicycles were not permitted on the premises, so for a small fee some people who lived near to the entrances allowed workmen to leave them in their gardens and side alleys. Doug Webb left his bicycle, complete with acetylene lamps, at the first house in Redcliffe Street. The going rate before the war was 3d a week or 4d if the cycle was put in a shed. Mr Knee, the newsagent opposite the London Street entrance, also made a few extra coppers by allowing cycles to be stored in his shop. As mentioned in the first chapter, the works was preparing for the accommodation of private bicycles in the late 1930s. I wonder what the impetus was for the department to invest in such facilities and permits, making the journeys so much quicker for many of its workers. The period between the mass dismissals in 1938 to the run up to war is not otherwise remembered as a time of concessions in favour of the men. Then some trades, like electricians, plumbers and others who moved about all over the site, were even allowed to use bicycles provided by the employer, in the course of their duties.

After work a lot of younger men ran out of the works to get ahead of the plodding mass. People standing at the exit end of the main tunnel said the sound of pounding feet coming towards them gradually built up to a thunderous roar. As is well remembered to this day, the wall of cyclists leaving the main exits was formidable enough to stop the traffic. Motorists and pedestrians in the know avoided certain routes when the railwaymen turned out. In 1950 the evening paper reported that the Swindon Accident Prevention Council were trying to involve local rail union officials in discussions about how potential accidents arising from the works spilling out into the town could be avoided. Dave Viveash said that Stan Lewington, his foreman on the finishing off gang, rode a horse to work. 'He came across the fields from Lydiard and left the horse in an outbuilding at Even Swindon Farm, which was near the entrance at the bottom of Redcliffe Street. Then he would work all day in his riding boots.'

The Swindon Corporation trams ran for the last time in 1929, and fifteen double-decker buses took over the local services. After the war, and perhaps before, Swindon Borough Transport ran early morning buses on weekdays only. No times were given in the public timetable, so perhaps they were workmen's buses. The other major bus company was Bristol Tramways, better known as the Bristol Bus Company. They definitely did run buses for the railway workers; after the war the timetable stated, "From Emlyn Square – GWR, on days when the BRWR (British Railways Western Region) are open." The bus company Queen of the Hills, also ran a service for railway workers. They carried travellers from, and home to, Wanborough and Bishopstone, stopping outside the Junction station and the Mechanics' Institute. Since before the war, most of the managers who lived any distance away would drive in by private motor car and park in the Fire Station yard.

Quite a number of men, and some women too, lived some distance away and had to travel in by workmen's train. Services converged on Swindon from five different directions: Wootton Bassett, Chiseldon, Purton, Highworth and Cirencester. Old factory men still talk about the scramble to make the connection at Old Town station (Swindon Town) in the 1950s. Two workmen's trains arrived from different directions: the Chiseldon train arrived first, then two minutes later, the train from Cirencester Watermoor. Rather than run round its train and continue on to Swindon Junction, the train from Cirencester connected with the other train. The workmen had a very short time to cross the footbridge and pack themselves in with the Chiseldon people and continue down to Junction station. The train from distant Cirencester had first run in 1925, when the Midland and South Western Junction Railway works there closed and the workers transferred to the GWR.

The last Christmas before he left school (1943), George Petfield was travelling from Wootton Bassett to Swindon to work as a temporary postman. He would catch the workmen's train laid on for the factory workers as members of the public were entitled to do. George was surprised to find it ran Christmas morning, and was quite full. Later he caught the 7.25 a.m. workers' train from Bassett regularly to get into work. Peter Reade also used this service: 'I cycled down from Broad Town and met George Evans, a bricklayer in the factory, and we travelled in together.' A lot of women used the service to get in to Wills's, Compton's and Garrard's, as well as some who were going to the railway works. Regular travellers used the same compartments every day and newcomers were made to feel uncomfortable if they took someone else's usual seat. These trains were pulled by one of the modern pannier types, usually a 57XX class, and two to four non-corridor coaches, depending on the service. 'The secondary stock that was used was still gas-lit up until about 1945. There would be four on from Bassett and it was usually pretty full. The Purton train only required two coaches,' said George.

THE MEDICAL FUND

The Great Western Medical Fund Society facilities were available to railway workers in the works and their dependents, as well as retired and widowed members. Through the 1930s the number local people eligible for medical treatment was between 36,000 and 39,000 at any one time. In 1941 the company said: 'The Society attends to the needs of nearly 45,000 persons.' I suspect that by then the criteria for membership had been expanded. A condition of employment was that employees pay into the Medical Fund in return for a whole range of medical, surgical and health services. It is often said that no other similar scheme operated anywhere else in the country. George pointed out that works' people living outside the town could not make full use of the services on offer, and he thought they may therefore have paid a reduced subscription.

The large building on the corner of Milton Road and Faringdon Road housed the dispensary and baths. There were facilities for hairdressing, Russian and Turkish baths, as well as a tone-up under the hands of an expert masseur. The large and small swimming baths 'compare favourably with any in the south-west'. One of them could be covered, after hours, and used as a dance floor or for rollerskating. The pool opened at 6 a.m., and some railwaymen would have a swim before work. During the war years, members of HM Forces stationed in or near the town were allowed to use the baths and washing facilities too.

Many children of Swindon railwaymen were given a regular spoonful of cod liver oil, followed quickly by the far more pleasant brimstone and treacle, to help them keep healthy. Mothers collected these preparations, which were available from the medical centre dispensary on prescription, in 2-lb jars. For collection of medicines and tablets, patients brought their own containers before the war. Staff dispensed about 16,000 prescriptions annually, and this did not include the requirements of the MF hospital over the road. The skilled task of making up the ointments, infusions and tonics for each patient individually was done by pharmacists. They worked seven days a week, Sunday being one of the busiest days.

The position of chief medical officer (also known as consulting physician and superintendent) was the most senior in the Society. Dr Berry, then from 1936 Dr Lowe, and after the war Dr Gibson, all held this post. They and their team of ten full-time general practitioners held surgeries in the Milton Road building, morning and evening. They made domiciliary visits and provided an emergency call-out service. There was a fully equipped dental department with three dental surgeons and a dental mechanics' workshop. All other standard medical facilities of the time were provided, including pathology, ophthalmology, physiotherapy and X-ray departments, and all were staffed by specialist medical staff and trained assistants. No additional costs were made for dental treatment, and spectacles were available on prescription. Medical requisites such as invalid chairs, crutches, bed-rests and hot water bottles were available for borrowing. Referrals to specialist hospitals and institutions were also part of the service with, if necessary, an accompanying nurse or attendant.

The 1936 surgical outpatients department round the corner in Faringdon Road was known by locals as 'the surgery'. Here they treated mainly minor accidents from 'inside'. Crushed or lacerated hands were common, as were burns and foreign particles in eyes. Mr Greenwood, and in 1940, his former assistant Mr Schofield, were the general consulting surgeons ultimately responsible for all the treatment given here. Until the 1940s, this building, at the top of Taunton Street, had been divided up for various uses. The west end was the Lime House and the rest had been split between a garage for the MFS hearse, a store for bath chairs and a rifle range. The horse-drawn hearse was provided by the MFS until the late 1930s; it was known by all as the Shillibeer.

The adjacent hospital also served as a dressing station for casualties coming in from the factory. Here too the operating theatre provided facilities for all types of surgery, but they could not always treat serious injuries or provide specialized aftercare. Jack Sutton had been an ambulance inspector at Swindon since 1944. This was probably a full-time post created during that period, when the ambulance organisation was enlarged. Mr Sutton's main role was to train the works first-aiders, and this he continued to do for at least twenty years. Another of his duties, mercifully rare, was to accompany seriously injured workmen by train, to one of the large London hospitals with which the GWR had an arrangement. For instance, penetrating eye injuries were taken to the Royal Westminster Ophthalmic Hospital. It was not unheard of for an up express to be stopped especially to pick up a badly injured man from the factory, and an ambulance to be waiting at Paddington.

The GWR cottage hospital was enlarged in 1927 with a temporary extension to become a forty-two-bed hospital. After other less ambitious plans had been explored, it was decided to build a four-storey hospital on the site, doubling the existing capacity. However, the economic depression took hold and the new building plans were abandoned. Gwendoline Mercer began her training as a nurse at the hospital in 1944:

> I remember there were a lot of Welsh girls working at the hospital. There was a great sense of comradeship among the junior nurses (immediately after the war some patients remember there being a shortage of nurses). We used to live in the nurses' home in Emlyn Square and were only allowed out on our one day off a week. There were several nursing sisters in the hospital but the probationary staff still got to do a great deal of nursing. In our second year we were allowed to put stitches in, and some nights there were only two probationers on duty for the whole ward. Although Miss Wood, the matron, lived in and was our back-up, it was 'on pain of death' if you called her in the night. Off-duty we were not allowed out of the nurses' home after 8 p.m., unless we had special permission.

Ex-patients all said the MF hospital was spotlessly clean with a strong smell of antiseptic everywhere. Many remember being wheeled straight into the operating theatre with no pre-medication, and seeing all the surgical instruments being laid out. A mask and a pad, soaked with ether, would be held over the face while the patient was told to count slowly to ten. Afterwards most would feel very nauseous. Children had tonsils removed and went home the same day, but patients recovering from appendectomy or hernia repair were not allowed out of bed for three weeks. The local Methodist minister and the curate from St Mark's came round to see inpatients regularly, and the Salvation Army came in to sing hymns on Sundays. Visiting was on Wednesdays, Saturdays and Sundays as well as public holidays. The amount of food and sweets given to patients was strictly monitored and underhand tactics might be employed as a result. A period of convalescence in one of the jointly run railway homes might be considered beneficial following inpatient care. The Great Western Medical Fund Society ceased to exist upon the introduction of the National Health Act on 15 July 1948. At the date of dissolution, 18,000 members were entitled to shares, amounting to just over 2s for each complete year of unbroken membership.

WORKSHOP ACCIDENTS

It is often said that health and safety, known then as welfare, was virtually non-existent in the works years ago, but this is not true. The railway companies were required by law to educate employees and take all reasonable precautions to protect them from hazards in the workplace. Certainly by the 1930s, when accidents did occur, it was usually due to one's own negligence.

In theory, the safety equipment provided was leather aprons and gloves in the 'hot shops', and welding shields and eye goggles where necessary. However, many men kept protective wares locked away for their own personal use, and newcomers found them hard to come by. Ordinary window glass was the only suitable transparent material available at the time for goggles, but it would stop a flying particle of some force. There were, before the war, 103 dressing stations (first aid posts) with a bell, with which the walking wounded could summon the first aider. In 1931 the staff magazine reported that 270 of the Swindon workforce were ambulance trained: just 2 per cent. Among the lowest rates were those of the CME department.

The man qualified to administer on-the-spot treatment in the foundry had a reputation for being heavy handed, so the casualties would get young Jack Fleetwood to treat them. He could remove a particle from an eye or clean and dress a cut with the minimum of discomfort, but this was highly improper and Jack was reported and told to stop. According to those who were there at the time, serious accidents were rare, although when researching the works as a whole over a period of thirty years, the impression is that such incidents were not so uncommon. The causes included loose clothing becoming caught in moving machinery or suspended loads slipping from lifting tackle. Slipping on oil could be dangerous too, especially when men were jumping over pits.

When a member of his department was injured at work, an accident report had to be made out and sent to the CME. Where the company judged itself to have been negligent, a man would receive compensation equivalent to his wages for the period of his incapacity. This was subject to a doctor's report, and sometimes the company's own medical officer would be called upon to give a second opinion. If the injury resulted in permanent incapacity but the patient was still able to walk well, the man might be invited to return to the works to undertake menial work. This would be dependent on whether the company had filled the number of places they were obliged to make available by law. One such fellow was employed to go round and disinfect all earpieces on the telephones; he, like others employed on a similar basis, would be paid as a labourer. From 1949, if a man who had twenty-five years or more adult service was reduced in grade owing to ill health or accident, he would receive the mean rate between that of the vacated post and the post to which he was reduced, up to a maximum loss of ten shillings a week.

During the early 1950s a rehabilitation workshop was set up at Swindon works to assist the convalescence of injured workers. Under medical supervision, suitable patients were put on light production work as physiotherapy. In 1957 two casualty centres were opened, one on the loco side and the other on the carriage side, for treating injuries at work.

THE STOREHOUSE

Most of the department's correspondence, staff records, plans, ledgers, files and accident reports that were settled, out of date or not currently needed were stored on the second floor of a detached three-storey building on the eastern side of the main offices. On the ground floor were male toilets; the metallurgists, who took over the first floor in the 1950s, had previously been in part of the laboratory in the Fire Station yard.

In the 1940s, a man named Reg Cook was employed to file and, if necessary, retrieve documents in the storehouse. George Petfield remembers that Reg only had one eye, possibly as a result of an injury from the Great War; this is likely to be why he was given such work.

Jack Hartley of the M&EE's personal staff remembers that, in the 1950s, the place was packed with dusty papers and files, with no resident staff. He and Ralph Dowding were offered overtime to go through it all:

We wore protective smocks and worked through an elaborate index system of all documents to see what we thought would never be needed again. Tommy Turner, the chief clerk, marked each set of documents with a tick or a cross and we junior clerks threw out anything with a cross on it. Of course some things, no matter how old, were not to be disposed of, such as accident reports or plans of water supplies and electrical installations. We were aware that it was all historically interesting, even in those days. As much as we got rid of, so more arrived and it remained packed solid. There were racks around all sides, which even covered the windows, and we needed ladders to reach the top recesses.

The running/motive power department records were also kept there, and to make matters worse, the contents of the C&W storehouse were moved here when their offices were gradually amalgamated and moved into the CME building from the early 1950s onwards. Management saw this huge store as a millstone; unless more room could be found, there was nowhere to put all the more recent paperwork which, from a business point of view, was far more important. With the uncertainty whether Swindon would survive the 'Main Workshops Future Plan' of 1962, all remaining caution regarding stored documents evaporated. Jack told me that Bill Harris of the M&EE staff, who had been keen to get rid of all but the most recent material, got authority to send it all to salvage. All that had survived the wartime salvage schemes, when the company had very efficiently combed out redundant materials, was to go. Only the staff record cards were to be saved: they went to the BTC archives in London. Some staff went through them and took their own cards before that happened. Even in those days, the loss of what was a complete business history of the works and the department was seen as terrible by Jack and others.

STEALING

A lot of ex-staff have stories of petty thieving during the period of this book, and no doubt it was a major problem for the company. The stores department was allowed costs for the secure storage of materials and general supplies, against theft. It went on at all levels, so it cannot be generally associated with hardship, even before the war.

One story that I heard more than once in the 1970s concerned a man who, many years before, had taken sheets of lead out by wrapping them around his body and covering them with his coat. He tripped over in the street, and the exertion of trying to get up with all the extra weight caused a fatal heart attack. Jack Fleetwood's neighbour boasted of his ill-gotten gains once too often, and his workmates convinced him the watchmen were going to pay him a visit one particular evening. He got a pass-out and hurried home to burn the plunder in the kitchen copper. 'You could burn anything in those things,' said Jack. The fellow was being wound up, but if he did take anything else, he never admitted it. For those who did a bit of model engineering or carpentry at weekends and supplemented the materials from the workplace, there was a constant risk of police spot checks. Tins of paint or tools were often seen hastily deposited along the approaches to the exits, when word came back that searches were being conducted outside. At some point the men's side of the Works Committee had somehow managed to argue successfully that they should receive prior warning when security purges would be carried out.

When the royal waiting rooms at Windsor station (my informant said Slough, but I can't find any evidence of royal rooms there) were no longer required for that purpose, several gangs of different trades on the carriage side were sent to clear them; this was about 1950. The royal furnishings and decoration came back to Swindon to be disposed of by the stores department. Anything that had royal decoration upon it could not be sold on to the workers, including a lavish carpet to which someone fairly senior took a fancy. After it was cleaned, it was carefully folded and packed on to a handcart, then covered with some purchased wood. The paperwork handed in at Webb's entrance described it as a pile of scrap blocks.

After demobilisation, Doug Webb returned to the factory, stripping out coach interiors. Of course he kept the coins found down the backs of the seats, to supplement his labourer's pay. On one occasion Doug found a gold cigarette case in a royal coach and handed it straight in; 'Never thought of doing anything else,' he said. Jack remembers that most of the men in the shops were very honest. Occasionally, however, he said that tobacco or snuff would disappear from a line of jackets hanging up. Anyone caught would be outcast and have his working life, and possibly his life outside, made unpleasant by his fellow workers. If a man claimed to have lost his wages, a whip-round was organised and would virtually cover his loss. Sadly, as time went on, it was suspected that this goodwill was being exploited and the practice gradually died out.

DISCIPLINE

According to the NUR conditions of service handbook for railway employees (of 1937), a man charged with misconduct, neglect of duty or other breaches of discipline would be forewarned in writing of the nature of his offence and the punishment he was likely to receive. He was allowed to call witnesses and state any extenuating circumstances in the presence of company officials, prior to a final decision being arrived at. At the interview the accused could be accompanied by an advocate, usually a representative of his union. Where doubts arose or where the case was sufficiently serious, it could be heard by a more senior official. If and when found guilty of a serious offence, he had the right of appeal to a superior officer. The company was keen to avoid appeals, but in the event of this happening, it should be done before punishment was handed out. It was usual to allow a standard day's pay in cases of men attending disciplinary inquiries.

Although the railway companies must have agreed to the above, the wording in the GWR's *General Rules and Regulations* of the same period gives a different version and offers the accused little hope of a fair hearing. It states that they may at any time 'dismiss without notice' or 'suspend from duty, and after enquiry, dismiss without notice'. No doubt the company assumed the tone was sufficiently forthright to deter serious breaches of the rules, but still a man's whole livelihood was at the mercy of the foreman or overseer's frame of mind. This must have been particularly evident at times when the company was looking to cut the workforce.

These then were the official processes: by the 1930s, though, some wrongdoings were handled with a little more discretion. According to local folklore, when a Swindon engineman was called to account and his story seemed far-fetched, his foreman, who had himself come up through the ranks, said, 'You tell me the truth, and leave me to tell the lies to the superintendent.' Another unconfirmed story heard by George Petfield concerned a worker from the carriage side who was unhappy about his pay. He arrived at the wages office drunk, caused a scene and threw a punch at George Tomes, the senior clerk in carriage wages. He missed and ended up on the floor. At this time, the late 1940s, Mr Tomes was allowed to exercise his authority and he summarily had the man suspended for a week, but didn't want him sacked. Jack said that in Great Western days, the local newspaper was regularly taken to the manager's office and scrutinised to see if any of the men had been in front of the magistrate. If they had, their names and details were recorded in a 'black book'. The book of names survives today, but Jack could only speculate as to whether any further action was taken against the entries.

ASBESTOS

The CME Department used asbestos to lag its boilers, steam pipes and locomotive cylinders against heat loss. It was soaked and applied as a paste and when dry, it was clad with steel sheets. Train heating and other pipework was wrapped in asbestos tape. This material was uniquely effective for insulation and fire-proofing; asbestos does not deteriorate, it does not corrode the iron and steel that comes into contact with it, and it was reusable. One fellow worked in a corner of A Shop, breaking down asbestos that had been scraped off locomotive boilers prior to overhaul. He was probably a 'green card man': a term used 'inside' for someone who had physical or mental health problems, said Dave Viveash.

If it was disturbed in a dry state, asbestos released fine particles into the air. This was particularly so when it was being scraped off after use. Workers inhaling particles would develop some scarring of the lining of the lungs, but there were usually no troublesome symptoms for many years. Tom Smith, a chargeman and first-aider in the AM Shop, developed the disease from machining brake bands containing asbestos, for the Road Transport Department. Wives of men exposed to this mineral were also at risk when washing contaminated overalls.

Because of the delay before a person became unwell, it took a long time to make a connection between asbestos and serious lung disease. It was well into the 1960s before it was generally accepted that people exposed to the airborne dust had a high risk of developing lung cancer, especially mesothelioma. Not until then were precautions offered against the inhalation of particles. It had been suspected for some time that there might be a parallel between asbestos and another mineral, silica, used elsewhere in industry. The lung damage caused by long-term exposure to the latter had been acknowledged years before. Because of the high rate of Swindon works men presenting with symptoms, the disease has become known locally as the 'Swindon disease'. George Petfield remembers paying out in A Shop on summer evenings when the sun's rays shone across the shop. He said: 'You could see the air was full of dust.' There is no doubt that some of the dust came from stripping and reconstituting asbestos. Jack Fleetwood said: 'Because of the finer particles, blue asbestos that was sprayed into carriage bodies in the post-war period was even more dangerous.' In the early 1960s, Swindon started using polyurethane rigid foam to insulate its carriages against noise and heat loss, and diesel-hydraulic locomotives were insulated with fibreglass.

UNDERGROUND FIRES

Much of the land that the works stood on had been built up to between 12 and 20 feet above the town level. The material used was coke, cinders and clay, and large areas to the west of the works and to the north of the junction station would burn. Following spontaneous combustion, underground fires would burn slowly and spread. The ground reached temperatures of 500 degrees Centigrade and the clay turned to brick. Sometime after the war, the works fire brigade had sunk pipes down and saturated the ground affected for weeks on end. Mr Sealy, the works' fire officer, said years later: 'The heat travels through concrete and steel very quickly and no amount of water will touch it. The only way to stop it is to remove it.'

Vague references had been made about the areas of burning ground since at least the 1920s by employees, but I could find nothing recorded on the matter until the 1950s. An article in the *Western Region Magazine* of that period said one area had been burning continuously for twenty-five years and contractors had resorted to bulldozing down to the original ground level. Bert Harber remembers trenches being dug and filled with sand to try to stop the spread. His father, a first aider, had been summoned to Redcliffe Street bank because men working there had been overcome by fumes. This was probably exacerbated by sludge from oil recycling that had been tipped in that area. Several official photographs were taken showing the burning land here in 1951.

In the early 1970s, when land affected had been sold off for redevelopment, the potential for structural damage to buildings and drains by this phenomenon was found to be considerable. When not burning, this ground produced an amazing abundance of wild flowers. This was particularly noticeable after the war when labour was short and remote sidings were not being weeded, said an article in the *Western Region Magazine* in 1949.

Men coming out of the carriage tunnel entrance in Station Road: a less often photographed scene than the main entrance up the road. The photographer was stood by what was known locally as Bullen's Bridge, long after the bridge had gone and the North Wilts' Canal it spanned, was filled in. (Author's collection)

A workman's weekly bus ticket from 1948, priced 10d. The back is endorsed with a CME Dept Swindon, Cash Office stamp. (Author's collection)

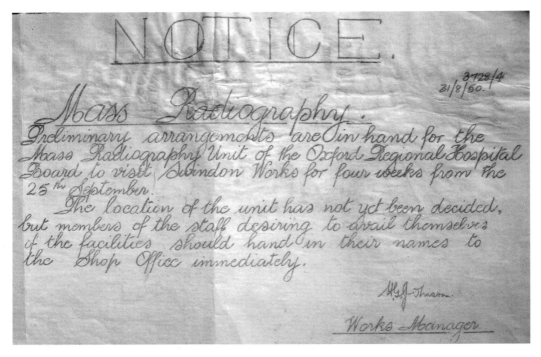

NOTICE.

3728/4
31/8/50.

Mass Radiography.

Preliminary arrangements are in hand for the Mass Radiography Unit of the Oxford Regional Hospital Board to visit Swindon Works for four weeks from the 25th September.

The location of the unit has not yet been decided, but members of the staff desiring to avail themselves of the facilities should hand in their names to the Shop Office immediately.

H.G.J. Johnson.

Works Manager

This is a poster advertising the "Mass Radiography Service" produced in the works. The staining is caused by paste residue on the back. From the wording it looks as if this year: 1950, was the first visit of the mobile van in which Works' staff could be X-rayed for tuberculosis. Yearly routine screening for TB was offered to railway staff thereafter and they would receive letters on the outcome. (Author's collection)

Ambulance training in the GWR mess rooms in London Street. A young Bert Harber acts as the casualty. (Bert Harber collection)

16

Leisure Time

Before the war the only extravagance for many men in the works was to go out the county ground and watch Swindon Town's home matches. Railwaymen made up a good proportion of Town supporters, and very occasionally the works closed early for a big game. This happened only once in the 1930s, in January 1938, when they closed at midday for an important cup match that evening.

Beer was around 4d a pint before the war; best bitter maybe 6d. It was cheaper in some of the working men's clubs such as the Monkey Club, one of the best remembered nowadays. This club was on the corner of Rodbourne Road and Redcliffe Street and is believed to have got its nickname from a Mr Monk, a steward who ran it sometime before the war. There were plenty of watering holes close by the factory, and they did a good trade. Jack Fleetwood had heard of the reputation of some even as a child. In the railway estate, the Cricketers Arms had a spirit licence, but the others were just beer houses. Until about 1936, children could go into public houses (but not working men's clubs) and collect beer for their parents in jugs and bottles. Some men spent more than they could afford on drink while their family went without. On the other hand, a few didn't drink for religious reasons or because they lived in fear of their wives, but most men abstained because they took their responsibilities seriously. They had become conditioned to a life of thrift long before taking on a family and were more likely to be found on their allotment in their spare time, supplementing the family budget. Few townspeople did any work at home on a Sunday, and some kept their children in for fear of disturbing the peace that descended on all the neighbourhoods that day. Jack Fleetwood remembers that he and his friends were not allowed to play outside a house of someone who had recently died.

Some railwaymen liked to keep pigeons, while others played bowls or tended their garden for relaxation. Amateur astronomy was quite a popular pastime in the 1930s, and Edwin Hopper spent his spare time scanning the heavens. In the back garden of his home in Kingshill Road, he built a 12-inch reflecting telescope, the largest in Wiltshire. Edwin worked in the works' tool room as a mechanic, and so would have been familiar with the principles of optical instruments. His telescope was set in a concrete base to avoid vibration from footsteps and road traffic. The whole structure was reckoned to weigh about a ton. The building of such a sophisticated instrument by a layman was thought worthy of two pages in the *GWR Magazine*.

ORGANISED LEISURE ACTIVITIES

With the co-operation of the company, a highly organised and competitive programme of leisure activities was developed over the years. Leagues for team games were organised at local and company level by the Social and Educational Union, which had evolved from the old Temperance Union. This in turn became the Staff Association in the mid-1930s. It was later claimed that the GWRSA was the largest industrial organisation of its kind in the world. The Mechanics' Institute was the home venue for most of the indoor games competitions. Skittles and whist drives were perhaps the most popular team games. For the less energetic, there were such things arts and crafts or horticultural shows to compete in.

The newly appointed assistant to the CME, Mr F. W. Hawksworth, became the Swindon branch president of the S&EU in 1932, the year they moved to a new headquarters at the Bridge Street Institute, on the corner with Holbrook Street. With the move, they inherited an integral theatre called the Little Theatre with seating for 180 people, albeit rather cramped and dilapidated. It was soon modernised so that the Great Western Players, the aptly named local dramatic section of the Association, could put on their full and one-act plays there. The Swindon branch of the GWR S&EU/SA had an impressive 4,000 members in the 1930s, thanks in no small part to Arthur Peck, who worked in the CME department. He was honorary secretary to this and the Swindon Amateur Musical and Dramatic Society. Later in life Arthur Peck was recognised for 'outstanding services rendered' by the Swindon and District Theatre Guild.

Outdoor sports such as football, cricket, hockey, bowls, miniature rifle practice and tennis were played at the GWR (Swindon) Athletic Association sports ground, which opened in 1931. The cost of the new sports ground, according to a monograph donated to the Swindon Central Library and written by R. T. F. Giles, came from an account set up to hold money paid for premium apprenticeships in the CME department. The CME's principal assistant, Mr Stanier, used his influence and, with others, managed to secure money from this account to provide a replacement for the GWR park, which was given to the borough in 1925. The timber sports pavilion here was rebuilt in the mid-1950s by carpenters from D Shop.

Like the other large GWR centre at Paddington, Swindon had respected classical and light operatic groups made up of singers and choruses, musicians and actors from among the works staff. Regular musical programmes were put on in the Mechanics' Institute concert hall, which included songs, soloists, choruses and humour, as well as the famous GWR Gleemen male-voice choirs. Many of these, and other classical and modern musical turns performed by the railway community, ensured that Swindon put up a strong showing at the GWR Music and Drama Festival, and a high proportion of the prizes came to the town. This annual festival did not take place during the war but, as part of the 'Holidays at Home' season, Swindon held their own musical festival. It continued after the war, mainly to inspire youngsters to develop their musical talents. A surviving programme from 1949 shows that the SMF brought together classical singers, choirs, speakers and musicians to compete in 49 categories. A large proportion of the competitors that had qualified, as well as officers and stewards, were works staff or were boys and girls who would go on to become employees. When dance music started becoming popular in the following decade, the festival finished.

The first full-length operas at the Mechanics' theatre started in 1930. Less than two weeks after the final performance that year, the building suffered a major fire. Renovation was completed in 1932 and the theatre reopened as The Playhouse; now the building had a concert hall and a dance hall. Some years later it was claimed that 'The Playhouse was equipped with facilities easily equal to any provincial theatre.' The Swindon College choral and orchestral classes, which became the Swindon Musical Society, gained respect throughout the music world for attempting lesser known operas, rather than staying safe with the popular productions. Jack Winter (bass baritone) and Ray Hatherall (tenor), together with Ray's wife Lorna Cantor, were among the best-known artistes from the 1930s through to the 1950s. Jack worked in No 1 Accounts Office and Ray was in W Shop working on loco frames. The latter was the first to bring the Russian operas to England, having them performed at the Mechanics' Institute. Soon the outside world heard about what was going on in Swindon, and VIPs such as the composers William Walton and Ralph Vaughn Williams were attending the shows, as was the head of the Royal Ballet. Despite the obvious home-grown talent, the theatre never managed to pay its way.

When performances were suspended during the war, Messrs Hatherall and Winter, together with Lorna Cantor, concentrated on their own travelling concert party called the Gay Cravats. They were accompanied by the musicians Charles Dommett on banjo, Gertrude Baden on piano, and George Reason, 'entertainer'. Another group called the Nobodies was started by Fred Powell, who worked 'inside' and lived in Birch Street. Doug Webb played the accordion and joined Bert Fluck's concert party in the late 1930s when he was only in his late teens. He remembers the group included Alf Salter, a baritone singer who worked in W Shop, the comedian Jack Wilkes, the comedienne Ivy Plyer and later, the singer Beryl Done. Beryl from Drove Road is known to have worked in the correspondence office in the 1950s, while her father was in the loco works' managers' office.

George Petfield remembers that 'Bert [Fluck] was a nice chap who played the piano and entertained the workers in the works canteens during the war.' As a piano accompanist, his name appears on countless local and company-wide concert programmes from the 1930s onward. Another was Miss Iris Rainger of the general stores office, who played the piano and could play several other instruments as well. By the time Mr Fluck had taken over the running of one of the two main mileage offices from Harold Lewis, his daughter Diana Dors was regularly appearing in the top British films of the time (1946–48). Gwendolene Binks worked in the CME offices for a time in the 1930s and 40s, possibly as a secretary in the offices of the running department superintendent on the ground floor. She too, was to become a parent of a famous showbiz personality, the musician Justin Hayward. Beryldene Hunt was a name that kept coming up in surviving concert programmes and cast lists of local stage productions and competitions, as did that of Mavis Gilbey from the correspondence office. Ms Hunt produced and acted in plays, was an elocutionist and gave concert recitals. As everyone in the offices knew everyone else, I asked Barbara Carter if she remembered her: 'Oh yes, she worked in our machine room. Beryl was tall and elegant and lived for amateur dramatics. She was a real eccentric, and even at work was rather theatrical.'

MECHANICS' INSTITUTE, EMLYN SQUARE

For a small subscription (see also Chapter 3) the local railway workers could become members of the Mechanics' Institute. As well as the main building in Emlyn Square, there were two smaller branches in the suburbs north of the main line that divided the town in two. Besides the most popular attraction, free holiday travel, the Mechanics' offered a lending and reference library, the only one in the town until 1943. The library held around 40,000 books and had an arrangement with the corporation whereby it was open to non-members. Alongside were reading rooms, which included a table reserved for wives and daughters of members. Visitors talk of the sense of quiet and tranquillity in these parts of the building, contrasting with the din outside from the railway factory across the road. With its polished tables, ornamental ceilings and classical plaster busts, the interior resembled a grand country house rather than a works' recreational centre. There was a smoking room, lecture hall and facilities for billiards, table tennis, chess and draughts. Upstairs there was a theatre large enough for 800 people, which was also used for dances (some people remember that this was called the Sunshine Ballroom in the 1950s).

The president and vice-presidents were all senior works managers, three of whom were also trustees. MI management was in the hands of an elected council of officials, men such as foremen, senior clerks and prominent works' committee members. The council members also served on various committees that managed the main activities of the Institute. The smaller branches in Gorse Hill and Rodbourne Road had reading, recreational rooms and libraries.

This grand Victorian building had very churchlike architecture and a well-known weather vane on top of the west pinnacle. The brass weather vane was added in 1902. It stood nearly four feet high and was quite clearly recognizable as the outline of one of Mr Dean's handsome 'single' locomotives. Unlike the one seen on the borough coat of arms, this loco was complete with its tender. After 1945 the facility, designed for the expectations of Swindon people a hundred years earlier, was struggling to attract sufficient membership. By the 1950s the concert hall was used for any local events that needed a venue, and other parts of the building were being used for storage. The library closed for good in 1959 or 1960.

THE JUVENILE FETE: 1931

One of the highlights for the railway community in Swindon was always the GWR Mechanics' Institute Fete, often referred to by the locals as the Children's Fete. It took place every year at the park in Faringdon Road, usually on the second Saturday in August. Permission had to be sought beforehand from the owners, Swindon Borough Council.

On the afternoon of Friday 7 August 1931, children from the nearby GWR estate were looking through the railings to see the steam wagons and horses towing trailers of equipment into the park as usual. It had been unseasonably cold and overcast, but this spectacle lifted the spirits and heightened the anticipation for the following day. The following morning there was a terrible storm while all the tents, sideshows, stalls and amusements were being erected by the touring showmen and caravan people. According to the *Evening Advertiser,* the ground soon became a quagmire.

The rain had stopped temporarily by the time the gates opened at 1.30 that afternoon, but it remained very dull and threatening. The threepenny admission ticket included ½ lb of cake and a ride on the roundabout or switchback for children up to 13 years. There was also free tea or a cold oatmeal drink for those who brought their own cup. So much cake was needed that a machine had been invented years before to cut it into squares to save time. Children invited from 'homes' received the treats too, on production of an admission ticket that was provided for them free of charge. How this was costed for the purposes of the accounts I do not know. The railway workers had, in years gone by, been asked to contribute a penny for the workhouse kids, so perhaps that arrangement still stood.

A variety programme of acts was performed on the temporary stage throughout the afternoon and repeated in the evening. Mr Wilkes and his orchestra accompanied the artistes; later they would move into the Drill Hall for the dancing. On show or within the sideshows were acrobats, comedy cyclists, 'the phenomena of Siamese twins', miniature horses, jugglers, Punch and Judy and contortionists. There were giant swings, slides, chairaplanes and bumper cars; the man in charge of the latter received electric shocks more than once as a result of the rain getting under the canvas canopy. The Swindon division of the St John Ambulance brigade were, as always, in attendance.

It was about 4 o'clock when everyone was forced to run for the trees, and soon some men were carrying their female companions across waterlogged areas to save their best shoes from sinking into the mud. The report in the evening paper on Monday said the mud was six inches deep by late afternoon. Because of the weather, only about a quarter of the normal 40,000 people paid to come in, and regulars were saying this was the worst Fete in living memory. By late afternoon the stage turns were stopped and, because the rain showed no sign of slowing, the fireworks display, which formed the grand finale, was postponed until dusk on Monday. All the leftover cake would be on sale then too. Probably because all the admission tickets had been collected and there was no way of knowing who had paid, admission to the rearranged fireworks was free for all.

It was a shame, too, for the president of the Mechanics', Mr Stanier, that the day had been ruined by the weather. He had worked hard to make all events put on by the MI a success, and attended the Fete each year. This would be his last, as he would be vacating all his posts to move north at the end of the year and become CME of the London Midland and Scottish Railway.

R. J. BLACKMORE

Anyone familiar with the GWR staff magazines or various Swindon publications from the 1930s up to the early 1960s will almost certainly know the name R. J. Blackmore. He would contribute pieces about lesser known aspects of the railway works where he was employed and the community around it where he lived.

Reginald John Blackmore was born in Armstrong Street near the Junction station in 1904. When the time came, he followed his father into the carriage works. From then on his leisure activities were organised around his workmates. Reg became a member of the 'Phifteen shop Gleemen', a male voice choir, one of at least two formed of works staff. Surviving family postcards show that he also played football and cricket for 15 Shop. Recreational pursuits were, however, restricted so as not to interfere with the Lord's Day.

The pre-war articles in the company magazine were rather restrained: informative rather than eloquent, in keeping with what was acceptable at the time, no doubt. Reg's writing was articulate and his subjects well observed. In 1931, at the age of twenty-seven, he won the gold medal for the best essay in the GWR Social and Educational Union Music Festival. This was no mean feat as the festival attracted a lot of gifted competitors and was consequently highly respected. From 1945 until 1955, Reg would tell children's stories he had written on the BBC radio programme *Children's Hour*.

The *Swindon Railway News,* which was published from 1960 until 1963, was written for the staff, by the staff. Most of the content, although informative, inevitably resorted to a tongue-in-cheek form of presentation. Stories, often of unfortunate human predicaments that circulated the workplace, were seized upon and retold in a satirical way. Here Reg excelled in his regular appeal on behalf of the National Savings Movement.

THE ANNUAL DINNER

With great skill and enthusiasm, the organisation secretary instilled motivation where necessary, and collected money for the annual dinner and social evening. These events were a traditional part of office life, and some workshops throughout the department. The foremen and inspectors also had their annual get-togethers, as did some retired groups of workers. A write-up of the larger occasions would often appear in the evening paper.

The staff of the central wages office would go to a local inn, such as the Crown at Stratton or the White Hart at Cricklade, for their staff Christmas dinner, said George Petfield. This was arranged for an off-peak period during work time. A corporation bus, usually a single-decker, was hired for the occasion. Annual staff dinners were popular inside and outside the works in those days, so it was sometimes not possible to book a specific venue on a specific date. From surviving programmes it can be seen that some time early in the New Year was usual, and most if not all the local hotels were venues for works dinners.

The chief mechanical engineer's personal staff held their annual dinner at the Goddard Arms Hotel, in the ballroom. In the 1930s, if not before, the rather solitary head of department, Mr Collett, did not attend these types of functions. All other senior CME staff, including the chief clerk and the principal assistant, did attend. Senior retired staff were also invited, but it was strictly men only. A professional photographer was hired to take the customary group picture, and we can see from these that upwards of sixty people were invited and expected to attend. After the meal, toasts were made to the reigning monarch and to the GWR Company, interspersed with a programme of light entertainment. The latter included songs, sketches and monologues, both serious and humorous. All the turns were performed by men from the works who were accomplished entertainers. There was always a chance that some of the entertainment would be considered unsuitable for women at that time, and presumably that's why they were not invited. Jack Hartley joined this department in the early 1950s and heard about the dinners of years gone by. He was told that Bert Fluck brought his daughter Diana along to do a turn one year. She sang and danced while her father played the piano. This must have been before the war when the future star was very young.

THE OFFICE OUTINGS

The outings were the highlight of the office social calendar and consequently the best supported events. It was a works sponsored day out, normally arranged for May or June, and would include a pre-booked evening dinner and perhaps luncheon en route. The calendar in the office was always marked well in advance with this occasion and the annual holiday shutdown in July. The only times these traditions were cancelled was in wartime. Programme cards were printed and distributed, giving the travel arrangements, the menus and the names of the organising committee. Some of the party would ask everybody to sign their programme, and which would be kept as a souvenir of the day. Seaside resorts, particularly those along the South Coast, and sometimes inland beauty spots were potential destinations, and each outing was men or women only. The itinerary and times made for a fairly hectic schedule, often arranged by people who were used to studying railway timetables and travelling about the country by connecting services using free passes. In 1936, 41 Office visited the Colchester and Clacton area. A visit to the East Coast was a popular one with Swindon railwaymen, as it gave them a chance to travel out of Fenchurch Street or Liverpool Street stations at a time when the railway network was of interest to most of them. Sometimes travelling via the capital would include a West End show on the way home.

The combined drawing and estimating office outings were taken on a Friday each June. In 1948 they bussed to Southampton for the steamer crossing to the Isle of Wight. The journey was always considered an enjoyable part of the day out, so on another Isle of Wight outing they went by train via Portsmouth and Southsea. The day was usually a long one, but with so many departments to accommodate in the month and the company insisting they be staggered, not everyone could get away on Fridays. Therefore many staff had to get into work the following day after arriving home in the early hours. Some offices and departments had been having an outing since the 1890s, and possibly earlier. The locomotive managers' office annual outing started in 1905, and by 1924, the ladies of the typists' section in that office were taking their day out on the same day. Presumably this was the arrangement from then on. From surviving group photos, it is clear that a river trip up the Thames from Caversham Bridge was a favourite for many groups of works staff, although pictures taken on the Thames may be more numerous than those of other destinations because this was probably the furthest the Swindon photographer was prepared to travel from his studio.

George Petfield remembers the outings from 1948. The south Devon resorts or Minehead were the most popular in the loco wages office, and they nearly always travelled by train. The party would often catch the 7.25 (5.30 off Paddington) Penzance via Bristol train. Some would bring bottles of beer, and it was a point of honour to sink the first pint before reaching Rushey Platt. There was a lot of drinking done throughout the day, but George doesn't ever remember any rowdy behaviour. Among the places they visited in the late 1940s and early 50s were Torquay, with a boat trip to Teignmouth for the pre-booked evening meal; in 1950 it was Sidmouth with a meal in the Fortfield Hotel; another year around this period it was Weymouth.

When returning from the South-West, a Swindon works party might have a private carriage, sometimes an open saloon, attached to the rear of an up train. Then it was usual to transfer the carriage to the 11.20 p.m. Wolverhampton parcels train at Taunton. Sometimes too, a carriage for a homeward ladies outing was attached here as well. One year, one of the vans on George's train developed a 'hot box'. 'You could see flames coming from underneath just short of Frome,' he recalled. Under normal circumstances they were due into Swindon Junction at 1.24 a.m. George lived in Wootton Bassett until 1955, and sometimes if the train slowed down through that station, he and others from the town would risk jumping on to the platform, thus saving the late-night taxi journey back from Swindon. Either way there were some very tired looking men in the office the next day.

On their way to Eastbourne in 1949, the nearest thing to rowdy behaviour in George's party happened on a London bus between Paddington and Victoria. As they passed the Royal Artillery Monument, one of the daytrippers, Frank Witts, who had been connected with this regiment in the First World War, leapt up and tapped the window with his walking stick. The window smashed, showering everyone with glass. Brighton was another favourite destination for works daytrippers, often including a meal on the way down on the Brighton Belle for 2s 6d a head. In the mid-1950s, the large group of wages staff were walking from the station in Brighton to the seafront and a local enquired, 'Are you holding a demonstration?'

Barbara Carter remembers her office outings being in May. 'They were always on a week day, the company giving us the day off.' As with the men, the ladies were also allowed free train travel, which did not affect their free pass entitlement. It did not, however, include the cost of any connecting coach or boat journeys. In the late 1940s the ladies of 40 Office visited such places as Hunters Inn on Exmoor, the Isle of Wight, and Minehead, which was the most popular destination, said Barbara. Yvonne Hodey only went on one outing, on a Friday in June 1953, when the ladies of 21 Office travelled to Southsea. The last of the sponsored office outings were in 1964, when the CME department became part of British Rail Engineering Ltd.

THE SHOP OUTINGS

In Jack Fleetwood's shop the men paid into a fund throughout the year, which covered the transport and the beer. The foreman didn't come along in the early post-war days.

They needed to keep a distance from the men so as not to feel uncomfortable maintaining discipline at work. Jack told me:

> We always hired a motor coach because if we used our free pass on the train, they were funny about the beer [this was not George Petfield's experience]. Workshop outings were taken on Saturdays, as parties of manual workers were not given a day off by the company. As a consequence, not every shop or section took an annual day out. Moulder Reg Dixon staggered off the bus at Portsmouth one year and laid out on the grass, the beer and the motion of the bus having taken its toll on him. 'Pick me up on the way back,' he said. After a day on the Isle of Wight, we found him still laid out in the same spot, on the way back. One 'kiddie', the chargeman labourer, always finished the evening with sea legs due to his affinity with Newcastle Brown. The driver would put him off outside his house in Faringdon Road and we would get him to the door, ring the bell and run.

Jack always referred to his workmates as 'kiddies'. This was not a Swindon term, so he may have picked it up from his mother, who was a cockney. As was George's experience, Jack doesn't remember any bad behaviour; a few bawdy songs on the bus perhaps, but that was all. 'Sometime later, the coach company wanted to discourage drinking on its tours. That, together with the increase in private motoring, killed off the annual workshops' days out,' said Jack.

Before the war the 15 Shop outings were called the 'golden road' because they used to go to London with the option of going on to the FA Cup Final. Harry Bartlett remembers Ron Franklin coming round for the 6d a week towards the 'golden road' day out, in the 1950s. By then they could only reserve blocks of tickets for the Amateur Cup Final. Electrician Bert Harber told me that by the 1950s his outing included wives and children. Sapperton Woods in Gloucestershire was the destination for one of Bert's days out.

The Mechanics' Institute main building in Emlyn Square in the 1930s. (GWR)

A production of 'Saloon Bar' at the Mechanics' Playhouse in 1945. (Swindon Society collection, courtesy of Bob Townsend)

The Great Western Silver Band outside the Mechanics' Institute: Mr Alder, holding the baton, was the conductor from 1930 until at least 1946. (Author's collection)

Staff Association billiards and snooker players outside the Mechanics' in the late 1950s. Left to right standing: Fred Haynes, George Jackson, Alan Hockin – 'loco side' fitter, Doug Mayhew, unknown, John Webb?, Jack Webber – Drawing Office electrical section, Ben Blackman - offices, unknown, Vic Davis, Frank Randall. Left to right seated: Herbert Brind – AM Shop, unknown, George Bees? Ken or Keith (Taffy) Williams – ASLEF shop steward, Len Sweet – Chargeman O Shop. (Author's collection)

The 40 Office outing to Hunters Inn on Exmoor in 1949. Identified are, left to right: Jean Claughan, Mary Shergold, Marjorie Gooding, Grace Turner, Gladys Ackrill, Barbara Dening, Phyllis ? The lady on the far right lived in Drove Road and Barbara remembers her getting a message at work, telling her to go home quickly as her house had been bombed. This was in August 1942. (B. Carter collection)

17

Trip: The Annual Holiday

I have tried to confine the content of this chapter to what went on at 'this end' up until the holiday trains left the town. For information beyond that, see Rosa Matheson's book *Trip: The Annual Holiday of GWR's Swindon Works*.

The applications for the works holiday train travel were dealt with by the admin section of the staff office in the works. The publicity and bookings were handled by a designated committee in the Mechanics' Institute; later they would issue the passes (tickets) and the travel details. Having all the special trains ready and at the starting and return points was the responsibility of the superintendent of the line's (traffic) department. They also had to dovetail those extra trains in with the normal timetabled services. A small army of staff at Paddington did nothing else but deal with alterations and additions (relief trains) to train services due to holiday periods, engineering work etc. Presumably they would not lose too much sleep over the extra works trains.

All employees of the GWR received free train travel at holiday time. All, that is, except the workers at Swindon works: they had to pay a nominal amount to be members of the Mechanics' Institute. Although membership also entitled them to an impressive range of recreational facilities, many only joined to take advantage of the holiday train travel.

Despite the subscriptions and the fact that the travel facilities offered were the company's own, the planning and especially the operational costs of getting the majority of the workforce and their families away and back each year must have been considerable. The CME department would pay the locomotive staff and running expenses, and the superintendent of the line's department would incur the operational costs of moving the train sets about the system.

Only at Swindon was it possible and beneficial to have a shutdown. Elsewhere the workers' holiday periods could be staggered, allowing them to travel by ordinary train services. Considering the sheer numbers involved, all travelling at the same time, there was no choice other than to provide trains exclusively for the Swindon workers. There were other drawbacks that the company had to bear too, such as the disruption to their goods and passenger services for the duration of the holiday period. No doubt some of the travelling public who took their holidays in the first part of July would be driven to travel by the Southern Railway or others, rather than share resorts crowded with Swindonians.

Back in the 1950s, R. J. Blackmore wrote at length about the rituals of locals in the lead-up to the works holidays. He had obviously listened with interest to stories of his parents' generation. Although referring to the early years of the twentieth century, the following extracts could equally apply to the 1930s and beyond:

And when it came to the summer holiday, then they all thought of Trip ; they all spoke of Trip ; they all prepared for Trip ; and so by degrees the air became charged with a sense of awareness of the approaching festival. The children began to chalk up the slogan: 'Roll on Trip' on walls in every part of the town. Cheap lines of shoes and holiday wear and indeed anything that could be squeezed into the category of holiday requirements, were marked up 'Special for Trip' (Later in his notes Mr Blackmore points out that businesses may do better in the run-up to the holiday but would suffer while most customers were away and, because of the works' pay arrangements, not do much trade for a while afterwards). The supreme question banded backwards and forwards a thousand times a day, was: 'where you going Trip?' Some old boys who had been asked once too often would reply 'ourgate', in other words, mind your own business . . .

The week preceding Trip was heady with excitement. The children cut paper streamers to release through the open windows of the carriages. There was an orgy of preparation throughout the town while, on three evenings, the lecture hall at the Institute was open to receive the holders of membership cards. Staff then dealt with the business of date-stamping the cards and issuing the required railway tickets and times of trains, to the respective applicants . . .

'Trip' morning had a magic all its own. There was little sleep the night before . . . With the grey dawning the doors began to open all over the town, and the holidaymakers streamed through the streets towards the special sidings where the trains were waiting; made up and labelled. Fathers carried bulging cases on their shoulders, mothers carried half-sleeping infants; children pale with excitement, milled around with their buckets and spades and toy boats. Barrow boys of all ages did a good business carrying luggage: later the taxi and corporation buses put them out of business.

At the entrances to the sidings the growing crowd was met by a variety of opportunists, mostly sponsored by firms seeking to advertise their wares. A publishing house handed out free copies of comics, while a well-known chocolate manufacturer gave away bars of chocolate, in each case, to the children. Reuben George, an earnest philanthropist, always took the opportunity of making a collection on behalf of the Poor Children's Fund: the money being used at a later date to finance an independent train outing for children whose parents did not receive a free ticket, and were too poor to pay the fare.

In the 1930s, the works closed for the annual shutdown at midday on the first Thursday in July, and reopened on the following Monday week. The local schools broke up at midday on 'holiday Thursday' too. The directors of the company provided what were officially called 'special trains' which took the Swindon factory workers away for a well-earned break. Long-distance trains were made up of corridor stock and left on the Thursday evening, travelling overnight; the rest left early the following morning. 'Trip Day' for railway families just going away for one day was the Friday and, for the town's traders and others, the following Wednesday.

The numerous arrangements with which thousands of trippers had to comply had been honed over the years and ran like clockwork by the 1930s. No doubt there were administrative hiccups, but this was a time when little, if any, of such things became known outside. To a large extent the previous years' arrangements acted as a template, with the only variables being dates and numbers travelling. I have seen notices that have been amended in biro: these must have been the previous year's copies that had been sent to the printer so they could alter sections of the type.

The first sign that Trip arrangements were under way in the factory was the appearance of the 'Application for Tickets Etc.' posters on notice boards. These stated that travellers must give particulars of destination, numbers of tickets required and whether they would be away for the day or the whole week. Bookings had to be made by the end of May, after which details of the holiday train arrangements were displayed on the noticeboards. The local paper also printed details of the numbers travelling. In the week leading up to the holiday, the passes were to be collected from the Mechanics' Institute along with any tickets for relatives and friends of employees not entitled to free or privilege tickets.

The holiday pass covered travel to any of the seaside resorts served by the Great Western and over lines run jointly with other companies. It also covered the steamer crossing for those going to the Channel Islands, as it was the GWR, and later BR, that owned the ships and ran the service. The nearest resorts, Weston and Weymouth, were the most popular with the day trippers; any further meant a long and tiring day. Devon and Cornwall were easily the most popular areas to spend the week away. The French polisher Jack Purbrick always took his family to Penzance. His daughter Joyce remembers him saying every year: 'Might as well get your money's worth out of 'em.' This was a not uncommon line of reasoning among GWR employees in the 1920s and 30s, apparently; my grandfather's family were reluctantly taken to the bottom of Cornwall as a result of the same mentality. According to the *GWR Magazine*, 27,416 people left the town in 1933, over 1,000 more than the previous year.

Trip was the unofficial term used by Swindonians and was known to every person who had heard about the way of life of this industrial community. From Christmas onwards, it was the most eagerly awaited event of the year for those involved. The mass exodus in July was on such a scale that all the Swindon and district folk who lived through it have particular memories of it. I have heard that some elderly residents of Exmouth and St Ives still refer to early July as 'Swindon week'. Because of the numbers of people and trains to be got away in a short space of time, the departure points varied: most left from the Junction station, where even the local branch platforms were utilized, for connecting trains. One or two trains left for the South Coast from the station in Old Town and meandered down the old M&SWJ, as it was still called. The remainder were all West of England-bound trains, which left from works' sidings on the down side of the main line. Local trains and buses were run in the early hours to bring people in from outlying districts to connect with the holiday trains.

Everyone wore their best clothes; if you were going to buy something new, you did it just before Trip . From photographs we can see that fashions changed over the years, albeit slowly. Before the war the men wore a suit and often a bowler hat or straw brimmer. They might also wear a bow tie, a handkerchief in the top pocket or perhaps a buttonhole flower. The young men, who might also take bicycles with them, usually wore an open-neck white shirt. For the ladies, a gaily patterned cotton dress and a raincoat, just in case. Gran, of course, would wear her best hat. Although the town was noticeably quieter, not every railway family went away at Trip . Those left would often stay up or get up early to wave their neighbours off: 'The key's through the letterbox on a piece of string . . . Don't forget to feed the budgie, will you.' That's assuming the bird and cage were not going too. Barbara Carter was a child in the 1930s and she was one of those who stayed at home: 'My father was a clerk in charge of an office, and so to offset the exodus somewhat, senior staff worked through the holiday. All I remember is how quiet it was everywhere and how difficult it was to get groceries.' Local grocers' shops had stayed open late before 'Trip Day' and 'Trip Week', and they then often took the opportunity to close when the majority of their customers were away.

For those families not travelling from the station, the situation was a novelty. They would enter the works' premises at the Park Lane and Station Road entrances and walk alongside the main lines, which were temporarily roped off. As it got light people would be looking out for neighbours and workmates. Dave Stratford remembers his father

Bert would be on duty with other watchmen to see no one wandered on to the running lines. Having to climb wooden steps which were placed up to the open carriage doors was another annual treat remembered by many who were children at the time, partly prompted by the often published Edwardian photographs. Jack Fleetwood remembered that some foundrymen had cast carriage keys for their own use. They would arrive a bit early to let them, their family and perhaps their neighbours in and have a compartment for themselves. Holidaying with friends and neighbours was very much a Trip tradition. Mothers had written in advance and arranged 'board and attendance' with a landlady who advertised in *Holiday Haunts* magazine, or more likely with whom they had stayed in previous years. A box full of vegetables from the allotment was often taken and put in the guards van with all the others. The landlady would cook them up with perhaps a bit of fish each day, as fish was cheap in seaside resorts.

By the late 1930s, with the start of paid holidays for the manual workers, the week away started after work on the first Saturday in July. In 1939, with the population of Swindon at 63,000, about 27,000 people filled the thirty holiday trains and another 600 or so went by ordinary train services. With such statistics, it should be remembered that a significant proportion of the workforce came from areas outside the borough. Many of the workers and their families were just getting used to the idea of staying away for the whole week when, from the first July of the war, Trip was cancelled for the duration. With all the extra work, a depleted workforce and the uncertainty of what lay ahead, it is surprising that the company did not cancel Trip until it was announced that the beaches of southern England were out of bounds to the public. As late as the 17 May 1940, the *Evening Advertiser* reported that 20,586 people had booked their Trip as usual.

Perhaps the splendid planning used to get so many evacuees away from west London and elsewhere in such a short period was modelled on Swindon works' holiday trains. The one-week holiday periods were now to be staggered throughout July, August and September so that orders, that had become all the more urgent, were not held up. Presumably this too was another last-minute decision. People were discouraged from travelling, and by the middle of the war the borough council arranged a programme of entertainment and attractions known as 'Holidays at Home' to cover the holiday period.

There was not the time or resources to reinstate Trip for 1945. The following year, with most of the shops on a five-and-a-half day week, the works resumed the pre-war arrangements whereby the holiday began at 12 noon on the Saturday. This was the first year of the two-week paid break. The last Trip train that day was away from Swindon by early evening; a few more trains left on the following Sunday, Monday and Tuesday. That year, 1946, 17,892 people were conveyed, but not all by the twenty-seven Trip trains. Some daytrippers travelled by service trains on week-days but were still entitled to the concession. When the Saturday shift was dropped again, the overnight trains for west Cornwall and north-west England left Friday evening, the rest early on Saturday, Monday and Tuesday.

The CME running department had the headache of finding spare locomotives, not least the shedmaster at Swindon, who found it advantageous to set aside certain engines in advance. I suspect there was a policy of using engines with high mileages for the holiday trains, just as they used run-down rolling stock. Other depots assisted by supplying locomotives, and sets of coaches were formed up and brought in from other areas too.

In 1950, the holiday shutdown was brought forward a week, but it returned to normal the following year. By now, because of nationalisation, the free holiday ticket could take the holder all over the UK and Eire. Most people, however, continued to visit resorts that the old Great Western had promoted. Pam Pinnegar had been a (steam) hammer driver 'inside' during the war. In the 1950s she and her husband and another Swindon couple (possibly her sister Peggy, also an ex-hammer driver, and her husband) moved to Paignton. They both ran guest houses and took in Swindon people during Trip weeks.

By 1954 it was said that only about 50 per cent of people in this country went on holiday by train. This was not the case among Swindon railway families, as in general they had little incentive to find alternative means of travel. Numbers had varied little since the 1930s, but after 1956 there was a reduction in the holiday specials as a result of trippers being diverted on to ordinary train services. Although the works was showing little sign of the coming decline, in 1957, the *Evening Advertiser* reported that the excitement of the annual holiday was 'not what it used to be'. Locals seeing friends and relatives away said many looked noticeably less enthusiastic than they used to. Perhaps they had heard of the bus strike that awaited them on their return. R. J. Blackmore wrote about the holidays in the 1950s, a time when the scale of the event had hardly changed at all. Interestingly he writes in the past tense, which seems to confirm what the local paper said. On the matter of the return journey he wrote, no doubt from personal experience:

> Somehow or another the return trains always managed to draw into the station, and it was a custom for many who had stayed at home, to congregate about the station approaches and witness the return of the trippers. Sun-bronzed (sometimes with peeling skin) tired-looking and a little jaded after the rueful goodbye to the sea and the long journeys, they threaded their way to their particular part of the town and to their own particular red brick dwelling. On Monday the hooter would bellow forth again, and the dreary monotonous workaday world would swallow them all up for another year.

Some shopkeepers still closed all day on Trip Wednesday at the start of the 1960s, catching out unsuspecting shoppers, but not anywhere near as many shops as in previous years. The holiday trains were gradually phased out with the rundown of the works, but the holidays of Swindon railway families are well remembered today, the journey as much as the seaside destination. This is because, like the Children's Fete, also organised by the committee of the Mechanics' Institute, it captured the imagination of the children who grew up in an era when their memories were to be sought and recorded.

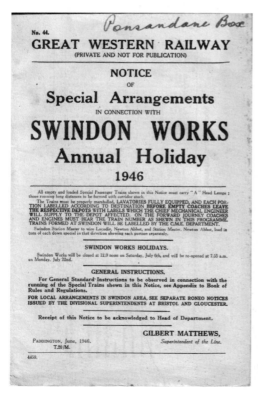

A poster for the annual holiday in 1946, giving details for those visiting resorts in other railway companies' territories. It is unusual not to have the company name or initials displayed. (Author's collection)

The Superintendent of the Line's Dept produced and distributed these comprehensive booklets each year. They gave details of each Works' holiday train to be run and operating instructions for its working over each section of the route. Similar sets of train arrangements were produced for station masters, signalmen and officials at Christmas, Whitsun and August Bank Holiday times as they needed to know about all additional or altered train services in their division. This booklet was issued to the signalmen at Penzance in 1946. (Author's collection)

Right: The timetable of the Bristol buses running between the trains and the outskirts in 1935. Swindon's second bus company used the unofficial but universally known term 'Trip': the railway company rarely ever did. The first buses to leave from Swindon left Regent Circus where, presumably, they had been parked-up from the day before. (Author's collection)

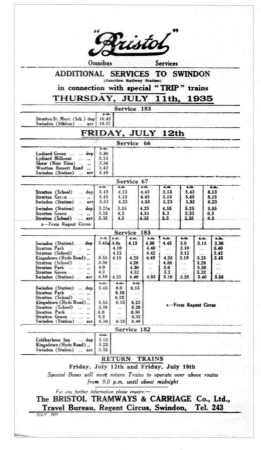

Below: Photographs of 'Trip' trains are quite rare apart from a series of views taken before the First World War by professional photographer, William Hooper. This is one of them showing a holiday train about to depart for Devon or Cornwall. This area was the original timber stacking ground adjacent to Rodbourne Lane signal box. These people would have come in via the entrance at the top of Park Lane. (Andrea Downing)

Top: Ready to depart for the west in, what was almost certainly, 1938: Tom and Gladys Ferris and their children Roy and Eileen have got their compartment in a Works' holiday train. This was the overnight train to St Ives waiting to depart from Rodbourne Lane down sidings. Tom Ferris was a gas fitter and plumber based in 15A Shop. (*Swindon Advertiser*, courtesy of Roy Ferris)

Middle: Families arriving at The Works at the start of 'Trip fortnight' in 1946. This was the first year of two weeks paid holiday but not all trippers stayed away for the whole period by any means. These people have just entered the gate at the top of Park Lane and are climbing the slope to the bridges over Rodbourne Road (better known by locals as Rodbourne Lane). On the left is Percy King; behind him is Reg Reeves; behind Reg is Tom Ferris and his son Roy; the man with glasses is George Rickards; the lady in front is Bessie Reeves; Ivy Rickards is on the extreme right. The Reeves of Clifton Street and the Rickards were friends and would be, no doubt, sharing a compartment on the same train. (*Swindon Advertiser*, courtesy of Roy Ferris)

Bottom: By sheer coincidence the Ferris family of Ferndale Road had their picture in the Evening Advertiser yet again, this time in 1947. The departing trippers are crossing the bridge over Rodbourne Road early on Saturday morning. The train in the background will be bound for Devon or Cornwall. It is probably the Paignton train because that's where the Ferris family were going that year. (*Swindon Advertiser*, courtesy of Roy Ferris)

Bibliography

BOOKS

Adams, Prof. Henry, *Engineers' Handbook* (Cassell & Company, 1908)
Bartlett, Harry W., *Wartime Swindon as I Remember It* (published privately, 2011)
Bryan, Tim, *All in a Day's Work: Life on the G.W.R.* (Ian Allan 2004)
Cattell, John and Keith Falconer *Swindon: The Legacy of a Railway Town* (English Heritage 1995)
Chapman, W. G., *Cornish Riviera Ltd* (George Routledge and Sons, 1936)
Cook, Kenneth J., *Swindon Steam 1921–1951* (Ian Allan 1974)
Freebury, Hugh, *Great Western Apprentice* (Wilts County Library & Museum Service, 1985)
Fuller, Frederick, *The Railway Works and Church in New Swindon* (Redbrick Publishing, 1987)
Gibbs, Ken, *Swindon Works: An Apprentice in Steam* (Oxford Publishing Company 1986)
Gourvish, T. R., *British Railways 1948–1973* (Cambridge University Press 1986)
Knox, Collie, *The Un-Beaten Track* (Cassel & Company, 1944)
Nock, O. S., *The History of the Great Western Railway, 1923–1947* (Ian Allan Ltd, 1967)
Peck, Alan, *The Great Western at Swindon Works* (Oxford Publishing Company 1983)
R. C & T. S. *Locomotives of the G.W.R. Part Eleven* (1956)
Reade, Peter, *A Good Reade – Memoirs of a Wiltshire Life* (published privately, 2003)
Rogers, H. C. B., *G. J. Churchward* (George Allen and Unwin, 1975)
Timms, Peter, *In and Around Swindon Works.* (Stroud: Amberley, 2012)
Tomkins, Richard and Peter Sheldon, *Swindon and the G.W.R.* (Alan Sutton and Redbrick Publishing, 1990)

GWR AND WESTERN REGION PUBLICATIONS

A Century of Medical Service. Bernard Darwin (Published for the GWR in 1947)
Dieselisation-Problems, Prospects and Progress. R.A. Smeddle CM&EE (B.R. Western Region, London Lecture and Debating Society, 1959)
Electronic Accounting, Powers-Samas (B.R. Western Region, 1957)
Gas Turbines. A.W.J. Dymond (Pamphlet No 217, Swindon Engineering Society, 1947)
The General Plan for the Future of Swindon works (BRWR. 1960)
Great Western Progress: 1835–1935. (Great Western Railway 1936)
Materials' Handling in Swindon works (B.R. Western Region, 1956)
Notice of Special Arrangements in Connections with Swindon works Annual Holiday (various years)

Safety Precautions for Railway Shopmen (1941)
Supplies and Contract Department (Materials Inspectorate, 1960)
Swindon works and its Place in British Railway History (B.R. Engineering Limited 1975)
A Visit to the United States (General Manager's Office, Paddington 1927)

NEWSPAPERS AND JOURNALS

The Evening Advertiser
The Swindon Advertiser
The Evening Advertiser Railway Supplement (November 1958)
The Swindon Messenger
The Swindon Railway News (1960–1963)
The British Machine Tool Engineer (April–June 1950)
Pamphlets of presentations read to the Swindon Engineering Society (1920s to the 1950s)

OTHER SOURCES

Steam Museum Archive
Swindon Central Library, Local Studies (previously the Swindon Reference Library)
Swindon Museum, Bath Road
County Records Office, Trowbridge
Unpublished notes of R. J. Blackmore